The French party system

edited by Jocelyn A. J. Evans

Manchester University Press
Manchester and New York

distributed exclusively in the USA by Palgrave

Published by Manchester University Press
Oxford Road, Manchester M13 9NR, UK
and Room 400, 175 Fifth Avenue, New York, NY 10010, USA
www.manchesteruniversitypress.co.uk

Distributed exclusively in the USA by
Palgrave, 175 Fifth Avenue, New York,
NY 10010, USA

Distributed exclusively in Canada by
UBC Press, University of British Columbia, 2029 West Mall,
Vancouver, BC, Canada V6T 1Z2

British Library Cataloguing-in-Publication Data
A catalogue record for this book is available from the British Library

Library of Congress Cataloging-in-Publication Data applied for

ISBN   0 7190 6119 9 *hardback*
         0 7190 6120 2 *paperback*

First published 2003

11 10 09 08 07 06 05 04 03   10 9 8 7 6 5 4 3 2 1

Typeset in New Baskerville and Stone Sans
by Carnegie Publishing Ltd
Printed in Great Britain
by Bell & Bain Ltd, Glasgow

To Barbara

Contents

List of figures and tables   *page* ix
List of contributors   xi
Acknowledgements   xii
List of abbreviations   xiii

Introduction   1

1 Stress, strain and stability in the French party system
  Alistair Cole   11

I The left

2 The French Communist Party: from revolution to reform
  David S. Bell   29

3 PS intra-party politics and party system change
  Ben Clift   42

4 The Greens: from idealism to pragmatism (1984–2002)
  Bruno Villalba and Sylvie Vieillard-Coffre   56

5 Managing the plural left: implications for the party system
  David Hanley   76

6 Beyond the mainstream: *la gauche de la gauche*
  Jim Wolfreys   91

II The right

7 The UDF in the 1990s: the break-up of a party confederation
  Nicolas Sauger   107

8 From the Gaullist movement to the president's party
  Andrew Knapp   121

9 The FN split: party system change and electoral prospects
  Gilles Ivaldi   137

III System context

10 Europe and the French party system
    Jocelyn A. J. Evans   155

11 Contemporary developments in political space in France
    Robert Andersen and Jocelyn A. J. Evans   171

    Conclusion   189

    References   201
    Index   211

List of figures and tables

Figures

4.1 Green membership by department   *page* 59

4.2 Green presidential election results (1981–2002)   63

4.3 Ecologist regional election results by department (1986 and 1992)   64

4.4 Green electoral strategies by department (1986 and 1998)   65

4.5 The main themes of the Green–PS programmatic agreement (1997)   70

4.6 Motions in the Toulouse Congress and regional assembly voting   72

4.7 Green presidential primaries in 2002   73

8.1 Votes for Gaullists and for all moderate right-wing parties at parliamentary elections (1958–2002)   129

11.1 Mean scores for attitudes in favour of immigration by party bloc   181

11.2 Mean scores for attitudes not in favour of the death penalty by party bloc   181

11.3 Mean scores for attitudes against homosexuality by party bloc   182

11.4 Mean scores for attitudes against privatisation by party bloc   182

C.1 Effective number of parties and presidential candidates in France (1978–2002)   190

C.2 Effective number of parties and presidential candidates on the left and right in France (1978–2002)   191

C.3 Total volatility in French legislative elections (1978–2002)   193

Tables

5.1 Vote–position ratio in first Jospin government   82
7.1 Party affiliation of single candidates fielded by the
     moderate right (per cent)   117
7.2 Party affiliation of moderate-right deputies (per cent)   117
8.1 The moderate right: presidential candidacies and share
     of votes cast (1965–2002)   123
9.1 The FN in national elections (1984–2002)   137
9.2 Change in the socio-demographic structure of the FN
     electorate (1984–97)   139
10.1 Assembly votes on amendment of Article 88–2 and
     ratification of Amsterdam Treaty by parliamentary group   157
11.1 Allocation of party proximity response to blocs   178
11.2 Demographic profiles (per cent) of party proximity groups
     in France (1988–97)   179
11.3 Average attitudes toward privatisation for extreme-right
     identifiers, by year and social class   184
C.1 2002 legislative election results (first round) and change
     (1997–2002)   192

List of contributors

Robert Andersen	Assistant Professor of Sociology, University of Western Ontario; and Senior Research Fellow at CREST, Department of Sociology, University of Oxford
David Bell	Professor of Politics, University of Leeds
Ben Clift	Lecturer in Politics, Brunel University
Alistair Cole	Professorial Fellow in Politics, University of Cardiff
Jocelyn Evans	Lecturer in Politics, University of Salford
David Hanley	Professor of European Studies, University of Cardiff
Gilles Ivaldi	CNRS *chargé de recherche*, CIDSP-IEP, Grenoble
Andrew Knapp	Senior Lecturer in French Studies, University of Reading
Nicolas Sauger	*Allocataire de recherche*, CEVIPOF, Paris
Sylvie Vieillard-Coffre	*Docteur en géographie*, CRAG – Université de Paris 8
Bruno Villalba	*Maître de conférences* in Politics, CRAPS – Université de Lille 2
Jim Wolfreys	Lecturer in French Politics, King's College, London

Acknowledgements

The editor gratefully acknowledges the support of the British Academy, the Association for the Study of Modern and Contemporary France (ASMCF) and the European Studies Research Institute (ESRI) at the University of Salford for their financial and logistical support in running the conference 'Changes in the contemporary French party system: internal dynamics and external context' at Salford in September 2000, the papers from which constituted the first drafts of the chapters in this book. He would also like to thank the Centre d'Informatisation des Données Socio-Politiques (CIDSP) – Banque de Données Socio-Politiques (BDSP), Grenoble, for providing the SOFRES/CEVIPOF datasets used in the empirical analyses in Chapter 11 and the conclusion. Finally, he would like to thank Tony Mason and Richard Delahunty at Manchester University Press for their help in producing this collection.

List of abbreviations

AC!	Agir ensemble contre le Chômage
AED	Alliance pour l'Ecologie et la Démocratie
AGM	Annual General Meeting [Green Party]
APEIS	Association pour l'Emploi, l'Information et la Solidarité
AREV	Alternative Rouge et Verte
ASSEDIC	Association pour l'Emploi dans l'Industrie et le Commerce
CAP	Convention pour une Alternative Progressiste
CDS	Centre des Démocrates Sociaux
CDU–CSU	Christlich–Demokratischen Union – Christlich–Soziale Union
CES	Convergence Ecologie Solidarité
CFDT	Confédération Française Démocratique du Travail
CGT	Confédération Générale du Travail
CNI	Centre National des Indépendants
CPNT	Chasse Pêche Nature Traditions
CRC	Coordonner, Rassembler, Construire
DAL	Droit au Logement
DD!!	Droits devant!!
DL	Démocratie Libérale
DLI	Démocratie Libérale et Indépendants
EA	Ecologie Autrement
EC	Executive College [Green party]
FA	Federal Assembly [Green party]
FD	Force Démocrate
FN	Front National
FNJ	Front National de la Jeunesse
GE	Génération Ecologie
LCR	Ligue Communiste Révolutionnaire
LO	Lutte Ouvrière
MdC	Mouvement des Citoyens

MEDEF	Mouvement des Entreprises de France
MEI	Mouvement Ecologiste Indépendant
MNEF	Mutuelle Nationale des Etudiants Français
MNR	Mouvement National Républicain
MPF	Mouvement pour la France
MRP	Mouvement Républicain Populaire
MSI	Movimento Sociale Italiano
NIRC	National Inter-Regional Council [Green party]
PACS	Pacte Civil de Solidarité
PCF	Parti Communiste Français
PPE	Partido Popular de Espana
PR [party]	Parti Républicain
PRep	Pôle Républicain
PRG	Parti Radical de Gauche
PS	Parti Socialiste
RCV	Radicaux–Citoyens–Verts
RI	Républicains Indépendants
RPF [de Gaulle]	Rassemblement du Peuple Français
RPF [Pasqua]	Rassemblement pour la France
RPFIE	Rassemblement pour la France et l'Indépendance de l'Europe
RPR	Rassemblement pour la République
SFIO	Section Française de l'Internationale Ouvrière
SUD–PTT	Fédération Solidaire, Unitaire, Démocratique des PTT
UDF	Union pour la Démocratie Française
UMP	Union pour une Majorité Présidentielle/Union pour un Mouvement Populaire
UNR	Union pour la Nouvelle République
UPF	Union pour la France
WTO	World Trade Organisation

Introduction

Jocelyn A. J. Evans

In the more recent literature on European party systems, emphasis has been placed squarely upon the notion that the overall cross-national trend is one of convergence and, by extension, stabilisation. Where new parties have appeared, they tend to have been absorbed into existing structures and very few have actually superseded older parties. Increasingly, European systems which had stretched from the two-party system of Britain to the polarised pluralism of Italy are coming to resemble each other. Whether or not the premises for such a hypothesis are accurate, the French case at first glance shows few signs of conforming to such a model. In 2002, the French party system seems to be demonstrating a fluidity, if not outright instability, equal to any period in the Fifth Republic's history. The question this book aims to answer is: to what extent does this represent outright change and to what extent shifts within a stable structure?

Looking at the supposed format of the system before the presidential elections of this year, the key elements were a plural but essentially cohesive governing left, and a hopelessly divided right. By the end of the presidential elections, commentators were speaking of a hopelessly divided left and a newly cohesive right, a state of affairs confirmed and reinforced by the legislative election outcome in June. Granted, the cohesion of the left had always been suspect – largely the outcome of elite compromise and in particular the leadership of its Prime Minister, Lionel Jospin. Similarly, the right's fragmentation, although conforming to certain ideological differences, was always due more to personality clashes within and between parties than to any gulf of doctrinal incompatibility. However, the interaction between certain conjunctural events in the pre-electoral period and key institutional changes also pre-dating the elections combined to rebalance the party system in terms of its components if not in terms of its overall structure.

Moving from left to right, a previously governing Communist Party which had seemingly survived the post-1990 collapse of many of its sister parties clung on with 4.8 per cent of the first-round vote and 21 deputies to form its own parliamentary group with little to spare. The previously governing Socialist Party saw its vote drop only by a relatively small margin, but the two-ballot system and relative absence of three-way run-offs – the famous *triangulaires* of 1997 – returned a paltry number of seats as a result. The Green Party remained on the fringes of the mainstream and of electoral success, unable to provide a credible alternative on its own, but hampered by its travelling on the Socialists' coat-tails. The Union pour la Démocratie Française (UDF), once the presidential federation, had now been relegated to 5 per cent of the vote and only just able to secure enough deputies for its own parliamentary group.[1] The Rassemblement pour la République (RPR) and Démocratie Libérale (DL) (plus two-thirds of the UDF), brought together under the banner of the Union pour la Majorité Présidentielle (UMP), formed the first right-wing party in France able to unite the right in a manner similar to its Gaullist predecessors of forty years earlier. Finally, the extreme right still loitered menacingly on the margins of the right with one in ten votes, but was incapable of winning a single parliamentary seat, even with the apparently immense political capital of its candidate having reached the second round of the presidential elections.[2]

The presidential element had a larger effect than normal on the legislative elections both for timetabling and constitutional reasons. Perhaps most importantly, the inversion of the electoral calendar to put the presidential elections first meant that no party wanting to run an effective electoral campaign could avoid fielding a presidential candidate. Quite simply, because of the presidential priority and its outcome, there was no legislative campaign to speak of. Sixteen candidates in the presidential first round indicated that few parties were ignorant of this logic, but in the process so fragmented the vote that, at least for the left, the starting line-up proved catastrophic.[3] Second, the recent reduction of the presidential term from seven years to five, partly as an obstacle to another period of *cohabitation* deadlock and partly as a rationalisation of an excessively long executive incumbency, has pulled the presidential candidates and their respective parties closer together. The effect of the five-year simultaneous mandates in terms of power distribution between president and governing parties is as yet unclear – what is clear, however, is that the tightening of the two executive branches helped to ensure the moderate right's effective unity and consequently its clear margin of victory.

However, despite the importance of these elections – indeed, all elections – in providing a benchmark for assessing the systemic array, the election results per se should not be looked at in isolation. Such changes are to be regarded as at least partly the result of shifts which have occurred in the French party system over recent years, and not simply the outcome of a combination of conjunctural effects and mathematical quirks. To address these, this book assesses the context to the current situation and the extent to which the array we find today is in keeping with the changes in the system and the players within it in recent years. The contributors concentrate principally on the period subsequent to the *quadrille bipolaire* – the four-party, two-bloc array vaunted as the French ideal type in the semi-presidential two-ballot majoritarian system – which is largely held to have 'peaked' in 1978, and begun its 'descent' very soon afterwards.

The changes since 1978 have been principally conjunctural rather than structural. The main feature at legislative elections since the final follow-on victory of the right in that year has been alternation. Held up as a dynamic to which to aspire by proponents of an Anglo-Saxon remodelling of the system, this has been taken to extremes which had probably not been envisaged. Simply, neither bloc has been able to retain incumbency since that date – six changes of governing bloc in six elections over a little under one-quarter of a century. At the mass level, this *hyper-alternance* [4] has had the greatest systemic effect, giving voters little to decide upon when making their electoral choice. For many voters, each side having had three periods in government and none having been seen as particularly successful, all mainstream parties look as bad as each other. When adding to this the periods of *cohabitation* where one has often been hard pressed to tell the two sides apart, Le Pen's parody of the left and right as *blanc bonnet, bonnet blanc* seemingly has some foundation. However, even a rapid succession of swings of the electoral pendulum does not equate to party system change per se: re-equilibration has largely occurred between two stable blocs, one each side of the centre. The unoccupied centre and the floating voters of a Downsian logic have consequently remained deciding elements to elections since 1978, conditioned by the level of turnout and fragmentation within electoral blocs.

Newer smaller parties, who conversely *do* represent potential structural change if relevant within the system, have also been affected by this logic. The Greens could only hope to win a small proportion of the electorate, namely the committed environmentalist voters, if they attempted to remain faithful to their 'neither left nor right' stance of the 1980s. Similarly, Jean-Pierre Chevènement's attempt to play a similar 'off the spectrum' republican card in the 2002 presidential elections led to disastrous results in both the presidential and legislative elections. In the former case, however, the decision to implant themselves firmly on the left reaped electoral rewards and a position in government. The other major player to reject the two-bloc labels was the Front National (FN). In terms of votes, this party was much more successful, winning 15 per cent at its legislative peak in 1997. Similarly, its *pouvoir de nuisance* allowed it to cause the moderate right severe problems in constituencies where it managed to advance to the second round together with the anticipated left and moderate-right run-off candidates. However, in representative and governing terms, again the two-bloc system prevented it from ever winning more than a single deputy at any one time.[5]

Lastly, the 'empty centre' of the two-bloc system rejected any attempt to fill it with a cross-bloc alliance – for instance, the failed attempt of Michel Rocard to include the Centre des Démocrates Sociaux (CDS) segment of the UDF in the minority Socialist government between 1988 and 1993. The left–right logic remained and remains inexorable, at least at the national level and in the mainstream. At the sub-national level, in the second-order European elections, and as Alistair Cole notes in the opening chapter of this volume, 'on the margins' – the extremes and, at the mass level, among the disenfranchised, disenchanted pool of voters who are casting protest votes or abstaining in apparently ever-greater quantities – a different set of circumstances pertain, given the differing electoral systems and a separate set of stakes. There, the moderate right has not been entirely cut off from the extreme right, illustrated in particular by the ill-fated compromise by four UDF regional presidents to rely upon FN support in their councils in order to ensure incumbency. Moreover, there is greater scope for compromise within the mainstream in local councils than at the national level. As Jean-Luc Parodi has termed it, this 'electoral accordion', whereby the party systems at the different electoral levels expand and contract according to the rules of the game and the political context more generally, should have some knock-on effect at the national level – when the accordion opens, it does not close again in exactly the same fashion (Parodi, 1997).

The voters choosing the extremist candidates or not voting at all compound these distorting effects by effectively rejecting the rules of the game. Survey after survey reveal numerous voters decrying left and right as anachronistic and the parties which place themselves in these terms as atrophied. A large proportion of the electorate in the presidential election demonstrated their disenchantment by voting for electorally hopeless candidates – *le vote inutile*. Useless, that is, except in terms of demonstrating to the mainstream that they could not necessarily rely on their vote and that, as a result, some of them might not reach the second round. Yet, this dynamic did not reproduce itself at the legislative elections, at least not in terms of those who voted (abstention set a new record). Despite an unprecedented 8,444 candidates in the first round, the actual changes in vote were relatively sober. Small parties failed, the mainstream hegemons remained or were resurrected, and *le vote utile* resurfaced. The latent extremist pool remains, however, as a potent source of future change.

The threat of change being replaced by politics as normal has not been restricted to the margins, however. For instance, the area upon which perhaps clear ideological differences have been most apparent – Europe – between the members of the moderate right led to the UDF and RPR–DL presenting separate lists at the 1999 European elections. Invoking the electoral accordion once more, one might expect this schism to have some effect on coalition-building at the national level in 2002. And in fact, if we look at the first-round legislative ballots, the UDF precisely would not present single candidates with the RPR. However, this dynamic of *rupture* was confounded by the formation of the UMP in the aftermath of the presidential first round. Thus, the fragmentation of the moderate right alluded to at the beginning of this chapter has at a stroke been almost eliminated. A split right no longer matters because the redistribution of votes between the two sections is sufficiently skewed to make one almost irrelevant. The major forces for change are thus less a mutation of the structural pattern to the system and more the shifts of power within essentially stable structures.[6]

The above elements are a synthesis of the principal areas covered by the authors in the chapters which follow. Perhaps the most important element discussed is that of the cyclical shift in the balance of power towards the left and then back to the right between the mid-1990s and today. In this respect, David Bell's chapter on the Parti Communiste Français (PCF) and Bruno Villalba and Sylvie Vieillard-Coffre's chapter on the Greens present the combination of strategic incentive and ideological disincentive that these parties have encountered in their role as props for the Socialist Party's government. The 1997 victory relied upon the Parti Socialiste (PS) presenting itself as a less arrogant party than it had been in the 1980s, and for this reason as well as for reasons of legislative necessity, it opened up to its 'extreme' and 'new' left flanks. The flanks have suffered as a result, partly due to their partners, partly due to their own failings. However, as Ben Clift notes, the success of Jospin in winning control of the PS in the mid-1990s despite competing factions within the party was not matched by an ability to ensure that similar cohesion extended in the long term to these two partners. The mutual intra-coalition sniping, the inability of the PCF to maintain an independent electoral following concomitant with a position of relevance and the Greens' almost pathological desire to assert autonomy from the Socialists have all contributed to the electoral defeat of 2002.

David Hanley's assessment of the years preceding this show the precariousness of the plural left entering the electoral campaign period, even when faced with the fragmented right and an apparently discredited president. Elite compromise may hold a governing coalition together, but at election time such coalitions demand more than just a consensus – which the *gauche plurielle* failed singularly to present anyway – among leaders. When such consensus is often absent on constitutional matters such as Corsica and on key aspects of economic and social policy, even the relative merits of the *gauche plurielle*'s incumbency can soon be overshadowed by negative elements. The PS's approach may have been both strategic and worthy in equal measures, but the remaining contradictions cost the left dear, providing division at the presidentials and no subsequent basis for cohesion at the legislatives.

Moreover, such a lack of cohesion is not restricted to the elite level on the left. One of the two key questions asked in the chapter by Robert Andersen and Jocelyn Evans is: to what extent is there evidence of greater mass ideological cohesion on the left in 1997 than previously? The answer is 'none'. Granted, the *gauche plurielle* was at the beginning rather than the end of its relatively short life in 1997, but the ability of the parties to compete and to form a government might suggest some antecedent convergence. Until similar data become available for 2002, we can only speculate as to the extent to which convergence during the *gauche plurielle*'s reign occurred – but the speculation is still 'not at all'. In terms of competitive space, there have simply been too many voices on the left. Now many of them have been marginalised, but this does not solve the mainstream left's problems – now who can the Socialists reasonably ally themselves with to oppose the newly unified right? The success of returning to the same PCF–Parti Radical de Gauche (PRG)–Green trio – Chevènement's Pôle Républicain (PRep) being a terminally chastened force – is not assured of success, despite perhaps being inevitable.

Nevertheless, as is often the case in democratic competition, one side only does well because the other side is doing badly. Success is relative although in electoral terms the outcome is absolute. In the French case, the right seems to be victorious and cohesive only now that the left is in disarray, and thus we should perhaps not be too certain that the right's troubles are a thing of the past. The *front républicain* to oppose Le Pen's second-round candidature and Jacques Chirac's subsequent call for a presidential majority party all build upon the conjunctural elements which we have already highlighted, but they are in no way based upon any amicable resolution of personality clashes within the right. Nor have the parties suddenly resolved policy differences – these remain in some areas, and in others have been resolved gradually over many years. Chirac has simply found a context allowing him to assert almost total dominance over the moderate right, at least in the short term.[7]

As Andrew Knapp's chapter on the RPR and its presidential successor shows, the interference of the president in his own party has been a common and not altogether welcome aspect of his first incumbency. The clashes in particular with Philippe Séguin, former General Secretary of the RPR, led to perceptions of considerable party disunity during the late 1990s. The latter's departure in 1999 may have led to greater Chiraquian unity within the party, but it did nothing to alleviate tensions with the UDF. Nicolas Sauger's chapter illustrates the way in which the departure of DL in May of the previous year deprived the UDF of one of its more proximate elements to the RPR. Consequently, DL's acceptance of the

UMP has left the UDF isolated between the unified moderate right and the chasm of the centre. Its future appears unsure, to say the least.

As we have noted, the shifts in the system have not been exclusively focused upon the shift in the balance of power between left and right governing blocs. One of the specificities of the recent period in French party development has been the rise of the extremes, most notably the extreme right but also the continued presence of the extreme left. Both have proved more successful at presidential elections, suggesting that personality may play a substantial independent role in vote preference at this election. Whatever the reasons, however, the success of the extreme left has been a perhaps surprising corollary to the decline of the moderate left. Jim Wolfreys emphasises, however, that the success of the extreme left has been as much through alternative action – the social movements and protest which reappeared in the mid-1990s – as through the ballot box. Arlette Laguiller and Olivier Besancenot can thus mobilise support in the single national constituency in a way that their parties, groupuscular in their constituency support, cannot.

Conversely, the right extremists' support has implanted itself precisely at the regional level and consequently built up to a national level allowing over 10 per cent of the vote consistently since the mid-1980s. The success in the 2002 presidential elections was based upon the core support that the party has relied upon from its earliest days – older voters in the Midi and Eastern regions, supplemented by the industrial areas of the North and Parisian belt. The party which subsequent to Bruno Mégret's departure to form the Mouvement National Républicain (MNR) in 1999 had been declared dead still finds a stable electoral pool upon which to draw. Gilles Ivaldi's contribution implies that the relative failure of the party at the second round of the presidentials and at the legislative elections after its leader's success in the presidential first round may mark a zenith in its success. However, there is still undoubtedly a large pool of voters who are positioned in such a way in French political space as to be receptive to this party's political supply.

The status of this pool is somewhat unclear – certain authors have granted it 'separate status' as a new bloc within the French system; others prefer to see it as an extreme flank, but still part of the right. Andersen and Evans favour the latter interpretation, arguing that the extreme right does represent the radical side of the right bloc in ideological terms, and has done since the 1980s. In some ways, the social composition may be different to that of the moderate-right bloc, but the definition of voting blocs by social composition alone seems somewhat circular as an argument – and in ideological terms, there is no evidence that the moderate and extreme-right bloc do not share similar ideological positions, differing only in intensity.

Though perhaps unwelcome to the moderate right, this emphasises that the differences between them and the extreme right are no more exacerbated in many ways than the differences between the moderate left and the extreme left (if socially less acceptable for many). In overall systemic terms, then, there appears to be remarkable stability in the bloc balance between left and right and between the elections of 1997 and 2002. Electoral flows are apparent in 2002, but these have principally occurred between the presidential and legislative ballots – from extreme left to moderate left; and from extreme right to moderate right. Given the landslide victory of the moderate right, some shifts from moderate left to moderate right are also likely. In many ways, this seems to correspond quite closely to the expected cyclical changes one finds in stable party systems – intra-bloc shifts and competition for the centre 'floating' voter. But one should not ignore that the extremes remain strong on the right, and have shown evidence of a pool of potential support on the left, even if this has so far been restricted to the presidential ballot.

A very similar conclusion is reached by Alistair Cole, who chooses to give the system the status of 'artificial bipolar multipartism'. In other words, the stresses between the parties and their leaders pull towards increased fragmentation within the system, but the institutional framework continues to force this into the two-bloc logic. Given consistently rising levels of abstention among voters turned off by the choice 'imposed' by the current institutional framework, revisions to this framework are likely to go beyond the changes in presidential incumbency to date. Commentators continue to talk of the formulation of a Sixth Republic, although whether this indicates full regime change or simply a substantial amendment of the Fifth Republic is unclear. Furthermore, the ardour of incumbents to change a system which has brought them to power is always dampened by incumbency itself. The extent of institutional and constitutional change remains to be seen.

However, the form that such changes take are crucial to the future dynamics of the system. Calls for the introduction of proportionality to the legislative elections would favour smaller parties and increased fragmentation of the system. This may mean that the party tensions finally produce significant structural change once released from their current institutional constraints. Concomitantly, the European 'issue' dealt with by Jocelyn Evans also suffers from institutional binding and may turn out to be a future element to party system restructuring, as well as representing a separate arena with which the domestic party system has little interlinkage. To reiterate, however: the shifts which have occurred since the *quadrille bipolaire* seem to have taken place within largely stable structures.

We will return to shifts across time in the system in the conclusion, contenting ourselves for now with a couple of elementary observations with which to introduce the authors' contributions. First, the hybrid status of the system – bipolar logic plus a certain level of latent polarisation – satisfies the Downsian model of an unoccupied centre and floating voters deciding the outcome to a certain extent; but the polarisation implies that fewer voters are to be found in the centre, many moving to more extremist candidates when the context is favourable. In this light, many of the chapters emphasise that while the parties themselves may lack the ideological keenness that we are told once characterised political parties, the electorate still wants to see such definition. While there may be the contented voter in the middle ground looking to sustain the status quo, this type is less prevalent than in other European systems. Parties can mobilise their electorates *if* they are able to take a clear stance on issues, and credibly so.

Second, and linked to this, the chapters on the mainstream parties all allude to the machinations that elites go through not only in their jockeying for individual influence within a party or a coalition, but also to be in a position to mobilise the electorates. Yet time and again, the elite manoeuvring hinders this aim, either because the electorate perceives this as elites putting their own careers before their representative function, and hence the electorate is turned away; or simply because the machinations fail, either due to internal intransigence or external pressures, and hence the electorate remains unmobilised. Two examples of this are well placed to conclude this introduction. First, the Socialists and the *gauche plurielle* – an electoral alliance designed from the vantage of opposition to encompass the various strands on the left and provide an electoral majority succeeded; but the same alliance in government singularly failed to back the supposed presidential candidate of the left or to secure its own return to power because elite manoeuvring could not disguise ideological dissent, and indeed often pandered to it. Second, the newly cohesive right and the UMP – parties seemingly destined to remain fragmented despite the best intentions of some elites – suddenly found themselves drawn inexorably together by the presidential framework and the need for cohesion in the face of an extremist threat, and consequently for many voters came to represent a credible governing alternative characterised by unity and effectiveness.

It is precisely such interactions between parties, electorates and the institutional framework – the supply and demand in the electoral market – that produce the outcomes which mould the party system. The chapters which follow will look at these three elements and their effects on each other in order to better understand the state that the French system finds itself in at the beginning of the twenty-first century.

Notes

1 With 22 seats won at the second round of the legislative elections, François Bayrou the UDF leader was confident that a number of former UDF deputies who had decamped to the UMP would return to the UDF parliamentary group. At the time of writing (summer 2002) the parliamentary group only numbered 29.

2 His stock was reduced somewhat by his crushing defeat in the second round of election, however.

3 The only main parties not to field their own presidential candidates were the MPF and the RPF – Philippe de Villiers was absent from the beginning, and Charles Pasqua withdrew his candidacy shortly after the beginning of the campaign.

4 A term coined in Evans and Ivaldi (2002).

5 Except for the 1986–88 period when the party won 35 deputies due to the proportional representation electoral system preceding this legislative term.

6 Remaining with the European theme, the transfer of power away from the domestic system is surely also a potentially influential restructuring factor. The effects on the domestic party system, as Chapter 10 shows, have to date been minimal, however; effects on policy-making, particularly in the economic sphere, have been much greater, but are evidently outside the remit of this book.

7 All 2002 post-election conferences have debated whether Chirac's destruction of his competitors on the right parallels a silent assassin or an accomplished demolition derby driver. No firm conclusion has yet been reached.

1
Stress, strain and stability in the French party system

Alistair Cole

Introduction

Political parties do not find a natural breeding ground in France. Portrayals of French political culture point to *incivisme*, individualism and a distrust of organisations (Crozier, 1970, Pitts, 1981, Gaffney and Kolinsky, 1991). Though these representations are overly impressionistic, a powerful strand of French republicanism has denigrated political parties as divisive, fractious organisations. This is best exemplified by the Gaullist tradition, within which the political movement facilitates a direct relationship between the providential leader and the nation, but does not presume to intervene in this privileged relationship. The distrust of parties is deeply embedded in the ideology of the republican state itself, where the state represents the general will, superior to the particularistic interests represented by parties, groups and regions. There is no natural sympathy for doctrines such as pluralism which emphasise the importance of the *corps intermédiaires* between the citizen and the state.

At the same time, French political parties perform such essential functions as political mobilisation, the aggregation of interests, organising political competition, feedback, public management and political recruitment. Our aim in this chapter is to give an overview of the evolution of the French party system in the first forty-five years of the Fifth Republic, to examine the principal changes since the 1980s and to identify the underlying continuities in the party system.

The structure and evolution of the French party system

The history of French parties prior to 1940 was one of fragmentation and regional specialisation. A complex mosaic of political factions existed during the Third Republic. On the centre and right of the political spectrum, party labels either did not exist, or signified distinct political realities in different parts of the country. More centralised, coherent and disciplined parties gradually began to emerge after 1945 – in the form of the Christian democratic Mouvement Républicain Populaire (MRP) and de Gaulle's ephemeral Rassemblement du Peuple Français (RPF) – but such parties were undermined by their internal divisions and by the corrosive effects of the Fourth Republican political environment. The situation was clearer on the left: since the Tours split in 1920, there had existed two well-organised rival parties, the Section Française de l'Internationale Ouvrière (SFIO) (PS from 1969) and the PCF. Historically speaking, these fraternal enemies of the left have experienced a relationship based on mutual distrust: long periods of internecine conflict and rivalry have been punctuated by much shorter episodes of left unity (the tripartite government of 1944–47, the 'Union of the Left' of 1972–77, the Mauroy government from 1981 to 1984 and the plural-left government from 1997 to 2002).

During the Third and Fourth Republics, the fragmented structure of the party system, along with the parliamentary basis of political power, had a direct and divisive impact upon governmental stability: no single party or coalition of parties could normally gather a lasting majority of support either within the country, or within Parliament to sustain majoritarian governments. Cabinets lasted an average of twelve months in the Third Republic, and seven months in the Fourth (Williams, 1964). This pattern changed abruptly with the creation of the Fifth Republic. After an initial period of confusion from 1958 to 1962 linked to the consolidation of de Gaulle's leadership, the party system became simplified between the 1960s and early 1980s on account of the bipolarisation process, streamlining parties into two rival coalitions of the left and the right. Beginning in earnest in 1962, the height of bipolarisation occurred in the 1978 parliamentary election. The structure of the party system in 1978 was that of a bipolar quadrille. Four parties of roughly equal political strength together obtained over 90 per cent of the vote and divided voter preferences evenly between the PCF and the PS in the left coalition, and the neo-Gaullist RPR and the liberal conservative UDF on the right.

There are several explanations for this process of rationalisation. The first relates to the institutional rules of the game. From this perspective, the enhanced prestige of the presidency as modelled by de Gaulle between 1958 and 1969, the bipolarising pressures of the direct election of the president after 1962 – only two candidates go through to the decisive second ballot – and the strengthening of executive government in the constitution of the Fifth Republic all operated in favour of a rationalised party system. The institutional argument emphasises the emergence of the presidency as the linchpin of the political system from 1958 to 1986 (Wright, 1989). Consequently, the key contenders for office gradually refocused their attentions upon the presidential election: to exercise influence, parties had to form part of rival presidential coalitions. The existence of disciplined, pro-presidential coalitions controlling the National Assembly for most of the period since 1958 was in stark contrast to the Fourth Republic, where governments were short-lived and multifarious, usually based on unstable coalitions and shifting party alliances. Until 1986, parliamentary majorities were elected to support the President. At the time of writing in the summer of 2002, the argument remains pertinent that the institutional architecture of the Fifth Republic and rules of the game favour a bipolarised party system, as we shall see later on when we briefly consider the 2002 elections. In historical terms, these institutional factors were even more important. With the emergence of strong, stable governments encouraged by the 1958 constitution, parties were deprived of their former capacity for Byzantine political manoeuvre in an Assembly-dominated regime.

A separate but related institutional argument highlights the role of the two-ballot electoral system in parliamentary elections (Bartolini, 1984). By its discriminatory effects against smaller parties, the two-ballot system forced the centre parties to choose between the Gaullist-led majority and the left in order to survive. The two-ballot system also provided powerful incentives for ideologically neighbouring parties, such as the PCF and PS, to form alliances, and it stalled minor parties, such as the Greens or the FN, at important stages of their development. While the discriminating effects of the majoritarian system are obvious, the electoral system has not in itself prevented the emergence of new parties. Electoral systems can operate in variable manners according to underlying political circumstances. While the two-ballot system has penalised centre parties for most of the Fifth Republic, it strengthened centre parties in the Third Republic (Goldey, in Bogdanor and Butler, 1982). One must also therefore bear in mind specifically political factors, most notably: the political leadership of de Gaulle; the historic impact of Gaullism and its role as a federating force of the centre and right; the survival instinct of the left-wing parties; the rejuvenation of the French PS and the rebalancing of the French left in the 1970s; the talented mobilisation of prejudice by Jean-Marie Le Pen during the 1980s and 1990s.

Finally, analysis of party system evolution must also incorporate a third series of explanations based on social change: these vary from neo-Marxist arguments relating to the emergence of the social class as the salient electoral cleavage, giving a sociological underpinning to left–right bipolarisation, to sociological analysis pinpointing the emergence of the 'new middle classes' as the central groups in post-war French society, favouring the emergence of broad-based parties such as the PS (Bacot, 1976, Mendras, 1989).

Since the mid-1980s, however, the structure of the French party system has become far less neatly balanced, giving way to a more complex pattern of uncertain and changing contours. There has been an increase in the number and a change in the nature of parties and the issues processed through the political system. The bipolar contours of the French party system have been challenged by the emergence of new political issues, such as immigration, security and the environment, and the difficulties experienced by the mainstream parties in articulating these new political demands. When observing the French party system in 2002, one is struck by the increasingly manifest opposition between a formal, bipolar and structured party system as represented in national political institutions (especially the National Assembly and municipal government) and an underlying multipolar, fragmented and *contestataire* pattern of party support.

The three main developments in the past two decades have been: the emergence of a series of minor but significant parties, and in particular the breakthrough, persistence and subsequent division of the FN; the changing dynamics of factional and coalition politics, perhaps most clearly demonstrated in the decline of the PCF and the emergence of the PS as the dominant party of the left; and patterns of growing electoral instability, namely increased electoral volatility (each election since 1978 going against the incumbent government) and a certain disaffection towards traditional politics, as demonstrated in higher abstention rates and the weakening of the parties of the 1978 bipolar quadrille. Overall, while the PCF, PS, UDF and RPR obtained over 90 per cent of the vote in 1978, in 1997 and 2002 these parties obtained around 67 per cent. While there are many enduring features of party system stability, which we will explore in the final section, we are primarily concerned in the subsequent section to identify stresses and strains and to map out the important changes that occurred in the 1980s and 1990s.

Stresses and strains in the French party system

The challenge of new parties

The emergence of new parties (or the breakthrough of previously marginal parties) and the reaction of pre-existing players to these party newcomers is the most obvious development. The most significant of these parties are the Greens and Lutte Ouvrière (LO) on the left, and the FN on the right (Cole, 1998). There has been a plethora of more temporary and marginal forces that have had a lesser, but real, impact upon specific elections, or across particular issues. Such ephemeral or marginal forces as La Droite of Charles Millon, the RPF of Charles Pasqua and Philippe de Villiers, the Mouvement Ecologiste Indépendant (MEI) of Antoine Waechter, and Saint-Josse's Chasse Pêche Nature Traditions (CPNT) fit this category. These movements testify to the importance of 'flexible specialisation' (Kitschelt, 1997) as issue-specific parties rise and fall to exploit the contradictions of broader-based structures. These marginal parties invariably define themselves as being against the parties of the political establishment and perform better in 'second-order' elections fought under proportional representation (regional elections, European elections) than in the decisive parliamentary or presidential elections. In the 2002 National Assembly election, a total of 8,455 candidates presented themselves in 577 constituencies, an average of 14.65 per seat, the highest ever.[1]

By far the most significant of these parties is the FN. With around 15 per cent in the 1995 presidential, 1997 parliamentary and 1998 regional elections, the FN could already claim to be the second formation of the French right. In the first round of the 2002 presidential election, Le Pen and Mégret, the two candidates of the far right, polled almost 20 per cent between them (16.86 per cent for Le Pen, 2.34 per cent for Mégret) outpolling the combined Socialist–Communist total in mainland France.

In party system terms, the success of the FN above all harmed the mainstream right, or, at least, it did until 2002. For almost two decades, the FN damaged the cohesion of the parties of the right by posing highly divisive dilemmas of alliance strategy, organisational discipline, political philosophy and policy adaptation. The tripartite structure of the French right (RPR–UDF–FN) has been its undoing ever since the breakthrough of the FN in 1982–83. We can illustrate the corrosive effects of the far right by comparing the 1997 and the 2002 National Assembly elections. In 1997, consistent with Le Pen's desire to defeat the Juppé government by fair means or foul, the FN maintained its candidates wherever it could on the second ballot. There were 76 left–right–FN triangular contests; the left won 47, the right 29. Given the closeness of the result, the FN's tactics undoubtedly facilitated the arrival in power of the Jospin government. In the changed political circumstances of the 2002 National Assembly elections, the far-right parties were less able to influence the outcome of the mainly bipolar left–right second-round contests (Cole, 2002). With a reduced first-ballot score in 2002 (11.33 per cent for the FN, 1.10 per cent for the MNR), the FN was less able to provoke the three-way contests that had been particularly damaging for the parties of the mainstream right in 1997. In 2002 there were only 9 three-way fights, down from 76 in 1997. There were 28 duels between the FN and UMP (from 56 in 1997) and only 8 duels between the left and the FN (from 25 in 1997). The right won back 43 of the seats it had lost as a result of three-way contests in 1997 (Jaffré, 2002). The main difference between the two elections related to the level of FN support, as well as the degree of unity of the mainstream right parties (low in 1997, high in 2002), a theme to which we shall return.

The real impact of the FN lay in its agenda-setting role. At its height, the FN forced issues such as immigration and security onto the political agenda and ensured that they remained there. If primarily detrimental to the mainstream right in party system terms, the FN had a corrosive impact on all existing parties, especially insofar as it skilfully exploited the theme of the political corruption of the pro-system parties, the RPR, UDF and PS.

From faction to party

One of the most striking developments of the 1980s and 1990s was the rise of internal factionalism in almost all major political formations. There is nothing new about party factionalism. Divisions within parties were inherent in the parliamentary organisation of the Third and Fourth Republics. In the Fifth Republic, the modern PS was reconstructed after 1971 as an explicitly factional party, with the right to free expression of factions (*courants*) guaranteed within the party's constitution. Initially the preserve of the PS, in the 1990s party factionalism became as characteristic of the RPR and UDF, not to say the PCF and FN.

The most intractable factional conflicts arise in relation to personal rivalries, political strategy and policy differences. Personal rivalries testify in part to the normal contradictions of human agency. They also respond to precise institutional incentives in the Fifth Republic, to the pivotal role of the presidential election and, recently, to the organisational incentives for ambitious politicians to stand as a candidate for the presidency.[2] Even more than personal rivalries, however, during the 1990s the main parties, and especially the RPR and UDF, were divided on the question of alliance strategy and in relation to specific policy issues such as Europe and immigration. Though there has been a narrowing of distinctive economic policy positions between the main parties, issues such as European integration and immigration have divided existing parties and cut across traditional lines of political cleavage. The neo-Gaullist RPR was divided over European integration; the UDF was split wide open by the question of immigration and alliances with the FN.

It is sometimes difficult to distinguish between personal rivalries, questions of political strategy and policy differences. During the late 1990s and into the new century, the existence of a myriad of structures fronted by innumerable second-rank party leaders – Madelin's DL, Bayrou's UDF, Pasqua's RPF, de Villiers' MPF, Chevènement's Mouvement des Citoyens (MdC), Baylet's PRG and so on – increased the impression of permanent, personality-based competition, even though each political formation occupied a distinctive position along the political spectrum and was engaged in a relationship with one or more of the main political families.

If the first twenty years of the Fifth Republic were characterised by a tendency for the emergence of broad-based coalitions, the last decade of the twentieth century sorely tested the capacity for *rassemblement* of the main political formations. Each of the main party families experienced a schism within its midst, as there was a general move from faction to party. This move occurred within the PS (the creation by Jean-Pierre Chevènement of the MdC), the RPR (the creation of the RPF by Pasqua) the UDF (the breakaway of Alain Madelin and DL) and even the FN (the split of December 1998 and the creation of Mégret's MNR). Paradoxically, the pitiful performance of all of these factions-*cum*-parties has reinforced the centrality of party and of the main political families. While factions can often exercise influence within a party, once outside of the party fold their influence is either negative and short-lived (as in the case of Chevènement in the 2002 presidential election) or non-existent. As the case of DL and Madelin's deal with the UMP demonstrates, ambitious politicians need to operate within one of the main party organisations.

The diminishing legitimacy of party politics?

Various converging forces allow us to pose the diminishing legitimacy of party politics as a central research question. However we interpret the success of the FN – as a modern variant of Fascism or as something else – the persistence at a high level of support for two decades of a populist far-right party reveals an ambivalent attitude towards existing political supply, and indirectly towards liberal democracy, among a significant minority of voters. The inadequacy of political supply can be measured in other ways, most notably by the diminishing support for representatives of the two main political families, PS and RPR, and by growing rates of abstention. In the 1994 European election, the two leading lists were reduced to a combined total of 40 per cent; in 1999, this figure was even lower. On the first round of the 1995 presidential election, the two leading candidates (Jospin and Chirac) polled just over 40 per cent of the vote, a far weaker proportion than in any other presidential election (Cole, 1995). In 2002, the two leading candidates (Chirac and Le Pen) did even worse: with 36.74 per cent of voters and barely over a quarter of those registered to vote (Cole, 2002)

France's historic political families were each challenged on the first round of the 2002 presidential election, at which Jean-Marie Le Pen won through to the second-ballot run-off against Jacques Chirac. Communists, Socialists, Gaullists, Liberals, Christian Democrats, even Greens performed under par. None of these candidates did as well as they might have expected and many voters were dissatisfied with all of them. The strong performance of the far-left and far-right candidates, the high abstention rate (at 28.30 per cent, a record in any presidential election) and the general dispersion of votes to candidates not generally considered to be genuine presidential contenders such as St Josse, Chevènement and others were all part of this trend. Chirac and Jospin, the prematurely 'preordained' second-round contenders, obtained only just over one-third of votes and one-quarter of registered voters between them.

The corollary of this is the development of parties and movements which have defined themselves against the existing political elites, such as the FN, but also LO and the Ligue Communiste Révolutionnaire (LCR). While these forces are marginal in the bipolar party system, they demonstrate the survival of a tradition of radical politics on the far left and extreme right, potently recalled on the first-round of the 2002 presidential election when the far left (10.44 per cent) and extreme right (19.20 per cent) captured almost one-third of votes between them. The persistence and strengthening of the parties of the far left and especially of the extreme right articulates a profound disillusion towards the 'parties of government' of all complexions on behalf of the popular (working- and lower-middle-class) electorate. More than ever, the Le Pen electorate in 2002 was over representative of those suffering from the most acute sentiments of economic and physical insecurity. Le Pen was the favoured choice of the lower-middle classes (31.9 per cent) and of workers (26.1 per cent), far outdistancing both the Socialist Jospin and the Communist Hue in working-class support.[3] The French electorate's vote on 21 April 2002 suggested an unresolved tension between French identity, the implicit promises of French citizenship (including the economic promises) and the uncertainty provoked by Europeanisation, globalisation and an unpredictable future.

A more general cause of fragility lies in the pessimism of public opinion, which has lacked faith in political parties, broadly defined, to resolve intractable policy problems. This has tormented each government since 1981. After the economic miracle of *les trente glorieuses* (1945–74), political parties in government have proved incapable of dealing with the perception of prolonged economic crisis. In comparative European perspective, the reality of the French crisis is debatable, but the perception of economic malaise has had a destabilising effect on all incumbent governments since 1974. The real yardstick against which governments have been measured – unemployment – has proved to be particularly intractable. Since 1981, every single decisive election (presidential or parliamentary) has gone against the incumbent government, in a manner that suggests the electorate's dissatisfaction with the performance of successive governments.

This lesson was repeated in 2002, when the Prime Minister of the outgoing plural-left government failed even to reach the second round of the presidential election. In a very real sense, the 2002 campaign was fought as a single-issue campaign, but this time over the issue of insecurity rather than unemployment. Events and campaign strategies converged to define the agenda. A concatenation of events – the Middle-East crisis, the aftermath of 11 September, and above all a set of particularly shocking murders and violent disorders in France itself – set the agenda for the two months of the 2002 campaign proper. In all other recent election campaigns, the theme of unemployment has emerged as the principal preoccupation of voters. Not so in 2002 – SOFRES polls demonstrated that from January 2000 insecurity had replaced unemployment as the principal subject of concern of French voters (Gerstlé, 2002). To some extent, Jospin was a victim of his own success in bringing down unemployment rates. The unemployment problem was perceived as less acute than in the past, surpassed in importance by the ubiquitous theme of insecurity, much less favourable political terrain for a centre-left candidate.

Political variables are equally pertinent in explaining dissatisfaction with existing political supply. For over two decades, the problem of corruption has been at the top of the political agenda (Mény, 1992). There is some evidence of endemic political corruption, and much media speculation around the subject. Political corruption has centred on the operation of local and regional government, the imperatives of party finance and organisation, the attribution of public markets and personal enrichment. In the classic schema, political parties have received occult commissions for attributing public markets; any firm must factor the party commission into its bid. Cases of personal enrichment are rarer, but there are several celebrated examples to demonstrate the enduring appeal of avarice (Evans, 2002). The problem of corruption is a complex one. Most corruption cases have involved raising finance to fight prohibitively expensive election campaigns. While corruption has probably always existed, new incentives have been provided by the decentralisation laws, which leave important powers of planning and the attribution of public markets in the hands of mayors and their *adjoints*. More cases of corruption have been uncovered as a result of the increased activism of the *juges d'instruction* (investigating magistrates). The negative political fallout of any hint of corruption is such that incumbent ministers, such as Strauss-Kahn in November 1999, invariably resign if they are investigated by the *juge d'instruction*, even before any formal allegations have been made.

The French party system was shaken to its core by problems of political, institutional and ideological coherence throughout the 1980s and 1990s. Party fragility was real, but there were also countervailing forces in play. In the ensuing section, we identify three underlying causes of party continuity: institutional incentives, flexible and adaptable party organisations, and the absorptive capacity of the main French political traditions.

Underlying continuities in the French party system

The prestige of the presidency, and the majoritarian effects of the two-ballot electoral system are potent institutional variables. In a formal sense, at least, the bipolar party system remains a structural variant of the rules of political competition in the Fifth Republic, though we observe an ever-increasing gap between formal bipolarity, on the one hand, and the underlying fragmentation of electoral choice on the other.

The electoral series of 2002 defied many basic bipolar rules of the Fifth Republic. The first round of the presidential election did not produce a run-off between left and right. The second round was a quasi-referendum for democracy that produced the largest victory for any candidate in any free election in recent memory. The changing role of the presidential election points to the danger of attributing eternal features to the operation of particular political institutions. Rather than supporting from the first round the candidate they ideally want to see elected president (as in the traditional slogan, 'Choose on the first round, eliminate on the second'), voters have begun treating the first round of the presidential election as a 'second-order' election, expressing a preference in the same way they would in a regional or European election. That the 2002 campaign was closed rather than open encouraged such a fragmentation of support. The belief that the first round did not count encouraged voters to support minor or extreme candidates, either through obstinacy or as a way of influencing the agenda of the candidate eventually elected President. There was certainly a lot of choice. With sixteen candidates in competition in 2002, the first round played the role of a non-decisive proportional election, with the bulk of voters firmly believing in a Chirac–Jospin run-off. That this outcome did not materialise deprived the second round of its usual left–right configuration.

On 9 and 16 June 2002, the French party system returned to something resembling its normal bipolar state. Two parties – the UMP on the right and the PS on the left – occupied almost 90 per cent of parliamentary seats, a far greater measure of bipartisanship than in recent elections. The hegemony of the UMP on the right was matched by a domination of the Socialists on the left, in votes as well as in seats. The far-left parties (2.83 per cent) were squeezed by the movement to use usefully for the Socialists, as was the PRep,[4] with just over 1 per cent, and, to a lesser extent, the Greens (4.5 per cent) and the Communists (4.8 per cent). The far right lost one-third of its electorate by comparison to 21 April (11.33 per cent for the FN, 1.10 per cent for the MNR) and was unable to repeat its spoiling tactics of 1997, when it had helped the left win the election. In elections fought under the single-member constituency two-ballot system, the four parties of the 1978 bipolar quadrille (PCF, PS,

RPR and UDF) have continued to dominate parliamentary representation. Only one deputy (out of 577) was elected in 1997 from outside the rival electoral coalitions and none in 2002. Because the vast bulk of parliamentary seats are confined to members of the left or right electoral coalitions, the ability to form alliances is crucial. Its isolation has deprived the FN of major national parliamentary representation except in the 1986–88 legislature.

In addition to the institutional underpinnings of the Fifth Republic, the cohesion of the French party system also rests upon the bedrock of municipal office (as witnessed by the longevity of the generation of mayors first elected in 1977) which has itself been transformed into an arena of (mainly) bipolar political competition. The bipolar basis of political competition in the Fifth Republic has spilled over into local municipal and cantonal elections fought under the two-ballot system; since 1977, municipal elections in the large cities have by and large been contested by rival left and right lists, a pattern confirmed in 2001.

Structural explanations, then, are important in identifying how the institutional rules of the game have shaped important aspects of party competition in the Fifth Republic. But they do not tell the whole story. They have difficulty in distinguishing between different types of party supply and they underplay the dynamic and unpredictable qualities of the party system, as demonstrated by the breakthrough of new parties and the adaptation of older ones.

The underlying stability of the French party system also rests upon flexible and adaptable party organisations. This is a double-edged sword. On the one hand, French citizens appear more reluctant to join party organisations than their northern European counterparts. Mass membership parties of the German or Scandinavian variety are rare; only the Gaullists and Communists have presented examples of mass parties and both are a shadow of their former selves. But this relative weakness of party organisation *stricto sensu* has certain advantages. The weakness of organic links with the trade unions or business, for example, has allowed French parties to reposition themselves more convincingly than their counterparts in certain other European countries. More generally, flexible organisational forms are well adapted to the particular structure of incentives in the French polity, focused on the exercise of power in municipal government as well as on the conquest of decisive (presidential and parliamentary) elections. Here we would again emphasise the importance of municipal government. For certain parties (PS, UDF), municipal government has served as a long-term substitute for a powerful party organisation; for others (PCF, RPR), municipal government has underpinned the illusion of a genuine party organisation. Once the municipal support is removed, the organisational chimera is laid bare. Even 'strong' parties, such as the PCF and RPR, rely more on the logistical infrastructure provided by municipal government than on their formal party organisations. This is demonstrated in numerous former Communist municipalities such as Le Havre where the PCF organisation has been severely damaged following the loss of the municipal council.

The weakness of party organisation is not necessarily synonymous with a lack of organisational efficiency. The renewal of the French Socialist Party in the 1970s was predicated upon an open dialogue with voluntary associations much more than upon a revival in party membership. Their cross-cutting membership served the interests both of the party and supportive voluntary associations, facilitating the exchange of policy ideas and personnel. In their own very different ways, the Greens and the FN learned a similar lesson in the 1990s. The organisational capacity of the French Greens has been strengthened by the strong links maintained with voluntary associations (not just environmental groups). In the case of the FN in Orange and Toulon, the far-right municipalities created a network of parallel associations under the tutelage of the town hall (McAna, 2001), somewhat along the lines of traditional Communist-run municipalities. These practices have positive and negative characteristics. They can be interpreted as embodying new forms of political participation. They can also contribute to a lack of transparent governance – municipally financed associations are sometimes little more than vehicles for the exercise of informal partisan influence.

Lastly, the robust character of the main political traditions principally underpins the stability of the French party system: French-style communism, socialism, liberal conservatism, Gaullism, Christian democracy and national populism. They can each trace their lineage back to the Second World War or much earlier, and have each demonstrated the capacity to reinvent themselves to cope with changing circumstances and political incentives. Even when threatened by the rise of new parties and by the manifestations of disaffection with existing political supply, over time the French party system has proved its absorptive capacity. The 'absorptive capacity' (Hanley, 1999a) of the French party system is particularly marked on the left. This is demonstrated by the ability of the PS to transcend internal divisions and changing ideological fashions, and retain its dominant position on the left. The emergence of the Greens as a post-materialist, new-politics party forces us to modify this appreciation, but only partially: the three Green deputies are entirely dependent on alliances with the PS.

It is rather more difficult to apply the thesis of the absorptive capacity of the party system to the French right. This has been hampered by its divisions ever since the decline of historic Gaullism and the creation of the RPR and UDF in the 1970s. In addition, the rise of the FN from 1983 onwards has posed acute dilemmas of alliance strategy and political positioning for the parties of the mainstream right. The FN was a problem because the right was divided, hence too weak to ignore the far-right movement. The failure of the RPR to stamp its authority on the French right during the 1990s was all the more damaging in that a Gaullist President occupied the Elysée palace from 1995 onwards.

In one important respect, the 2002 electoral series represents a return to the sources of the Fifth Republic. Once re-elected President, Chirac imposed the creation of the UMP as a presidential platform to which all existing right-wing parties would have to subscribe. UMP candidates had to accept to sit in the same parliamentary group in the National Assembly, to support the President and to participate in the creation of a vast new party of the French right in autumn 2002. A committee containing representatives of the three main pro-Chirac parties (RPR, DL, part of the UDF) but heavily weighted in favour of the RPR distributed UMP candidacies in the parliamentary contest. François Bayrou led the resistance of a centrist rump, retaining the title UDF and pledging critical support for Jacques Chirac. The presidential party strategy worked exactly to plan. This strategy involved not just providing a majority for the President, but also engineering a realignment within the right in favour of the RPR, to sweeten the pill of the dissolution of the Gaullist movement into a much broader conservative party.

The 2002 elections represented the first time since 1973 that there had not been at least two major parties on the French right. Right-wing unity paid off handsomely. The UMP won an overall majority (399 seats out of 577), only the third time in the history of the Fifth Republic that a single political formation has held an overall majority.[5] In 2002, the UMP formula masked a new domination of the RPR. With the election of an overall majority for a single formation of the mainstream right, the French party system again resembles in part that of the 1960s, whereby a dominant presidential rally is flanked by a small centre party, a 'reservist' force of the right whose existence is barely tolerated.

However, the capacity for absorption is limited to the formal party system, as measured in decisive elections fought under the second-ballot system. It can account neither for fragmentation of party support in second-order elections, or for the evidence of dissatisfaction with political supply and demand that we uncovered in the previous section. One explanation of party persistence might be that parties gives expression to deeply embedded cleavages. Joachim Schild (2000) summarises the principal cleavages in French politics as being positional (left versus right), existential (religious versus lay), ideological (cultural liberalism versus authoritarianism), socio-economic (class conflict) and issue-based. We have argued elsewhere that these *variables lourdes* have lessened in significance since the early 1980s (Cole, 1998). The left/right cleavage remains pertinent in certain respects, but its mobilising force has been diminished as a result of the Mitterrand presidency and the decline of the PCF. The religious-lay cleavage retains the capacity to mobilise opinion on specific issues such as the defence of, or opposition to *écoles libres*, but the relation of cause and effect is uncertain. We demonstrated above that ideological cleavages can cut across party lines, as can those based on issues. Voting patterns corresponded far less neatly to social class identities in 2002 than they did in 1978 (Cole, 2002, Capdevielle *et al.*, 1981, Perrineau and Ysmal, 1998) . The electoral volatility of the new middle classes and the strengthening of the FN among the working- and lower-middle-class electorate explain these cross-cutting pressures. Moreover, as the issue of European integration demonstrates, party structures do not always correspond neatly to divisions over issues or ideologies. Traditional cleavages have clearly lessened in importance, as France has undergone multiple internal and external changes, but they remain as cognitive maps within the collective memory. While there is no easy relationship between political attitudes and behaviour, partisan lenses can provide one way of comprehending and reinterpreting a changing environment.

Conclusion

The decline of parties is not terminal; it is contingent on underlying political and economic circumstances. We can draw three main conclusions from the partially contradictory evidence presented in this chapter. Party system change is the first one. That the French party system has undergone strains and stresses is obvious. The challenge of new parties, the decline of certain older parties (notably the PCF) and the limited capacity of existing parties to articulate new political issues have had an impact on the number and the nature of parties. The issues processed by the party system reflect a changing policy agenda. On the one hand, new political issues such as the environment and immigration have forced their way onto the agenda. On the other, governmental realism and the end of 'lyrical illusions' associated with the abandoning of a certain type of left project under Mitterrand have refocused elite attention on public policies, rather than competing visions of society. Partisan discourses have not proceeded apace. The resulting distance between political discourse and policy achievement has created disillusion and demobilisation among many French voters.

This is one of the most convincing explanations of the public disaffection with political parties during the 1980s and 1990s. This aspect of the crisis of party politics is more apparent in France than in comparable countries. Because partisan discourses are deeply embedded in French republican political culture, public expectations have been higher and the electoral retribution for failure has been harsher. This is the specifically French dimension of a broader pan-European phenomenon, whereby established party families have had to adapt to a series of internal and external shocks over the past two decades, cognisance of which has preconditioned their ability to survive and prosper.

Indeed, this absorptive capacity of the main political families modifies the first conclusion. While the traditional parties were at times unnerved by the new-issue politics, the resulting new parties such as the Greens and the FN failed to replace the existing players. The Greens owe their political survival to the PS. Over a long period, the FN has articulated a powerful strand within French public opinion and indirectly influenced the political agenda. Without allies, however, it has failed to translate its electoral potential into full political capital and has lacked second-round credibility, both in the 2002 presidential contest (where Le Pen polled 17.85 per cent against 82.15 per cent for Chirac) and in parliamentary elections, where the FN usually fails to hold on to its first-round vote in those rare constituencies where it can fight the second.

The existing parties absorbed the fluid centre of gravity of French politics. They occupied a strategically and organisationally privileged position to adapt to and interpret a changing internal and external political agenda. The same process transformed the leading parties, and especially the PS and RPR, in important respects both by the exercise of domestic power and by the changing European and international policy agenda.

We conclude thereby in the persistence of a rather artificial bipolar multipartism, the left and right coalitions functioning most effectively when one party assumes a dominant role – the Gaullists from 1962 to 1974, and the PS from 1981 onwards. This leads naturally to our third and final conclusion. To the extent that two blocs provide the mainstay of political competition across most European countries, French party competition has moved closer to the mainstream European model. As in most West European democracies, the mainstay of political competition is between left of centre and right of centre parties and their respective political allies. The pattern of party fragility in the 1980s and 1990s was not specific to France but in many respects formed part of a pan-European adjustment to the end of post-war prosperity. The form that such fragility took in France – the rise of the extreme right, increased abstention, a weakening of party identity – was nationally specific, but similar phenomena could be observed in comparable countries such as Italy (where the entire post-war party system collapsed under the weight of political corruption), Germany (where the 'new politics' prospered on the failure of traditional social democracy) and Britain (where the electoral swing of 1997 broke all post-war records).

To achieve a just measure of the balance between party stress and party stability, we can learn from longitudinal historical and cross-national comparison. Longitudinal comparison suggests that there is no real equivalent to the party system stress of the Fourth Republic in the late 1940s, when the PCF and RPF – forces openly antagonistic to the regime – obtained the support of half of the voters. We must not lose a sense of perspective. From a cross-national perspective, while allowing for nationally tinted referential frames and for the discursive traditions of the main political traditions, we observe that the pressures on the French party system are broadly consistent with those observed elsewhere.

Notes

1 The inflated number of candidates in 2002 was mainly attributable to the rules on campaign finance, which allow parties to obtain state funding on the condition that they field candidates in at least 50 constituencies.
2 Candidates obtaining the signatures of at least 500 elected officials (mainly rural mayors) are eligible to stand for the presidency and participate in the official campaign, which gives them free media coverage. Candidates with over 5 per cent of valid votes get their campaign expenses reimbursed, up to a limit of 7,460,000 euros.
3 Figures from the Louis Harris–*Libération*–AOL post-election poll published in *Libération*, 23 April 2002.
4 This was the name given to Chevènement's presidential rally. Pro-Chevènement candidates stood in over 400 constituencies in the parliamentary election, but fared poorly.
5 The Gaullists from 1968 to 1973 and the Socialists from 1981 to 1986 are the other examples.

I

THE LEFT

2
The French Communist Party: from revolution to reform

David S. Bell

Introduction

Under the Fourth and Fifth Republics the Parti Communiste Français (PCF) was one of the most important forces in the shaping of the party system. This status only began to diminish in the 1980s with the victory of François Mitterrand in the presidential and legislative elections of 1981. Although the Communist Party is a shadow of its former self, the shape of the party system and its behaviour over the post-war period is explicable only in terms of the PCF's historical comportment. No discussion of the French party system is possible without taking into account the size and nature of what was, for most of the cold war, the biggest Communist Party in the western world.

French Communism has had both negative and positive effects on the party system. It was, on the one hand, the great party of the left dominating the parts of society which in other western countries were social democratic. It was tightly organised and ran unions, societies and associations which it used for its own purposes and it had a press and publishing empire of some size. It is not surprising that this power in the service of a revolutionary cause provoked hostility and even fear in both its allies and opponents. In the Fourth Republic, this negative influence kept the centre parties together, in the Fifth Republic, it helped to consolidate the conservative right into alliance. It was very difficult to ignore the Communist presence in most social areas until the Party's influence began to decline in the 1980s. By the same token the waning of the Communist Party's influence in the 1980s had ramifications across the party system, reducing confrontation, enabling realignments but also abandoning part of the extreme-left spectrum. At the same time, there were social changes which undermined the sense of the working class on which the Party depended. This was the start of the transition from a society of 40 per cent 'workers' in 1950 (broadly defined) to one of

27 per cent 'workers' in 2001 [1] and in addition to a working class which was fragmented, better educated and part of which took on middle-class aspirations. The Party did not comprehend these changes, and for a long time acted as if they had not happened.

The PCF continued its 'saw tooth' decline throughout the 1980s and 1990s. In the presidential elections of 1995 the Party's leader Robert Hue polled only 8.7 per cent to the Socialist candidate's 23.2 per cent. After the 1995 elections, a coalition of the left, led by the Socialists, was put together and the Communists participated along with the ecologists, the MdC, the left Radicals and some independents. In the 1997 snap general elections, the Communist Party's candidates polled just fewer than 10 per cent and won 34 seats, dwarfed by the Socialists' 242. In purely electoral terms, the Party's decline continued over the Parliament and by 2002 it was slipping into irrelevance. Its candidate Robert Hue polled a marginal 3.37 per cent in the presidential elections (its worst ever) not qualifying for reimbursement of his expenses and coming below two of the three Trotskyite candidates, Arlette Laguiller and Olivier Besancenot. French Communism only kept an edge through its force in local government although that had been further weakened the previous year. This local implantation explains its slight revival to 4.7 per cent of the vote in the ensuing general elections in June. However, it lost seats (including that of its president Robert Hue) and with 21 deputies crossed the threshold enabling it to form a parliamentary group by only one seat.

The three aspects of Communism

There are three aspects of the Party relevant to what it currently is in the French party system and from which it has to break free. First, the PCF was devoted to the Soviet Union where the 'Revolution' had taken place and to the USSR which was building Socialism. Even if 'mistakes' had been made on the way, the belief was that the elimination of private property and the central planning of the economy was the route to Socialism ('Just because there were spots on the sun, it did not mean there was no sun'). Hence, in France, Communism was seen as the *parti de l'étranger* and as promoting Socialist society with its queues for essentials, Gulag and nomenklatura (Duhamel and Jaffré, 1997).

Second, the Party was a 'party of a different sort'. It was the framework for the new society and the advance guard of the Revolution. Unity was at a premium enforced through 'democratic centralism', which can be summed up as obedience in the ranks and militaristic top-down command. The structure of the Party, divided into cells at the base and supervised by superior organs, facilitated discipline. But the main force in the Party was Lenin's 'professional revolutionaries', the employees of the Party dedicated full-time to its organisation. It was the 'bolshevik' core of the Party that enabled the Communists to magnify their influence in unions or in institutions which had been infiltrated.

But Communist Party voluntary activists and fronts, organised professionally, disciplined and spread throughout 'capitalist society', have also been one of the Party's resources. It claimed to have 275,000 members at its 29th Congress though the number could be as low as 100,000.[2] Yet the proportion of members under 30 has also fallen from 25 per cent in 1978 to 10 per cent in 2001 and the percentage of workers dropped from 47 per cent to 31 per cent over the same time. The Party newspaper *L'Humanité*, once part of a large publishing group and essential to activists, has had to seek private capital to keep going.[3] Of the other satellite front organisations very little remains. Only the Confédération Générale des Travailleurs (CGT) is a force to be reckoned with but that trade union is also in a tense relationship with the Party hierarchy: if the CGT is to revive, it needs to free itself from the Party but the Party needs the CGT to prop up its own flagging influence.

Third, the Communist Party had commandeered the cultural high ground of revolutionary Marxism and had imposed its own brand, Marxism-Leninism, as the orthodox version. By the 1990s, Marxism itself had become a negative factor in the Party's repertoire and, of course, linked with the 'Stalinism' of its recent past, something which, in its constant use of 'Communist', it continues to remind people of (Duhamel and Jaffré, 1997). Robert Hue's (1995) exercise in homiletic excess, *Communisme, La Mutation*, does not distinguish the new Party from the old one in a convincing way. In his opening to the 29th Party congress in 1996, Hue asserted that the roots of the Party are in the French Revolution of 1789 and that the PCF represents a long and continuous French tradition dating back to that time. But, of course, the Party has in its ranks people who remain devoted to the 'Communist idea' and they would be demoralised by any change of name.[4] Hence, to some extent the Party has returned to the young Marx to open up themes of justice and rights and of the once rejected 'humanism'. But the Communist Party remains a critic of 'capitalism' (though now referred to as 'market totalitarianism' or some similar term) and the ills of society are attributed to rampant 'neo-liberalism'.

Un passé qui ne passe pas

In Western Europe, the principal line of cleavage has been between left and right in the post-war period (Gallagher *et al.*, 2001: 95). Coalitions of parties have lined up facing each other across this divide. The norm has been a bipolar system with the main struggle for the centre ground – the middle or 'floating voter' – and a centripetal dynamic has been evident over the long term. It was the intrusion of the big Communist Party into the French Party system that frustrated any such bipolar development in the Fourth Republic (though not to the same extent as in Italy).

The Communist Party emerged from the war benefiting from the legitimacy of its part in the Resistance. At the Liberation, the French Communist Party was one of the big three political parties along with the Christian democratic MRP and the Socialist SFIO. It came to be seen as a national party: as patriotic, reformist and 'modern' while its rivals – notably the Socialists – were afflicted with a 'cultural cringe' when faced by the PCF's penetration of working-class milieux. By the October 1946 general elections, the PCF was the biggest party in the system polling 26.2 per cent to the Christian democratic MRP's 25.9 per cent and the SFIO's 21.1 per cent. It had participated in governments under de Gaulle and its leader, Maurice Thorez, made a serious bid to become Premier, falling short by only 51 votes. But the onset of the cold war meant that by 1947 the principal cleavage in the party system divided the Communists from the Socialists. It pushed the Socialists into alignment with the MRP and with other moderate and centrist groups willing to participate in a centrist programme and the Communist Party's self-imposed isolation became a ghetto from which it could not escape.

This 'polarised pluralist' format came into being and prevailed through the Fourth Republic until 1958 (Sartori, 1976). Parties which supported the Fourth Republic in the centre were attacked by anti-system parties from the two sides of the ideological continuum but the anti-system parties were kept out of power and had no incentive to moderate their attacks or to accommodate the political mainstream. Parties in the centre found it increasingly difficult to provide solutions to contemporary problems and the *régime* fell when faced by the Algerian crisis of 1958.

Alliance politics

For the French Communists, the main change in strategy was in 1956 with Khrushchev's 'parliamentary road to Socialism' in Western Europe: western parties were to use elections to gain power in the European situation that was then unpropitious for revolution. However, there was a tension at the heart of the strategy that the PCF never overcame. It was necessary to downplay the 'Revolutionary' aspirations (which were the Party's *raison d'être*) in order to find allies and get elected as part of a coalition.

However, communist parties sought allies and for the PCF this meant the SFIO had to be wooed. French Communists, still the principal party in France, and attracting one voter in four after the 1956 general elections, made overtures to the Socialists (Rioux, 1987: 260). However, the Communists remained excluded from the majority and their position in the ghetto was confirmed after the Soviet repression of the Hungarian uprising in November 1956. Communists persisted in seeking an alliance with the Socialists, but their reintegration into the party system was postponed (Schlesinger and Schlesinger, 2000: 136–7).

It was the return of de Gaulle to power in 1958 that transformed the party system. De Gaulle's politics also gave the Communist Party the real opportunity to promote the coalition of the left it had demanded after 1956. What the Communists wanted was an alliance of the left, of the Communists, Socialists and Radicals along with whatever other small parties could be persuaded to join. Communist leaders no doubt assumed that they would dominate it. This domination might not be obvious, and non-communist politicians would be the facade, but the Party's size in vote and membership, its resources and its command of the unions and its political resources would guarantee its authority over the left.

Potential allies feared the same thing and there began a long 'hesitation waltz' as non-communist parties sought a way of managing the PCF within an alliance. Matters were, however, hastened by de Gaulle's creation of a modern conservative party federating the parties on the right and forcing the small centre parties to chose between the right and the left. De Gaulle's politics started to move the party system to a bipolar one of confrontation between government and opposition with the centre divided between them. By the end of the 1960s the centre was already part of one or other of the coalitions.

As the 1960s and 1970s progressed, the choice between de Gaulle's conservative coalition and the left along with the Communists became sharper and was seen by many as one of choice of society and *régime*. But a new factor in allocating dominance on the left came from outside the Communist Party (and the Socialist Party) and that was presidential politics. In the competition for the presidency, the Communist Party could not hope to win although a candidate from the left might win with their support. Party leaders decided to avert a humiliation at the polls by not putting up their own candidate and chose instead to participate in (and legitimise) the presidency by supporting the independent Mitterrand. As the big organised party of the left it experienced an influx of members from the 1965 presidentials and it had taken an important step towards its objective of creating a coalition of the left. Under the leadership of Thorez, then Waldeck Rochet and then Marchais, the PCF's revolutionary ardour was muted and they bargained with the main representative of the non-communist left whom they helped to build up as a viable interlocutor.

However, despite the onset of bipolarisation between 1965 and 1973, there was the possibility that it could be rejected by the left and the centre as much as by the conservatives. On the Communist side, the changes made little difference and the search for an alliance around a joint platform continued. For the Communist Party, the apotheosis of the 'Union of the Left' around a 'Common Programme' came in June 1972. This platform was extensive and unique in French party politics, which was more used to coalition bargaining between leaders in the National Assembly than to manifesto politics. French politics polarised, and the fight, or so it seemed, for the future of the Republic became more divisive and also more mobilising.

What happened after 1972 and the conclusion of the 'Common Programme' was unanticipated: it was the Socialist Party which became the beneficiary of the coalition's advances. Within the left, the Communist Party lost its preponderance as the Socialists gained members and voters. The presidential elections of 1974 after President Pompidou's death were revelatory. In these, the Communist Party played an exemplary role supporting the Socialist candidate Mitterrand but making few demands. After that election, almost all the benefits went to the Socialist Party which began its rise in the polls and Socialists took the major winnings of the left at by-elections. This was a situation to which the Communist Party did not find a response. It started an open quarrel with the Socialists, which ended only in 1994 with a new leader.

The year 1977, it transpired, was a crucial year for the development of the party system and the Communist Party's place in it. Local elections held in March that year saw a further bipolarisation of the party system into left and right coalitions. Old 'Third Force' alliances that had subsisted between Socialists and centrists (against both the Gaullists and Communists) were finally ended and replaced in most cases by Communist/Socialist/Radical 'Union of the Left' alliances. There were 204 of these 'Union of the Left' lists in the 221 large cities and they won 156 of these contests. In the big cities (over 30,000) the Communists gained 22 and held in total 72 to the Socialists' 81. From the Communist perspective, the local elections provided tangible gains for the first time in the alliance and the number of Communist councillors in large cities almost doubled from 1,560 to 2,306.

But the worm had entered the bud. Communists were forced to share power even in their strongholds and the local victories pushed power down from the central Party apparatus to mayors. At its origins, Communist politics had gone counter to the trend of localised politics typical of France and instituted a central control of party politics. In 1988, panic measures taken in response to the collapse of its vote in the presidentials promoted local figures but made it more vulnerable to dissidents. In addition, its need to keep local power in order to survive as a national party bound them securely to the Socialist Party. These factors were to become crucial in the comportment of the PCF in the 1990s as the demands of the alliance pulled it in one (governmental) direction away from its revolutionary roots and militant supporters.

Anti-system to system politics

In September 1977 the negotiations to update the 'Common Programme' failed and the alliance was formally ended. As in the past, the PCF coupled a domestic hard-line with international solidarity with the USSR. In the development of the party system, 1978 was the year in which the role of dominant party on the left passed from the Communist Party to the Socialist Party. Thus in 1968 the Gaullist Party had been the dominant party in the system and had outdistanced the Communists by 46 per cent to the PCF's 20 per cent. In 1978, during the bipolar quadrille party system, there was a left–right division with each camp split in half. In the 1981 election, the Socialists polled 37.8 per cent, the neo-Gaullists 20.9 per cent and the Communists took 16 per cent. A Socialist and Left Radical total of 285 seats gave them an absolute majority, but the PCF's 44 seats did not give it leverage. Whether 1978 was the start of the decline or not, the process of sliding to the margins was inherent in the party strategy of 1978.

Over the rest of the 1980s and until the collapse of the USSR the Party's position steadily worsened. When Mitterrand won the presidency, the Party acceded to the demand to support the Socialist Party and, constrained by its own supporters, it took the four minor ministerial posts offered. However, it determined to make use of its position in government to associate itself with successes and criticise failures. This ambiguous tactic proved no more attractive than outright criticism and its slide continued. In 1983–84 it was even rivalled as a protest party by the FN. By 1984, the Party had decided that criticism of the Socialists from outside the coalition was the best strategy and it left government.

Communist hostility to the Socialists was unremitting from then until 1994. However, in terms of relevance, the PCF was close to slipping out of the party system (Sartori, 1976: 122–3). Yet, because the Party was hostile to the 'reformist' Socialist Party, and clung to the old certainties of state socialism, it was unable to capitalise on a probably unrepeatable opportunity. In 1993 the French Socialist Party collapsed. There were indications that the former Socialist space was open to conquest. One of these was the rise of the ecologists who were credited with 20 per cent in the opinion polls at one point (though their disorganisation prevented them from capitalising on this) and Le Pen also picked up left-wing support (Perrineau, 1997). A 'Downsian' reaction by the Party moving to the centre would, at this point, have led to a change in ideology to compete for the available votes.

As it was the PCF decided to stand pat. All the same between 1992 and 1994 the Communist Party survived. It reoriented its message using the Maastricht referendum of 1992 to a nationalist and patriotic one defending the working people of France from the perceived European threat. Communism in France had always emphasised its patriotism, affiliating itself with the national spirit and with the nation (Lavabre, 1994). In the past the Communist Party actively worked to bring together a mixture of working-class, peasant and intellectual communities to give them a common identity. What this means is that the PCF has taken up the defence of social and welfare rights against the inroads of an 'aggressive neo-liberalism'. This is the point at which Communist Euroscepticism comes to the fore and joins the Party's long-standing anti-capitalism. Europe is, in this view, the vehicle for a market-oriented liberalisation of France and for the dismantling of the welfare state. Yet they are limited by the alliance with the Socialist Party and by competition from the extreme left (and from the FN) for its voters.

In January 1994 at the Party's 28th Congress, Georges Marchais, who had effectively led since 1969, gave way to the unknown apparatchik Robert Hue. Hue changed the terminology of the Party, notably renaming the Central Committee the 'National Committee' and the General Secretary the 'National Secretary' but also replacing the old Marxist vocabulary and distancing the PCF's discourse bit by bit from the old-fashioned 'bolshevism' that was its heritage.[5] Robert Hue decided to promote a friendly rather than combative image and by 1995 the leader was held in record-high regard (35 per cent good opinions) and Hue raised the Party up with him. After the presidential election campaign the Party had ratings of 32 per cent good opinion (54 per cent bad) although the opinion polls did not translate directly into real votes (Duhamel and Jaffré, 1997). Hue ended up with 8.7 per cent of the vote and took only 1.7 per cent more than Lajoinie in 1988. Hue's vote was concentrated in 28 departments – in the Paris region, the north-west, the centre and the Mediterranean littoral. Even so, Le Pen outpolled him in some places. Local elections followed and proved worse for the Party, which lost its last big town (Le Havre), and seven towns of over 30,000. Robert Hue's strategy was to seek alliance with the Socialists while renewing the Party's doctrine as much as possible (given the old guard's reluctance to move). This was welcome to a Socialist Party which, under Lionel Jospin, had revived and sought allies on the left and the reward later was to be ministerial posts.

Party system possibilities

French Communists have rejected any amalgamation with the Socialist Party to join what was split in 1920. But, given that the Party had neglected the opportunity to transform itself in the early 1990s, its main problem has been to remain as an active participant in the French party system. Its strategic dilemmas turned on this problem of exerting some power in the constellation of small parties around the PS and it is one of influence. In other words, the Communist Party has lost its place in the Soviet empire and it has not found a replacement strategy. With the arrival of Robert Hue at the head of the Party, questions about what the Party's role might be and whether the Party is in any position to play it have become insistent. However, finding a new role for a party, which has historically had the strongest sense of direction of all parties, has run up against its own nature and that of the Party's partners.

There are broadly three views about what the Party's strategy within the party system should be and these all have ardent supporters. Communism in France has called on a sufficiently wide range of strands in the past for each position to claim some legitimacy and to be able to portray itself as the authentic continuation of French Communism. In itself this public quarrel about the Party's role is a novelty and one which the old generation of Communists are not used to. The leadership's idea prevails, but because of the tripartite division in the Party's hierarchy. These three strategies are: (1) the so-called 'alternative' strategy; (2) the 'hard-line'; and (3) the leadership's middle way as developed by Hue and supported by the National Secretary Marie-George Buffet.

The 'alternative' strategy

Inside the Party the biggest minority is probably the 'alternative' strategy promoted by, among others, the late Marseilles deputy Guy Hermier, Party ideologue Lucien Sève, the historian Roger Martelli and the journal *Futurs*. They want to see the Party developed as the conscience of the left taking up the rights of minorities, extending the welfare state and leading the attack on the Front National. A 'radical pole', it is argued, could be developed by bringing together the small groups of the extreme left along with ecologists and that would regenerate the Party. A revival would enable the Party to deal with the Socialists as an equal but the strategy is not, in the short term, friendly to the PS. This route seemed to be opened by the strikes of December 1995 that paralysed the country for some days and in appearance mimicked the old 'militant working class'. Much was made of the Gardanne by-election of October 1996 at which a Communist supported by a 'rainbow coalition' was elected against a strong challenge from the FN. There is intellectual support for an 'alternative left' and the opposition to the all-pervasive free market liberalism is popular at the grass roots.

This strategy runs up against several problems. The small parties of the left and the *gauche plurielle* are not harmonious and are competing – as the European campaign and the 1998 regional elections showed.[6] The Communists and the Trotskyite parties are competitors and the extreme left has historically made its way in opposition to the PCF. There were a few Communist/Trotskyist lists in the local elections of 2001 (one in Bègles against ecologist leader and 2002 presidential candidate Noël Mamère) in towns where local disputes led to defensive alliances but there were many more confrontations. On the ecologist side, the compatibility with the Communist Party is by no means evident and they have their own agenda some of which (opposition to nuclear power, for instance) is antipathetic to the PCF. On the post-Communist issues, like the promotion of women, the Pacte Civil de Solidarité (PACS) and soft drugs the party has not led the way and the other parties are more liberal. There is the additional risk that the radicalisation of the left will alienate it from the Socialists and that would pose problems for the continuance of the Party at local level.

The hard-line strategy

Some of the ideas of the strategists of an 'alternative' are echoed by the hard-liners unreconciled to the evolution of the Party away from its long-held positions. They are the Leninists who believe in the anti-capitalist, anti-imperialist, anti-American 'party of the working class' hostile to 'bourgeois' institutions, including the PS. A number of Georges Marchais' former associates, like Maxime Gremetz and the doyen of the Assembly elected in 2002, Georges Hage, are resistant to the 'social democratisation' as they see it of the PCF and there are others nostalgic (like Jacques Karman) for the days of the USSR. Most of the hard-liners can be found in the Honecker Committees and around the journal *Co-ordination Communiste*. These people adopt a hostile stance to the coalition of the left and the deal with the PS, which they see as a repeat of the mistake made in the 1960s. This is not a small group and it is important in federations like the Pas-de-Calais. As far as can be discovered, it has support in the apparatus of the Party although that remains loyal to the leadership and it also has its divisions (Duhamel and Jaffré, 1997). It is, however, looking backwards and not to a strategy for the future.

The leadership's middle way

More important is Robert Hue's 'middle way' between the two competing groups avoiding a schism but rejecting both a new 'Common Programme' and a competitive radicalism on the left and looking for allies to bring the Party into the mainstream.[7] These allies for practical purposes are the PS. Under Hue, the Party has tried to set itself up as the left of the Socialist–Communist alliance: in government but at the same time a popular tribune. Without being as aggressive as in previous years, this continues the 'Ministry of the Masses' to harass the government but combines it with governmental prestige and keeps close to the PS. Hue's balance is possible as long as it does not make moves that endanger the special relationship with the Socialists, but that means that the Party has limited freedom. When the Party was active in demonstrations for full employment (with the extreme left in October 1999) or when the Association pour l'Emploi dans l'Industrie et le Commerce (ASSEDIC) was occupied in December 1997, its position in government is liable to be questioned.

There are many drawbacks to Hue's strategy. It is difficult to avoid either toppling into opposition on the one hand or mutely following the PS on the other. It has to maintain its distinctiveness but at the same time deploy its resources in support of the government of which it is part. Participation in government requires a degree of solidarity and prevents it, for example, from using anti-Europeanism to rally its supporters, officials and activists. Thus, opposition to the Maastricht Treaty used as a campaign theme before the 1997 elections was dropped in the interests of electioneering with the Socialists. By the same token, the criticism of privatisation which surfaced in *L'Humanité* was also muted and the swallowing of some hard choices – like the privatisation of Air France – has had no pay-off in votes

Even where the Party makes a distinctive radical mark it is always liable to be outbid by the extreme left or even the ecologists. There is a space open to exploitation on the protest left as the Trotskyist LO has demonstrated by polling 5.3 per cent in the 1995 presidential elections and the 10 per cent taken by the three Trotskyists in 2002. In 2001 the Trotskyist parties have made advances in local elections (where they are usually weak) and there were some serious challenges to the Party's hegemony in its strongholds. With competition on the extreme left it is more difficult than it was in the 1980s for the Party to retain a position in government and keep its radical electorate. Its compromises in government (despite the occasional concession made by the Socialists) made it difficult for the PCF to claim to speak on behalf of the working class or the disadvantaged.

However, the payout from following the line Hue has chosen was clear. Most important is the continuation of local government strongholds and these include (even after March 2001) an important network. It still holds 90 town halls in towns over 9,000, it took 11.2 per cent of the vote in the cantonal elections in the 1,639 cantons where it was well represented and has 131 councillors. This is a network of some substance and it will be years before it is entirely lost. By the same token, it will be many years before the Greens (or the Trotskyists) can rival it. It also keeps the Party in the mainstream, at the centre of affairs and involved in bargaining. It can negotiate concessions in government and in committee and its supporters in the unions and state industries can be helped. Short of accepting a position on the outside looking in on the left and perhaps losing its role in the party system altogether, it has to stay in alliance.

What is lacking in Hue's line is a view of where the Party is going and how it differs from its partners. This proved fatal to Hue's campaign in the 2002 presidential elections. Hue was unable to give a convincing account of in what way the PCF had changed or even inflected the course of the Socialist government of 1995–2002. Hue's stance as the 'left of the left' did not look credible and it was tested by more extreme and outspoken candidates during the campaign with the result that the Party looked opportunist and jaded. Although the humiliation of Robert Hue in the presidential election caused a leadership crisis there was still no response to the key question of what new line the Party should take and its dilemma of how a 'revolutionary' party should behave was unresolved.

Conclusion

Little attention has been devoted to the resilience of the French party system and the way that it could accommodate a radically anti-system party which did not accept the rules of the game and wanted to change the nature of society. By incorporating the PCF into the party system, the mainstream left marginalised it and reduced its potential for destabilisation. However, its predominance on the left enabled other parties to play on fears of 'Reds' and its role helped an extreme right-wing opposition to emerge.

Despite the absence of an international Communist threat, it is not clear that this Communist effect, which promotes centrifugal competition, is played out. With the end of the cold war, however, the Communist–democratic cleavage became less salient and it became possible for other parties to define alternative lines of political division. In addition, Communist penetration of society has diminished on a number of dimensions. Party identification has dropped in France (as elsewhere in Western Europe) and the PCF has been dependent on this sense of party as no other. It could also be noted that class voting has also declined (although in France it has always been below the mean) to the lowest in Europe (Gallagher *et al.*, 2001: 250–61). This, for what was the self-defined 'workers' party', is a factor in its diminishing cohesiveness. New parties, or previously marginal ones, have entered the arena and rival the Communist Party for its own traditional electorate.

For the Communist Party, which knew where it stood and which had a vicarious participation in a greater project, adaptation to the new circumstances has proved unusually difficult. Yet French Communism, having been the dominant force on the left for the formative years of the Fifth Republic, remains a distinctive force on the left. It is rooted in French life and in its political culture, it is still highly structured and an effective organisation at local level as well as a potential government partner. But the Communist presence does not drive the party system and its position in the 'plural left' is more like that of a small 'hinge' party than an anti-system force. It has also proved unable to keep the extreme-left supporters inside the coalition of the left and its hegemony over the forces to the left of the Socialist Party was negligible in 2002.

On this last point, the weakness of the Socialist Party means that, as things stand, Socialist leaders will have to rely on Communist support to compose governing coalitions. Thus the PS also has an interest in the continuing existence of the PCF, even in a weakened condition, but only as one of the components of the 'plural left' and as one of a number of partners. For the Communist Party it means living with the tension between participation in government or in alliance with the PS (with the solidarity that implies) and retreating to the margins as a critical protest party (invoking the anti-system politics at which it is an adept). Both these positions have their partisans in the Party (and both positions have their dangers) but the leadership has so far opted for an alliance or government role. With the continuing vertiginous decline of the Party, the temptation to outbid the extreme left (perhaps using the CGT) and regain its radical electorate must be strong. However, the Party is too weak to be other than a minor part of any new coalition of the left led by the PS.

Notes

1 INSEE statistics.
2 *Le Figaro*, 15 April 1997.
3 *L'Humanité*, 22 May 2001.
4 *L'Humanité*, 28 January 1997.
5 *L'Humanité*, 7 May 1996.
6 *Le Monde*, 27 April 1999.
7 *Le Monde*, 14 July 1996.

3
PS intra-party politics and party system change

Ben Clift

Introduction

Approaches to the study of party system change tend to emphasise, on the one hand, broad electoral trends, such as disaffection with 'governmental' political parties, or increasing electoral volatility and, on the other, institutional developments, such as changes to voting systems. Such 'macro'-level analysis can at times treat parties as unitary actors, possessed of one 'response' to their changing environment, an approach which underplays analysis of the party itself. This chapter offers a two-tier analysis of the interaction between developments within the party system as a whole, and the internal politics of the French PS.

At both levels, an appreciation of both structure and agency is vital to understanding how both the PS and the party system have recently evolved. The first section illustrates the institutional constraints of the French party system, and how its competitive demands helped to structure the internal organisation of the PS. Subsequent sections show how, in turn, the PS has shaped the development of the French party system. The French party system is not a particularly rigid structure, destabilised by numerous changes to the electoral 'rules of the game', changing patterns of voting behaviour, and changing constituent parties over the last twenty years. As for agency, the set of actors shaping electoral strategy within a party can change rapidly. Furthermore, the internal organisational rules governing internal power relationships are themselves prone to evolve, affecting to what extent one particular strategic vision can achieve ascendancy within the party, and beyond it.

Disaggregating beyond the level of the party, and the party's response to a changing environment involves two dimensions. First, party disaggregation involves analysing different strategies from different factional groupings within the party. This leads in turn to considering a set of

42

intra-party structure and agency relationships in order to understand how factional interaction is mediated by the internal organisation of the party. Understanding these relationships is important, since which set of perceptions are in the ascendant within a party crucially affects the interaction with the party system and relations between competitor parties. The role of internal developments, as either a barrier or a precondition to the emergence of a more coherent electoral strategy in the late 1990s, is illustrated below.

Second, parties must be treated as *in*dependent variables, which actively interact with and constitute the party system. This is because political strategy involves both which competitor formations should the PS seek to ally with (and what should be the nature of those allegiance arrangements) and how the PS should seek to restructure the electoral system, thus reshaping the balance of forces within the French party system. This chapter considers how PS factionalism and organisational changes structure the internal debate, and shape the PS approach to the two dimensions of political strategy. The final section examines a series of significant episodes in the PS's development in the 1990s and explores the processes of interaction between intra-party politics and opportunities for party system change.

The French party system, the logic of *rassemblement*, and the *union de gauche*

The advent of the Fifth Republic brought with it a new electoral system for presidential and legislative elections, specifically designed to preclude the perceived systemic weaknesses of the Fourth Republic. The two-ballot majoritarian system contained institutional constraints requiring parties to reach a 12.5 per cent[1] threshold in the first ballot of parliamentary elections, and the rule that only two candidates progress to the second ballot of presidential elections. These presented a hurdle to smaller parties, and unleashed systemic incentives for larger parties, in the second ballot, to gain votes transferred from those eliminated after the first. The majoritarian two-ballot system thus favours both alliance candidates from the first ballot, and agreements of the weaker candidate to stand down between the two ballots.

At the same time, the extraordinary 'catch-all' success of the Gaullist Union pour la Nouvelle République (UNR) (Kirchheimer 1990: 54–5) encompassed most of the right, but extended into the centre and even to elements of the working-class left electorate. This is a case of Kirchheimer's catch-all thesis skewed by de Gaulle's success within a bi-polar presidentialised party system. Mitterrand appreciated the need to exploit the possibilities of *discipline républicaine* – or the need for a transfer of votes from other left groupings to the most likely winner between the two rounds. To this end, ideological distance from the PCF had to be reduced in a party system bipolarised by Gaullism. There was thus none of Kirchheimer's 'de-ideologization' and no 'drastic reduction in the party's ideological baggage' (1990: 58). On the contrary, there was a reaffirmed turn to the left.

Appreciation of these systemic factors lay at the heart of Mitterrand's strategic vision. Arguably, the reconfiguration of the left culminating at Epinay in 1971 was designed almost purely to exploit electoral opportunities of the Fifth Republic. As Hanley notes, 'the whole enterprise of creating the successful post-1972 PS stemmed from realising what the new electoral system involved … a new-look Socialist party had to be put together out of the SFIO and the oddments of the "non-communist Left"' (1999a: 61). Bergounioux and Grunberg note that the PS is 'more a juxtaposition of *courants*, traditions, and personalities than a genuinely unified party' (1992: 293). This federating process, however imperfect, was a necessary precondition of the *union de gauche* – the marriage of convenience which formed the linchpin of Mitterrand's strategy. The centrifugal tendencies of the French left endured (Bartolini, 1984, Bell, Chapter 2 of this volume), but such countervailing institutional constraints often overwhelmed such tendencies.

Thus the make-up of the PS bore the imprint of the functional requirements of the Party system. Internal proportional representation and the factionalism it institutionalised was also functional to the process of *rassemblement* required by the electoral system, enabling the PS to broaden its catchment area and bring together a more diverse electorate at the second ballot than would be possible, for example, with the monotheism of the PCF. Indeed, Sferza and Lewis (1987) argue that PS factionalism in large part explains the advances made in the 1970s. Schlesinger and Schlesinger's recent study attests to the effectiveness of the aspect of the PS as an electoral machine (2000: 142, table).

The competing institutional and electoral logics of the French party system

French political life involves many different electoral systems, electing the numerous representative bodies within the French polity. Elections, according to Machin, 'are too numerous and frequent, different electoral systems encourage different and sometimes conflicting competitive strategies and electoral systems are often changed' (1989: 76). Different electoral rules in effect demand conflicting electoral strategies. In order to assess whether a party designed to operate under the second-ballot *rassemblement* logic of the 1970s successfully adapted to the competing proportional and majoritarian logics at various levels, we should first briefly outline the significant changes.

'Decisive' presidential and parliamentary elections remain majoritarian penalising small parties, and encouraging the formation of coalitions. 'Intermediary' elections, however, have become increasingly proportional, encouraging parties to stand up and be counted. First, proportional European elections were instituted in 1979, with a 5 per cent threshold, and the country treated as one constituency. Second, in 1982, municipal elections became semi-proportional with 50 per cent of the seats awarded to the majority (or plurality) in the second ballot, but with the other 50 per cent of seats shared in proportion to votes cast. Third, at the time of the one-off proportional parliamentary elections in 1986, the first elections of the regional councils took place, 96 departments became multi-member constituencies, with a 5 per cent threshold, and seats distributed on the 'highest average principle' (Machin, 1989: 75).

This external turbulence of changing rules of the game in the party system coincided with a (slightly) calmer internal atmosphere within the PS as a result of Mitterrand's unchallenged supremacy until 1988. This ensured that his strategic vision prevailed. Although genetically programmed to operate under a majoritarian system inducing *rassemblement* in the second ballot, the PS proved adept at pursuing other strategies for different kinds of elections. This was facilitated by the party's flexibility, a by-product of its 'weakness' – the party has comparatively low membership, a small bureaucratised national office, and a tradition of local autonomy. For example, differential candidate selection procedures *within* the PS afford different degrees of influence to the national and local organisations.[2]

Part-cause and part-effect of the flexibility and 'weakness' of the PS is the hold that local *notables* – what Mény calls the 'Republican aristocracy' (1995) – have over the national party organisation. This tradition of local autonomy is highly significant in terms of electoral alliances, given the differential local performance of some of the PS's allies. An established *notable*, taking account of the relative strength of potential electoral allies in his or her locality, will decide the appropriate strategy accordingly, with scant regard for national strategic directives to the contrary.

Such localised strategic variation means that few generalisations can be made about national electoral strategy, since it varies in accordance with local electoral realities. Here again, the importance of developments within PS factionalism are significant. At the height of the factional skirmishing in the late 1980s and early 1990s, coordination was difficult to achieve. This was because of geographical variations in the strength of support for a particular faction. Certain federations operate as power bases for particular factions, and thus in an area where one faction predominates, it was difficult to impose a strategy too closely associated with a factional rival.

As the strategic context of PS electoral strategy became more complex, with the range of and variation in strategic options increasing, such organisational malleability enabled the PS to reconcile divergent positions. These are variations which the national organisation has neither the ability, nor perhaps the inclination, to counter. This organisational flexibility was thus a pressure valve releasing some of the tensions caused by the competing logics of the various electoral systems.

Lastly, in the last twenty years, the public opinion climate in France has been characterised by a crisis of representation for governmental parties, evidenced by electoral trends towards 'protest' voting, abstention and increased volatility (Boy and Mayer, 1997). The coincidence of disaffection with the political system, and the governmental parties within it, and with the electoral system changes outlined above is significant. None of the larger parties (PS, RPR or UDF) has sustained claims to 'catch-all' party status (Kirchheimer, 1990), in part because smaller parties benefited from protest voting. Proportional representation greatly increased the effectiveness of such expressions of disaffection. Furthermore, even in majoritarian elections, the impact of volatility has been significant, with no incumbent government having won a legislative election since 1978 – the so-called *hyper-alternance* (Evans and Ivaldi, 2002).

That said, we have not seen the triumph of smaller parties over governmental parties. The PS, even in its darkest electoral hour, still received more support than any other left political grouping. While the hegemony of the governmental parties has receded in the face of increasing volatility and abstention, the smaller parties have no more than dented large party support, unable to make the advances that some analysts predicted for them. In this situation, the PS cannot succeed alone, but remains the most important single left grouping. The need for electoral allies is clear. As Charlot puts it, 'this combining of forces between forces necessarily close at the level of ideas and political interests ... finds its cement in the institutional constraints which make the abandonment of union politically costly' (1992: 23). Thus for all the evolutions, continuity in decisive elections means a familiar logic continues to structure the party system.

PS factionalism – structuring the debate over political strategy

Parties are not unitary actors. They should be treated more as arenas, incorporating competing groups of actors, and a number of competing strategies in the face of a given structural context, as well as different suggestions for reform to that context. Intra-party differences over how to play the hand dealt by the strategic context of the French party system, and what structural changes to the system would further the party's ends, must be taken into account. This necessitates unearthing the intra-party political mechanisms, particularly pressing in the study of the PS where internal proportionality institutionalising 'presidentialised factionalism' has structured the party's development since its foundation at Epinay (Bell and Criddle, 1988, 1994, Cole, 1989).

Hine's framework for the analysis of party factionalism identifies structural incentives to factionalism. Following Sartori (1976: 94–104), Hine places considerable emphasis on the role of internal PR, arguing that, 'the use of proportionalism can have an important impact on the nature of intra-party conflict and, when introduced, can make actions more rigid and draw more individuals into their ambit' (1982: 45). It has been argued elsewhere that the importance of these structural incentives to factionalism has been overstated (Cole, 1986, 1989, Clift, 2000). This point is best illustrated by charting the fluctuating levels and intensity of factionalism within the PS since 1971. There were periods of very intense factional infighting, notably 1978–80 (Cole, 1989) and 1988–1992 (Dupin, 1991, Clift, 2000) which were interspersed with *relatively* calmer periods. Such fluctuation leads us to search for other factors influencing factionalism, since the system of PR, in operation throughout, cannot explain the variation.

Focusing almost exclusively on internal proportional representation tends to crowd out analysis of conjunctural incentives to factionalism, linked to different strategies pursued by factions depending on the political context. This political context is affected by such variables as the proximity of elections, and whether the leader has achieved internal hegemony within the party. Equally, it will be affected by changes in relations with competitor parties, and perceived opportunities for changes in electoral strategy. The set of non-structural incentives to PS factionalism considered here are the differences between factional camps of strategy and tactics both over what changes to the institutional parameters of party system should be advocated, and how to play the hand dealt the PS by the French party system and electoral context.

Electoral strategy is a key battleground of factional struggle. For example, one reading of the 'two cultures' thesis sees the fundamental schism within French Socialism as not a philosophical battle pitting Bernstein against Kautsky, but a purely *strategic* divergence over whether or not the PCF constitute appropriate electoral allies. The broad outlines of the two dominant strategic choices have remained constant, that is either *ouverture* towards the centre, or *Union* towards the left, and including the Communists. In 1985, the split between Rocard and Mitterrand centred on PR, with Rocard resigning in objection to Mitterrand's relatively (but not entirely) successful electoral manipulation of the 1986 elections. Criticism and counter-criticism of these competing strategies, and such electoral engineering, continued to dominate discussion of electoral strategy in the post-Mitterrand era.

Internal disagreement passed through the channels of the *courants*, which shaped the debate and limited the range of options. As we saw, the party's structure facilitated the uniting of the diverse groups behind the left's *présidentiable*. At the same time, however, each of the factions was afforded the luxury of their own *présidentiable* who could fight his or her faction's doctrinal corner, play a prominent role in internal party life, and in the longer term could groom themselves and position themselves as Mitterrand's heir apparent. Each *courant* leader – or 'elephant' as they are not-so-affectionately called in the party – must be the first signatory to their *courant*'s motion or general political statement (containing clues as to their electoral strategy position) which is presented at a conference.[3]

Courants, the received wisdom goes, are a positive and enlivening element of internal debate when they bring forth new ideas and engage in debates. However, those tasks, which were performed admirably in the 1970s have been superseded. In the mid to late 1980s, *courants* – with their own finances, offices, and newspapers, behaved increasingly like parties within a party. The title '*courant de pensée*' became decreasingly appropriate as the doctrinal role diminished, leaving only the organisational, power-brokering role. Rennes, the apogee of the *courant* system as a gladiatorial power struggle, made this drift all the more apparent. There ensued, in the years after the Rennes Congress, a sea change in the approach to internal pluralism, with a shift away from formal organisation along the 'parties within parties' lines, and towards Rose's 'stable sets of attitudes' model (1964). This has been accompanied by institutional changes, reducing the reliance on internal proportionality, and a revived convention of synthesising the major positions *before* congress, with all the major groupings effectively forming one *courant* (Clift, 2000). These internal changes, which ultimately underpinned Jospin's internal hegemony (see below), were accompanied by changes in the PS's electoral context, presenting some novel strategic challenges.

Episode 1: 'New politics', new cleavage formation?

In the later 1980s and early 1990s, support for political ecologism in France (the principal formations being Génération Ecologie (GE) and les Verts – the Greens) increased dramatically. After a 10 per cent showing in the 1989 European elections, the Greens polled 15 per cent of votes cast in the regional elections of 1992. The fact that one polling institution put ecologist support at 19 per cent in January 1993 did little to dampen ecologist hopes (Boy, 1993:161). In the context of the declining electoral fortunes of the PS and adverse public opinion, a factional debate between Mauroy (First Secretary from 1988 to 1992) and Fabius (First Secretary after Mauroy's resignation in 1992) centred on how to approach this new political formation.

The debate had two dimensions. On the one hand, it concerned contingent relations between the two parties, involving traditional debates about whether to sign non-aggression pacts, to agree not to stand in certain seats, or *désistement* between ballots in favour of the best-placed first-round candidate. On the other hand, there were debates about what structural changes to the French party system the PS might advocate either as carrots to encourage the ecologists to the negotiating table, or in the party's own interest. If the various forces of French political ecologism could be shepherded under the same umbrella as the PS, the speculation went, then this might represent a sufficiently powerful electoral force to keep the right out of power for the foreseeable future.

Fabius spoke in the preparation for the 1992 regional and cantonal elections of the need to work with 'the Mouvement des Radicaux de Gauche, *France Unie*, the two ecologist parties, the Communist renovators, other communists ... all those who form the Left and the progressives in the 1990s in all their diversity'.[4] However, the offer of an early electoral pact foundered in the absence of structural changes to the electoral system to facilitate ecologist progress.[5] The 'all-conquering' Greens were resolutely unimpressed by such offerings.

Fabius may have overestimated PS strength, or lacked the strategic vision to see the possibilities of a left–Green alliance. Perhaps he was reluctant to contemplate changes to the electoral system which would have the epiphenomenal effect of advancing the FN's cause. Fabius nonetheless played his hand badly. He attempted to repair bridges by 'greenwashing' the party's discourse,[6] then took the extraordinary step of deciding to withdraw unilaterally from second-round ballots in seats where the ecologists were ahead after the first, despite a lack of any electoral pact (Boy, 1993: 164–5). After this abject failure, Mauroy attacked Fabius and held the courant system responsible for the ill-adapted electoral strategy of 1993. 'The *courants* ... made us forget a realistic and adapted strategy ... We refused to understand that the only possible dialogue with the ecologists had to start with the adoption of a mixed electoral system, responding to the demands of democracy given the new political configuration.'[7]

Whether Mauroy would have handled things any differently, had he remained First Secretary a little longer, we will never know. The point, however, is that the intra-party debates over relations with electoral allies dealt with issues of such fundamental importance to the operation of the French party system as whether or not an offer of electoral system reform should have been made to the ecologists. Had Mauroy, not Fabius, presided over the negotiations, the shape of the French party system might be very different. If the smaller political movements of the left in all its diversity could have been brought under the same umbrella, could the catastrophic defeat of 1993 been avoided? Probably not, but the PS might have avoided plummeting quite as low as it did. The overall vote polled by the ecologist movements was 10.8 per cent in 1993. Had the PS been able to count on some of that support in the second ballot, it could have drastically reduced the scale of its defeat.

Episode 2: Rocard's 'big bang' – the attempted restructuring of the French party system

In the wake of the crushing defeat of French Socialism, the PS's relationship with the French party system underwent a series of fairly rapid changes. In order to understand fully the shifts in direction and rationale which ensued, we must look to the ascendancy or otherwise of various factional groupings. Fabius resigned, leaving his factional rival Rocard with scope to redesign the party's electoral strategy. Rocard's proposed big bang claimed to tap into secular changes within the French electoral context. The big bang sought to take account of the changes both in voting behaviour and the socio-economic structure of society. This was an electoral strategy designed to work in the context of what Gérard Le Gall, the PS chief electoral strategist, has called 'sociological quasi-indeterminism' (1993). Heightened electoral volatility and the declining relevance of socio-economic position to voting behaviour, had been factored in to Rocard's analysis.

The PS would, he hoped, ride the waves of these changes, and herald a restructuring of the French party system. Having criticised PS's traditional 'submission' of its allies, Rocard envisaged a 'vast movement, open, modern and rich in its diversity, ... [which] will encompass the reformism of ecologists, the loyalty to a social tradition of *centrisme*, and the authentic renovatory impulse of communism.' To facilitate the construction of this movement, Rocard advocated institutional changes to the French party system. 'Attached as I am to the majoritarian system, I think it indispensable to add to it a dose of proportional representation into the present system', Rocard implored all concerned to confront the obstacles to 'the political big bang to which I aspire'.[8] Rocard's radical project caused a stir, not least because it seemed to threaten the end of the PS. Rocard was proposing a *rééquilibrage* – redesigning the political landscape and reinventing existing political parties (Charlot, 1994: 270). The explicit advocacy of alliances with the centre had long been the Rocardian political strategy of choice, but his conversion to electoral reform gave the big bang a novel air.

In 1993, Rocard's position as both president of the party and *candidat naturel* for the presidency suggested that a *rééquilibrage* along these lines could have been possible. However, Rocard's idea never really weathered the storm that followed the 1993 defeat. The centrists firmly associated themselves with the parties of the right, some joining the Balladur government, others dissolving their own parliamentary group. Thus the realignment was only likely to happen *within* the left, since the centrists had raised the drawbridge. However, even this smaller-scale realignment was hampered. The spectacular failure of Rocard's gamble is largely explained by intra-party fighting, and the ongoing factionalism within the PS. Mitterrand was determined to derail Rocard's big bang,[9] part of his implacable opposition to Rocard's bid to succeed him as President. Mitterrand's friends within the Party accordingly backed Tapie's *Energie Radicale* list in the 1994 European elections against Rocard's official list. This split in the left vote helped the PS list plummet below 15 per cent – a humiliating result even given the PS's very low expectations in the wake of 1993.

Even before the European election results finally destroyed Rocard's political credibility, however, his intended redrawing of the political landscape was not proceeding entirely as he envisaged. Competing factional visions endured within the PS over the party's point of insertion into the French party system, who were the best allies, and on what ideological territory to meet them. Rocard's ambition for the *Assises de la transformation sociale*, a set of meetings with all potential allies, and supposedly the first institutional manifestation of the big bang in action, was to approach civil society groups and centrists. While Rocard happily involved Communist 'renovators' such as Herzog, he did not aim to reconstruct the *union de gauche*. However, those organising the *Assises* – Jospin, a disciple of *mitterrandiste* political strategy, and Cambadélis, a one-time Trotskyist and loyal Jospin ally – did not share Rocard's strategic vision.

Although marginalised in the party and contemplating leaving politics at the time, Jospin saw the *Assises* as an ideal opportunity to explore the potential of the *Rouge–Rose–Vert* coalition. Rocard became aware that the direction being taken by the *Assises* deviated from his vision, but Rocard's lack of a hegemonic position within the PS analogous to that enjoyed by Mitterrand when steering the party's political strategy in the 1970s meant that he could not impose his vision. Furthermore, Rocard's lack of hegemonic authority within the party was mirrored by the PS's lack of hegemonic authority on the left of the French party system. Fabius's experiences with the Greens prior to 1993 indicated that the PS elite was no longer at liberty to dictate the terms of relations with competitor formations. In the period 1993–94, articles in the PS weekly *Vendredi* on electoral strategy contain the disclaimer, 'in the spirit of partnership, exempt from any desire for hegemony, and respecting the autonomy of each formation'.[10]

How genuine this newfound modesty really was is questionable, but it nevertheless hints at a real impediment to the desired restructuring process. The PS did not seem the appropriate body to orchestrate the *rééquilibrage* because it was too tarnished and powerless a body to deliver on any pacts it formed with other political formations, not least because changing the electoral system requires being in government. Both internally within the party, and externally within the party system, Rocard was not in a position to deliver his big bang. Indeed, the late Pierre Guidoni argued that bargaining only really began from a position of relative strength, in the wake of Jospin's creditable 1995 presidential election defeat, which was a necessary precondition of re-establishing alliances. 'In reality, we pursued our alliance strategy *only when* we regained electoral hegemony, it was at that moment that we could start offering presents.'[11]

Episode 3: The birth of the *gauche plurielle*

Internally, the context of factionalism changed after 1995, when the prize everyone was fighting for – the presidency – was lost. Jospin ended 1995 as defeated presidential candidate, but also the unassailable leader of the left in France. Jospin converted his political capital gained by his 'successful' defeat into security of tenure and an hegemonic position within the PS by becoming (before the process had reached the party's statute book) the first directly elected PS first secretary (Clift, 2000). At that point, just as had happened earlier under Mitterrand, a ceasefire descended, making coordination of electoral strategy much easier. In stark contrast to the early 1990s, once Jospin's internal (and external) ascendancy was assured, his hands were freed to proceed as he wished in shaping PS electoral strategy.

In hindsight, the *Assises de la transformation sociale* in 1993–94 constituted vital groundwork which paid dividends when Jospin was re-elected first secretary. The four programmatic conventions under Jospin, and the programmatic elements for the meetings with the PCF and the ecologists, were all traceable back to the *Assises*. The dynamic of recovery set in train by 1995 heralded a renovation, with significant modifications, of the *union de gauche*. In its *rassemblement* of the whole of the left, Jospin's political strategy displayed some Mitterrandist continuity, but, with the addition of the Greens, the *gauche plurielle* represented a novel structuration of the French party system.

Within the PS, Jospin's internal hegemony represented an enormous asset in dealings with potential allies. Jospin's orchestration of candidate designation (a process facilitated by the haste-inducing surprise dissolution) for the 1997 legislative elections leaving room for alliance candidates clearly demonstrated this. The trick was to 'organise the legislative elections *as if* they were proportional elections'.[12] This attested to a degree of centralised organisation which, as Rocard found, is difficult to achieve when the de facto leader of the party does not enjoy widespread support within the party. The spectacular failure of Hollande's *gauche unie* in June 2002 can be traced in part to his lack of his internal hegemony analogous to Jospin's. Protracted, ill-tempered PS–PCF–Verts–PRG electoral negotiations eventually achieved only 34 single candidacies, not the 577 that Hollande had hoped for, with an additional 136 'partial agreements' involving a candidate 'wearing the colours' of at least two of the four formations at the first ballot.[13]

Internal developments within the PS's ally formations were also important preconditions of the *gauche plurielle*. This point, which further highlights the importance of analysing *intra-party* politics when considering party system change, can be illustrated by briefly considering the case of the Greens and the PCF. In the mid-1990s, Voynet and Cochet overcame internal opposition, and the Greens emerged as the dominant force in French political ecology (O'Neill, 1997: 195–209). Under Voynet's direction, the Greens came to abandon their 'neither right nor left' stance in the face of electoral difficulties at grass-roots level. The modest performance in the 1994 cantonals, no seats in the European elections, and the difficulties they had fielding candidates on a national level[14] further underlined what Daniel Boy (1993) has termed the 'coming back down to earth' of the ecologists in the period after 1993. The eschewal of all alliances contradicted the institutional logic of the system. When only Dominique Voynet made it to the second ballot of the 1993 legislative elections, these difficulties were brought home to the Greens.

With PS recovery after 1995, the Greens realised there was no longer the political space available. This very different political context, facilitated, prior to 1997, the first alliance being concluded between the PS (supporting 29 Green candidates) and the Greens (supporting 77 PS candidates). In terms of *structural* changes, Jospin made encouraging noises about PR to woo the Greens. In 2002, four of the single *gauche unie* candidacies were Green, and the PS supported 59 Green candidates (albeit in safe right seats), who in turn supported 94 Socialists. Despite increased Green first-round vote share (from 3.6 per cent in 1997 to 4.5 per cent), the vagaries of the electoral system left them with only three deputies.

The significant developments in the PCF's internal politics were threefold: ongoing decline, the increasing importance and autonomy of the PCF 'red' *notables*, and the change of leadership. The PCF's continuing decline shifts the terms of trade against the PCF, reducing its room to manoeuvre (despite the surprisingly resilient return of 21 deputies in June 2002). Second, as David Bell has noted in this volume (Chapter 2), local politics has become of increasing importance to the PCF as it declines nationally. The need to retain 'political reality' at the local level constrains the PCF at the national level, due to the autonomy which local *notables* derive from their local power bases and consequently allows them to pave the way in areas where alliance is mutually advantageous, for closer PS–PCF cooperation. Thus the PCF is condemned to the Union.

Third, with the arrival of Robert Hue some foresee a steady reduction in the distance between the two historic rivals. Such predictions paper over certain significant cracks – the pace of reforms and European policy, for instance, not to mention the legacy of eighty years of hostility. Nevertheless, the PCF has few other strategic options, beyond a dangerous radicalisation which, as Bell has also noted in this volume (Chapter 2), could result in the destruction of the left's electoral coalition. As a result of partial 'social democratisation' under Hue, and the shifting terms of trade in the Socialists' favour, the fundamental differences which produced the *deux cultures* have dissipated as the price to pay for union with the PCF reduced.

Conclusion

Early in the 1990s, the PS attempted root-and-branch restructuring both of itself and the French party system. The restructuring failed, for both external reasons, in the form of adverse electoral results, and internal reasons, namely the falling from grace of the strategy's key proponent, or the sabotage of the strategy by factional rivals. The success of Jospin's post-1995 restructuring owes a great deal to the fact that, internally, despite recent structural changes, the basic institutional logic which once underpinned Mitterrand's dominance of the party underpinned Jospin's *incontournable* position within the PS. Furthermore, externally, a similar strategic vision which once inspired the *union de gauche*, rooted in the 'institutional cement' of the rules of the game of the French party system, was seen by Jospin as a sine qua non of political success and underpinned the *gauche plurielle*.

The *gauche plurielle* owed a great deal both to Jospin's internal hegemony, and to the reestablishment of PS electoral hegemony on the left. The 2002 defeats may reopen debates about increased proportionality, which could fundamentally alter the institutional logic which cemented the *gauche plurielle*, creating uncertainty about the future shape of, and strategies within, the left pole of the French party system. The first attempt at a successor strategy, the *gauche unie*, proved incompatible with the institutional logic of dual-ballot elections, and failed given record abstention, the continued decline of the PCF, disappointing results for the Greens and increased fragmentation of the left, which could not agree to cohere around a damaged but still dominant PS. In its wake, it is unclear whether the conditions exist to rebuild a governing coalition of the left within the French party system.

Notes

1 Set at 5 per cent of those voting in 1958, revised to 10 per cent of the registered electorate in 1966, which was in turn raised to 12.5 per cent of the registered electorate in 1976.

2 The proportional list elections (regional, European) involve a high degree of central input into list construction. For cantonal and municipal elections candidate selection is, on the whole, decided at the section level. For parliamentary elections, candidate selection takes place at the departmental or federation level, where the degree of national-level interference also varies (see below).

3 The strength of any given *courant* is determined by the votes its motion receives. The bottom line is a mathematical equation between proportion of votes obtained and proportion of internal positions of responsibility. The federal structures mirror the national, where, at the departmental level, all factions are represented proportionately on the Federal Executive (Bell and Criddle, 1988: 210–16 and Figure 10.1).

4 PS Info no. 512 (18 April 1992) – proceedings of the Comité Directeur 12 April 1992.

5 In part as a means to appease the Greens, the multi-party Vedel Commission had been convened in 1992 to look at electoral reform, ultimately recommending a compromise position of a mixed AMS (German-style) system, with 10 per cent of National Assembly seats decided proportionally. Prime Minister Bérégovoy (a close associate of Fabius) decided not to proceed with electoral reform ahead of the 1993 elections.

6 Fabius claimed Bérégovoy's government was engaged in a model of growth he called 'eco-development … nothing less than an ecological restructuring of society' *Journal Officiel de l'Assemblee Nationale*, 8 April 1992, p. 381.

7 PS Info no. 544 (17 April 1993) – proceedings of the Comité Directeur, 3 April 1993.

8 All quotes taken from Rocard's speech at Montlouis-sur-Seine, 17 February 1993.

9 Despite personally favouring a shift to proportional representation, for example in the 1993 elections (Favier and Martin-Roland, 1991: 266, 383).

10 See. e.g., *La Lettre de Vendredi* no. 31, 21 October 1994; *communiqué commun* PS/PCF 18 October 1994.

11 Interview with Pierre Guidoni, PS National Secretary for International Relations, 24 September 1997.

12 *Ibid.*

13 The PS agreed to withdraw from 105 constituencies, 13 in favour of the PCF and 33 in favour of the PRG. In exchange, the Socialists benefited from Communist support in 36 constituencies, and from the PRG in 515 constituencies. Of the 34 single candidacies, 14 were PS, 12 were PCF, 4 PRG and 4 Greens (*Libération*, 18 May 2002).

14 Only 37 per cent of constituencies had a green candidate in the cantonal elections, and they gained only 3.9 per cent of the vote.

4
The Greens: from idealism to pragmatism (1984–2002)

Bruno Villalba
and
Sylvie Vieillard-Coffre

Introduction

'Utopia has come to French history', declared René Dumont on 26 April 1974. Conscious of the necessity of establishing such a utopia, he was of the opinion that the newly founded ecologist movement should 'organise so as to establish itself permanently as an influence in French political life' (Dumont, 1974: 5). Twenty-five years later, this utopian movement has been replaced by a complex organisation. In a quarter of a century, the Greens have had the opportunity to try out a number of organisational approaches and to test various electoral strategies and to develop novel internal practices based on their own particular motivations and identity. Gradually, however, they have been forced to accept a dose of political reality and adapt their membership practices in the interests of electoral success. In carrying out our organisational, electoral and ideological analysis, our aim is to explore how the Greens have tried to maintain a coherent identity while facing up to the new responsibilities which have recently been placed at their feet.

Structure and membership

The democratic formality of the party is an attempt to save the Greens from oligarchic tendencies as well as to establish the following principles: free engagement, enshrined in membership regulations; free expression within the party, to fight against the tendency of the individual to disappear under the force of militancy; and the revitalisation of democratic practice, in particular participatory democracy. The organisational structure is meant to lower the boundaries between politics and civil society: the 'movement' should remain a policy tool and nothing more. The Greens abide by these founding principles, maintaining a collective memory of the party's origins as well as transforming it to cope with contemporary political challenges.

Building a 'different' party

Comparative analysis has revealed that, in general, ecology parties in Western Europe abide by similar principles in their organisational structures (Richardson and Rootes, 1995, Vialatte, 1996). Their organisations are based on five principal characteristics: plural leadership; rotation; limitations on multiple office-holding; the absence of a professionalised leadership; and regulated gender parity (Rihoux, 2001: 123). Their aim is to build a 'different' party whose rationale lies in the importance of grass roots democracy (Poguntke, 1993: 136–48).

For the French Greens, the organisation should formally ensure equality for all members, regardless of their function or power within the movement. Four principles derive from this: the primacy of regions (regions have complete autonomy as to their organisational structure); collective decision-making (the National Inter-Regional Council (NIRC) and the Executive College (EC)); direct democracy (by means of internal referenda); and gender parity. Between 1984 and 1994, the regions directly appointed three-quarters of the NIRC, the legislative body of the movement with over 100 members. The Annual General Meeting (AGM) was the sovereign body of the movement within which policy direction was decided and the remaining quarter of the NIRC were elected by proportional representation. The NIRC and EC were both bound by its decisions, demonstrating the importance of the equality principle for each member.

New statutes were passed in 1994, in order to provide a more effective policy tool. The main change was the abandoning of the AGM, to be replaced by a meeting of regional delegates every two years. This congress occurs in two stages. First, a 'decentralised AGM' where national and individual motions are introduced and voted upon takes place at the same time and with the same agenda in all the regions.[1] Delegates to the Federal Assembly (FA) are also elected at this stage, by proportional list vote. The second stage takes place one month later. During the FA, the delegates vote on motions which have not yet been passed or validate amalgamations of different motions. They also designate the remaining quarter of the NIRC (around 30 delegates) by a proportional list vote. However, there is still a regional AGM which meets annually to consider matters and motions pertaining to that region. Every two years, the regional members of the NIRC are elected. The list of delegates to the national council is consequently based upon local alliances.

These statutory changes were accompanied by a change in membership activity. In terms of finances, the Greens experienced a major boost in the mid-1990s. Between 1984 and 1989, membership dues had been the main source of income,[2] the Greens refusing company or other groups' contributions. From 1989, the pooling of representatives' allowances, and in particular those of MEPs, increased revenues. However, the major step up occurred with the new party finance regulations that began to be introduced from 1988 onwards. From then on, all parties were financed by the State according to their results in legislative elections – worth around $1.7m for the Greens in 1997. Moreover, like all parties they had benefited since 1995 from the public financing of campaigns which substantially increased the budget allocated for this purpose. Overall, in 2001 the Greens' budget was around $3 m. This has given the Greens the opportunity to employ a small internal bureaucracy, and to give its members stipends somewhat beyond the token gesture they had previously been paid.

The increase in members' participation within local bodies has led to a more professionalised and effective operation (Boy, *et al.*, 1995). This institutional structure has also established membership somewhat at a distance from their original participatory principles (Villalba, 1996: 149–70). The Greens may have tried to establish a democratic framework, but they have progressively adapted this to try to integrate themselves more fully into the political system. Certain basic rules (no multiple office-holding, rotation of positions, non-professionalisation, collective decision-making, and so on) have all been compromised, with the key exception of gender parity.

The importance of militants

At the moment of the creation of the Green Party in 1984, membership was low and spread across only about twenty departments (Vieillard-Coffre, 2001: 122–30).

High-population density is the first reason for this unbalanced spread (see Figure 4.1).[3] Attachment to ecological ideas is particularly strong in urban areas, due to greater consideration being given to improvement in the quality of life. Second the presence of leaders with strong local support can contribute to membership size (for instance, Antoine Waechter and Solange Fernex in the Haut-Rhin). Lastly, mobilisation around important environmental issues (infrastructure routes, nuclear power plants, inter alia) can also explain higher membership, although not entirely (for instance, anti-nuclear protest has little purchase in the Seine-Maritime department).

In 1986, nationalising the party was a principal concern of the Greens. A transformation of the party's internal functioning was necessary to do this, particularly in integrating unwilling local groups into the national framework. It was also necessary to reconcile ideological differences

FIGURE 4.1 Green membership by department

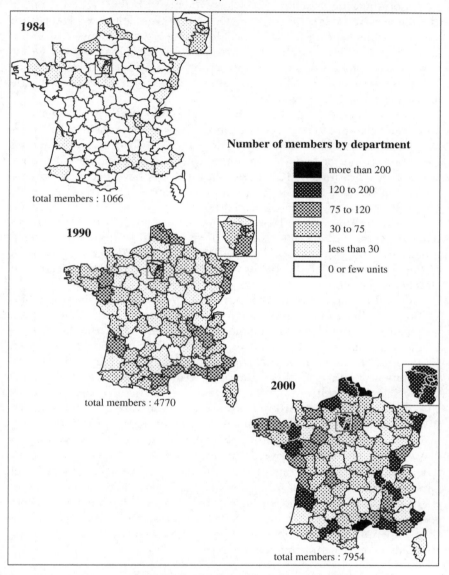

Source: Bennahmias and Roche (1992), and Green Party official figures
All maps produced by Sylvie Vieillard-Coffre

between the various regions. Electoral campaigns provided the main
means of slowly nationalising the party. By the end of the 1980s, there
had been an increase in the number of members across practically the

whole country, even if the increases themselves were as unevenly spread as the original membership. The departments with the highest number of members were the 'historic' zones (Nord, Pas-de-Calais, Haut-Rhin and Bas-Rhin, Rhône and Drôme, the Breton departments, Gironde,[4] Paris, Essonne, and certain Mediterranean coastal departments). Other regions have 'gone greener' more recently – Franche-Comté and Corsica in 1989, for example, the latter after an electoral alliance with the nationalists led by Max Siméoni.

However, since its creation, the membership body has undergone important changes. The Greens have to live with a high level of membership turnover (30 to 35 per cent per year) either because of fluctuating electoral fortunes or because of internal wranglings (31 per cent left after Waechter's departure in 1994). Significant drops have been particularly noticeable in Haut-Rhin and some Alpine departments such as Alpes de Haute-Provence or Hautes-Alpes, although certain areas have been on the up (in the Jura, where Dominique Voynet is based). When the Greens manage to present a clear vision of their political project, membership usually rises, as was the case between 1987 and 1993 after the adoption of the autonomy principle, or since 1994 when the party has placed itself clearly on the left.

The end of the 1990s marked a new stage in the movement's stabilisation. The effects of the split had largely disappeared, and public opinion was once more open to Green themes. From 1994 onwards, the clarification of the party line, closely linked to the institutionalisation of the Green Party after its entry into the National Assembly and into the Jospin government in 1997, solidified the party structure. Since then, all departments have had their own local affiliates,[5] even if these are still unequally spread. For instance, the Ile de France has more than 2,000 members, Corsica only 44, out of a total of 10,372 members in April 2001.

Sociologically, the Greens are essentially taken from the least popular classes. Workers and employees only represent 15 per cent of members. Their education level is higher than the national average, with 22.7 per cent of members holding a Masters or equivalent qualification. Many of them proclaim themselves to have grown up in a left-wing household which 'talked politics'. More broadly, many members live in a milieu of friends and partners sharing their ecologist convictions and having frequent contact with other members.[6]

A hesitant electoral journey

A relatively unstable electorate

The Green electorate is very close to the party membership in terms of its sociological profile. In the 1970s and early 1980s, the bulk of the ecology electorate lay in the middle classes, educated, with medium to high incomes and on the edge of the intellectual set. At the beginning of the 1990s, it began to display a more popular profile (Boy, 1990). Increasing numbers of blue- and white-collar workers began to vote this way, but with important fluctuations according to the period – 28 per cent in 1989, 19 per cent in 1993, and with an overall drop towards the end of the 1990s. On the other hand, retired and inactive voters are no more known for their ecology vote than small business owners and farmers. The gender split was roughly equivalent to that of the population as a whole between 1984 and 1990, with a feminisation in the mid-1990s. As concerns age, the Green electorate is on average younger than other party electorates. The 1990–95 period accentuated this rejuvenation, except in the 1995 presidential election, and since then younger voters have again become more important; 79 per cent of the Cohn-Bendit list voters were less than 49. Along the left–right continuum, the majority of voters place themselves on the left, followed by in the centre, and some elections have reinforced the leftist position – for example, the 1988, 1995 and 2002 presidential elections. The bulk of voters will choose a left-wing candidate in the second round, if one is present.

At the level of issues, voters are principally motivated by environmental concerns, a facet which has remained relatively stable across time. The questions which concern them are less along the lines of mainstream politicking.[7] However, geographical analysis of the spread of this electorate shows that there is no simple correlation between the occurrence of a local environmental crisis and a strong vote for the Greens. Beyond the purely environmental, the vote is motivated by considerations about the nature of democracy, for instance participation, or derives from circumstance – the decline of the PS at the beginning of the 1990s, a rejection of the traditional political system, and so on. Lastly, many votes derive from exchanges with neighbouring parties, notably the PS and sometimes the right (Boy and Chiche, 2002).[8] Consequently, the development of the ecologists remains heavily dependent upon the situation of other political actors. Together, these factors at least partly explain the high volatility of this electorate.[9]

The 2002 presidential election reinforced this pattern. Noël Mamère may have won 350,000 votes more than any previous Green candidate, but the national result was not up to Green expectations. The party was unable to exploit electorally the various environmental disasters which had affected France in recent years.[10] Furthermore, the extreme-left parties had fought the Greens for part of their electorate. Lastly, one cannot ignore the unfavourable internal situation within the party which had demoralised the membership during the campaign. In the subsequent legislative elections, the total national vote had risen by a little more than 200,000 votes since 1997 (4.5 per cent as opposed to

3.6 per cent in 1997) but the Greens lost four deputies from their 1997 total of seven.

The instability of the Green vote weakens the party's competitiveness and in 2002 particularly opened it to the problems of high abstention and tactical voting. The back-to-back timetabling of the elections helped to minimise the importance of the ecology vote in a context where the right was mobilising for a presidential majority in the National Assembly to put Jacques Chirac's programme into action. Within the left, the absence of Lionel Jospin from the second round of the presidential election provoked a backlash in favour of the Socialists in the legislatives to the detriment of the other *gauche plurielle* members.

The electoral learning-curve and managing competition

Despite its short life to date, the Green Party has tried out a number of electoral strategies. By carrying out an independent campaign or by participating in more or less ephemeral alliances, they have gradually mastered their electoral technique. However, one can still ask questions about their territorial implantation. The departments with the highest ecology scores in presidential elections between 1981 and 2002 give an interesting picture of the party's regional strength (Figure 4.2).[11] The areas of predominance are from Brittany to the north of Pays-de-la-Loire and across to Basse-Normandie, together with Alsace, Vosges, the Jura and the Arc Alpin.

This map shows certain areas of weakness as compared with the membership bastions, in particular Nord-Pas-de-Calais and the Mediterranean coastal departments.[12] On the other hand, other areas, such as the Alps, see strong electoral support despite the weaker membership presence. Clearly, there is no necessary connection between level of membership activity and level of electoral success, nor is there any evidence of a link between areas of electoral strength in the most recent elections and those which preceded it. PR regional election results broken down by department provide a good example of this (see Figures 4.3 and 4.4).

The results show strong contrasts among themselves. In 1986, some departments in Corsica, Aquitaine and Poitou-Charentes did not have a Green list, and overall these elections mark a fall-back from the position at the previous elections. This coincides with the end of the construction of political ecology (1974–88). René Dumont obtained 1.4 per cent in the 1974 presidential election and the ecologists won 4.4 per cent (2.2 per cent across the whole of France) in the 1978 legislative elections. With 4.5 per cent at the European elections of 1979, two formations contested the 1984 Europeans and won 3.4 per cent (Greens) and 3.3 per cent (Entente Radicale Ecologiste pour les Etats-Unis d'Europe, led by Brice Lalonde), respectively. The 1986 regionals, despite being

FIGURE 4.2 Green presidential election results (1981–2002)

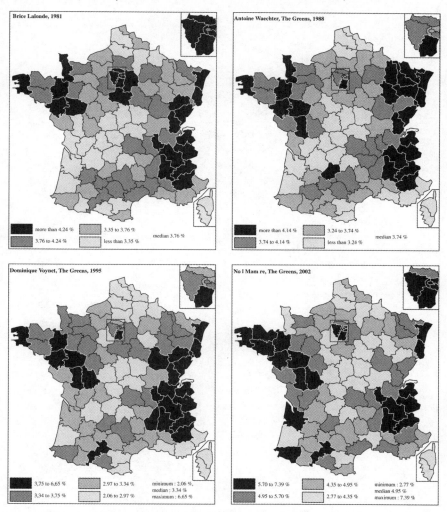

Source: Sainteny (2000), and Green Party official figures

held under PR, were hardly more favourable with 3.4 per cent in departments where a list was presented, and 2.4 per cent and three councillors nationally – Didier Anger in Manche, Antoine Waechter in Haut-Rhin and Andrée Buchmann in Bas-Rhin.

The end of the 1980s marked a turning point for the Greens with good results in the March 1989 municipal elections – 8.1 per cent in towns with more than 9,000 inhabitants. By this time, the Greens held a virtual monopoly of the ecology label, and benefited from a favourable

FIGURE 4.3 Ecologist regional election results by department (1986 and 1992)

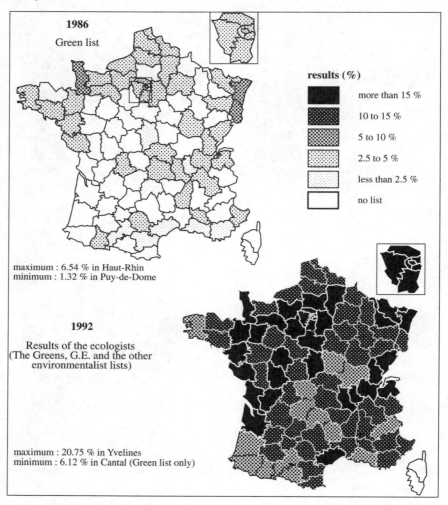

Source: Official Green Party figures

cultural and institutional context (Sainteny, 2000: 117–42). Politically, the PS was particularly weak after a litany of scandals, incumbent weariness and the experience of cohabitation between 1986 and 1988, and part of its electorate turned to the ecologists.

The creation of GE in 1990 by Brice Lalonde aimed to create a competitor for the Greens, developing an ecological perspective closer to that of the PS and presenting an image of 'realistic reform'. The

FIGURE 4.4 Green electoral strategies by department (1986 and 1998)

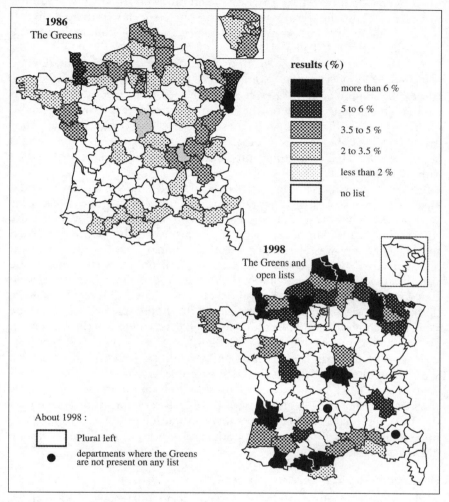

1986
The Greens

results (%)

more than 6 %

5 to 6 %

3.5 to 5 %

2 to 3.5 %

less than 2 %

no list

1998
The Greens and
open lists

About 1998 :

Plural left

departments where the Greens
are not present on any list

Source: Official Green Party figures

March 1992 regional elections bear witness to the success of this action, with GE and the Greens obtaining almost an identical number of votes – 7.1 per cent and 6.8 per cent respectively. The best scores were won where the two lists were in competition.[13] Where the Greens were the only ecology list,[14] their results were better than in 1986, but weaker than the combined GE–Green scores in the previous departments. For example, in Haut-Rhin the Greens won 14.6 per cent of the vote, whereas in Bas-Rhin, the Greens' 11.14 per cent and GE's 7.25 per cent represented almost 18.4 per cent between them. In Nord-Pas-de-Calais, the Greens, led by Marie-Christine Blandin won their only regional presidency. For the party, this region was henceforth treated like a political laboratory, to test and prove their capacity of functioning at the institutional level (Villalba, 1999).

For the 1993 legislative elections, the Greens and GE united. The so-called 'Ecology Entente' won one of their best results under the two-ballot system, with 7.9 per cent of the vote, and around 11 per cent in the constituencies where they fielded candidates. However, these elections also indicated the weakness of the ecology label. Many other groups calling themselves ecologists suddenly appeared a few weeks before the first ballot and ate into the Entente vote (Dolez, 1997). The same was true of 2002.

In the following cantonal, 1994 European and 1995 presidential elections, with scores of 3.5 per cent, 2.9 per cent – their worst ever European result – and 3.4 per cent – with Dominique Voynet as the sole ecology candidate (Szac, 1998) – respectively, the Greens returned to the electoral wasteland. The 1995 municipals were also deemed 'unsatisfactory' by the Greens themselves, returning 6.5 per cent in the constituencies where they stood. Evidently, the ecologist split between the Greens and GE and the split within the Greens themselves were both partly responsible for the drop. In September 1994, Antoine Waechter created the MEI[15] but was unable to challenge the Greens in elections, despite the ideological challenge.[16] For its part, GE progressively moved towards the liberal–Gaullist right, a process which caused significant internal divisions[17] and inexorable electoral decline – 2 per cent at the 1994 Europeans; no presidential candidate in 1995; little presence in the 1997 legislatives; and only three councillors elected in the 1998 regionals. GE's remnants placed themselves in DL's orbit before once again attempting an independent electoral strategy, but with no greater success.[18]

Electoral results in the *gauche plurielle*

At the AF in Le Mans in 1995, the Greens decided to engage in a strategy to federate the ecologists on the left. After difficult negotiations and statutory modifications, the Parti Ecologiste, parts of the Alternative Rouge et Verte (AREV) and of the Convention pour une Alternative Progressiste (CAP) and the CES were integrated between the end of 1997 and the beginning of 1998. The unified programme reinforced the central position of the Greens as the principal representative of political ecology. GE was unable to turn itself into a centre- and centre-right-oriented ecology pole for the 1997 legislative elections. Nevertheless, the Greens were not the only repository for the ecology vote. A series of small formations also contest this vote, among others AREV, CAP and the rightist Ecologie Bleue, composed of old members of GE who intended promoting environmental issues from inside the UDF. These formations only obtained weak results but showed that there is an available pool of ecology voters who will move to 'independent' ecology candidates (Boy and Villalba, 1999: 143–62).

The 1997 legislative elections opened a new electoral phase, with the Greens engaging in an alliance with the PS while simultaneously trying to maintain an autonomous political strategy. At the first round, the 455 Green and Green-endorsed candidates won just over one million votes, or 5.1 per cent – at the national level, 4.1 per cent. But hundreds of Green candidates did not reach the 5 per cent threshold. In the 1998 regional elections, the Greens tried to adopt a strategy of alliance, as well as maintaining the principle of autonomy for the regional federations in the electoral procedure. Fifty-four full *gauche plurielle* lists and five partial ones were entered. The 37 other lists presented by the Greens were the so-called 'Green and open lists'. In all, they won 5.6 per cent (Boy and Villalba, 1999). The map of the ecologists' results reflect this double strategy. The results of the Green lists are less good than those of the ecologists in 1992 (Greens plus GE plus other ecology lists) but only just below that of the 1992 Green lists on their own (Figures 4.3 and 4.4). In terms of representatives, the Greens lost 38 of the 105 seats won in 1992. Without doubt, then, this is a downward trend. At the cantonal elections, they obtained 7.6 per cent in the 718 cantons where they fielded candidates. Finally, in the 1999 European elections, despite a head of list with a strong media presence, Daniel Cohn-Bendit, a number of salient environmental themes – GM crops, 'mad-cow disease', etc. – and weaker competition from other ecology lists, the 9.7 per cent score was still below the 1989 and 1994 results.

For the municipal and cantonal elections of 11 and 18 March 2001, the Greens repeated this double strategy, presenting 180 independent lists (which won an average of 14 per cent) and taking part in around 300 full or partial *gauche plurielle* lists. The ensemble of 'left' lists (the *gauche plurielle* without the independent Green lists) won 36.4 per cent at the first round and 38.84 per cent at the second in those communes with more than 3,500 inhabitants. At the final count, the Greens won over 1,000 municipal councillors, including around 40 mayors. Only four mayors were elected on independent lists – three in the Ile-de-France and one in Territoire de Belfort – and 25 were elected on 'communal interest' lists,[19] mostly in communes with fewer than 3,500 inhabitants. Thanks to the *gauche plurielle*, the election of mayors in the largest communes, such as Les Mureaux, Saumur, Lyon I or Paris II, reinforced the credibility of the programme, addressing local politics from their own perspective. The Greens also presented more than 700 candidates in the cantonal elections (and endorsed 100 *gauche plurielle* candidates).

They obtained 13 general councillors, bringing their total number of elected representatives to 17 (excluding the Parisian councillors who follow a slightly different procedure). Of these 13, 9 were supported by the other parties from the governing majority.

Since 1974, then, political ecology's electoral results have alternated between phases of growth and phases of decline. Overall, the Greens can only rely on 5–7 per cent of the vote. Well managed within the alliance, these votes have brought important benefits. The peak at the end of the 1990s, when they returned to results on a par with those at the beginning of the decade, resulted from their taking into account both the weight of the Fifth Republic's majoritarian logic and of the left–right cleavage, and even more so the importance of environmental themes to public opinion. Even though the Greens still suffer from a lack of credibility outside the environmental field, their participation in government and strategy of agreements with the *gauche plurielle* have more than made up for this programmatic weakness.

However, they do not seem to have known how to exploit their governmental participation and presence in the National Assembly in the 2002 elections. Although they presented an unprecedented 451 candidates, only 11 of these broke the 30 per cent barrier, with 22 winning more than 20 per cent. For the Green leadership, even a ministerial candidate had no guarantee of success with Dominique Voynet and Guy Hascoët both being defeated in their respective Jura and Nord constituencies. Only Yves Cochet, the former minister for the environment in his new Paris seat and Noël Mamère in Gironde managed to win re-election, together with Martine Billard, also in Paris. Billard, the only new deputy, ironically comes from the left–libertarian stream of the Greens, which had been very critical of its own party's time in government.

Partner within the *gauche plurielle* government

To understand the relationship of the Greens with the plural-left majority between 1997 and 2002, it is necessary to look at the changes in the party's political and ideological priorities.

Implantation on the left

In 1984, the Greens hesitated over the strategic direction that their party should take. For two years, certain influential figures within the party – Jean Brière, Yves Cochet and Didier Anger – prudently shifted their focus towards the left. However, the strong 68 per cent support for Antoine Waechter's motion, 'Ecology is not for marrying!' placed the Greens in a position which proclaimed the irrelevance of traditional political cleavages ('Neither right nor left'), the important of alternative values (the importance of the environment, the alternative challenge to economic growth) and destined the party to fight for a new 'cultural majority' in France. This radical vision may have allowed the Greens to occupy their own niche in political space and, despite their marginality, to hide a thin manifesto demonstrative of its ideological weaknesses. Gradually, however, this approach became more and more contested by those with a more pragmatic view of political action. Indeed, by 1993, the Greens had ceased to consider the autonomy principal as an absolute block on any political alliance. Waechter was repudiated. Henceforth, the Greens have clearly presented themselves as part of the left. The AF of Le Mans in 1995 discussed the predictable political compromises necessary for agreement with the left – the PS, PRG and PCF – and even future electoral compromises. From January 1997, the Greens and the PS divided up constituencies, agreeing unanimous acceptance of Green leaders, desistment pacts and, last but not least, the financial considerations linked to state financing of parties.

The Greens benefited from the programmatic agreement with the PS in being allowed to promote certain themes which had always formed part of ecology's discourse (see Figure 4.5). Unlike in 2002, the agreement between the Greens and its partners was predicated upon a negotiation of programmatic contents. Particular attention would be given to job-sharing, an issue to be found in Waechter's 1988 campaign, and which was also a fundamental part of Dominique Voynet's (Voynet, 1995). Overall, the contract dealt more with social than with environmental issues.

This strategic development won the Greens national posts: seven Green Party or Green-affiliated deputies sat in the National Assembly[20] and Lionel Jospin gave the Ministry of Territorial Management and the Environment to Dominique Voynet. On 8 April 2000, Guy Hascoët was named Secretary of State for the Interdependent Economy (Economie Solidaire). The Greens had thus passed a further threshold of legitimation. This approach seems to have satisfied ecology members. In 1998, 79 per cent of them thought that governmental participation was a positive thing. The members believed that their representatives had principally been influential in the areas of the environment (70 per cent) and gender parity (61 per cent) (Boy and Villalba, 2000). As far as ideology was concerned, the Greens were seen as presenting a radical front which went beyond the current policies or intentions of the *gauche plurielle* – for instance, 67 per cent wanted the naturalisation of all illegal immigrants.

The European election campaign was an opportunity to show the extent of Green ideology. Cohn-Bendit initially focused his campaign on issues of concern to him, and notably the 'liberal–libertarian' vision of ecology (Cohn-Bendit, 1999). Under pressure from Green members, however, he reoriented his campaign to focus more upon social issues and problems high on the French agenda – pensions, youth development,

FIGURE 4.5 The main themes of the Green–PS programmatic agreement (1997)

• **Economic and social clauses**

Wholesale reduction in working hours via a law on 35-hour working week with no salary reductions; further decrease to 32 hours by 2003; creation of a 'tertiary sector' of social and ecological utility; minimum income guarantees for 18–25 year-olds

• **Democracy and citizenship clauses**

Suppression of article 16 of the constitution; no multiple office-holding; gender parity; adoption of statutes for local representatives; reinitiation of decentralisation of the regions; re-establishment of asylum law and *droit du sol*

• **International clauses**

Social and environmental charters to be introduced into a new Maastricht Treaty; establishment of sustainable development criteria for single currency; elimination of weapons of mass destruction

• **Territorial and environmental clauses**

Moratorium on building of nuclear reactors and MOX production until 2010; closure of Super-Phoenix reactor programme; reduction of nuclear waste stocks.

Reviewing of waste treatment in the Hague, and no new contracts signed by France; an energy law by 2005 at the latest; development of the rail network; moratorium on motorway construction; review of taxation on fossil fuels; introduction of eco-tax on pollutant energy sources; abandoning of Rhine-Rhône canal project; implementation of 'Natura 2000' directive

---

minimum income guarantees, etc. Nevertheless, he continued to promote his 'third left' perspective as his own political strategy.

After the spring elections in 2002, the Greens asserted their desire to revitalise the left camp via ideological renovation – 'reaffirming left-wing values' and in particular those concerning social and environmental policy. The influence of the electoral results and the need to reorganise the balance of power on the left will have important consequences for the internal development of the party.

Factional influence and its limits

Internal debate within the Greens has remained a source of tension between factions ever since the party's creation. They represent the support of certain members for the leaders, and are based upon ideological or strategic concerns. Increasingly, however, factions are becoming a means of attacking other candidates or securing membership benefits. At the

Toulouse Congress on 11–12 November 2000, six main factions vied for power.[21] The ideological differences were sometimes difficult to discern, and it was particularly on matters of electoral strategy that divisions appeared. In fact, the unequal geographic distribution of members strongly affects the political influence of the factions (Vieillard-Coffre, 2001: 147–50). Thus, certain departments had an effect on the vote – Dominique Voynet won in the Jura, of course, but also in six of the eight regions where membership is high, and in particular in the largest, the Ile-de-France (see Figure 4.6).

But the result at Toulouse was also in part due to the confrontation of two major and fairly similar factions: Maison Verte and Dynamiques. The first opposed Dominique Voynet's strategy, while the second chose to ally with her. The Maison Verte list led by Marie-Christine Blandin and Stéphane Pocrain won in the Nord-Pas-de-Calais with half of this region's votes and just over 100 in the Ile-de-France. In contrast to this list, the one led by Noël Mamère and Guy Hascoët was important not in the regions of its two leaders, but in those with the most members (251 votes in Ile-de-France and 122 in Languedoc-Roussillon, as opposed to 63 votes in Aquitaine and 80 in Nord-Pas-de-Calais). The weight of a faction thus comes from its success in the regions with the most members, even if the faction itself does not win.

The primary to elect the ecology candidate for the 2002 presidential election demonstrates the limited use of factions. Five candidates took part. A 21-year-old candidate, Alice Crété, was supported by ALV – she won 12.59 per cent. Verts Ecolo and Dynamiques put their support behind Etienne Tête (9.71 per cent) and Noël Mamère respectively. The writer and regional councillor, Yves Frémion, was not supported by any faction and won 8.20 per cent; nor was Alain Lipietz, although he is considered to be a member of Dominique Voynet's inner circle. In the first round in May 2001, Mamère won 42.78 per cent of the vote, with Lipietz taking 25.55 per cent. These two candidates insisted that their candidacies did not reflect a game playing upon the support of different factions. Alain Lipietz won the surprise victory, managing to gather a majority of the second-round vote without the official support of a faction or of the Green leadership. He won 3,528 votes against Mamère's 3,183. Lipietz's victory was based principally on the level of constancy in the different regions' support for him. While Mamère scored highly in certain regions, Lipietz at least doubled his score in every region (see Figure 4.7).

However, Lipietz's candidacy did not satisfy certain national leaders. Making good use of certain media *faux pas* committed by Lipietz, the party apparatus forced him to submit to a second approval process by the members. On 29 October 2001, with 81 per cent of the vote demanding his removal, Lipietz stood down in favour of Noël Mamère. At this stage, it is less the factions and more personal rivalries and media

FIGURE 4.6 Motions in the Toulouse Congress and regional assembly voting

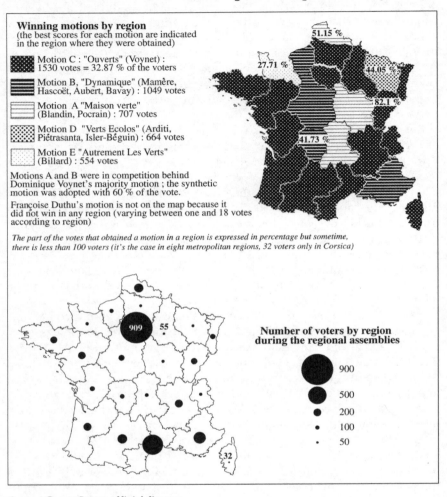

Winning motions by region
(the best scores for each motion are indicated
in the region where they were obtained)

Motion C : "Ouverts" (Voynet) :
1530 votes = 32.87 % of the voters

Motion B, "Dynamique" (Mamère,
Hascoët, Aubert, Bavay) : 1049 votes

Motion A "Maison verte"
(Blandin, Pocrain) : 707 votes

Motion D "Verts Ecolos" (Arditi,
Piétrasanta, Isler-Béguin) : 664 votes

Motion E "Autrement Les Verts"
(Billard) : 554 votes

Motions A and B were in competition behind
Dominique Voynet's majority motion ; the synthetic
motion was adopted with 60 % of the vote.

Françoise Duthu's motion is not on the map because it
did not win in any region (varying between one and 18 votes
according to region)

The part of the votes that obtained a motion in a region is expressed in percentage but sometime,
there is less than 100 voters (it's the case in eight metropolitan regions, 32 voters only in Corsica)

**Number of voters by region
during the regional assemblies**

900
500
200
100
50

Source: Green Party official figures

scrutiny which determine the balance of power within the party. From
now on, membership support will not be a guarantee against the party's
interests as perceived by the Green leadership.

Conclusion

For the first time in their history, the Greens are able to assess their
participation in a governing coalition. They had ceased to be a marginal

FIGURE 4.7 Green presidential primaries in 2002

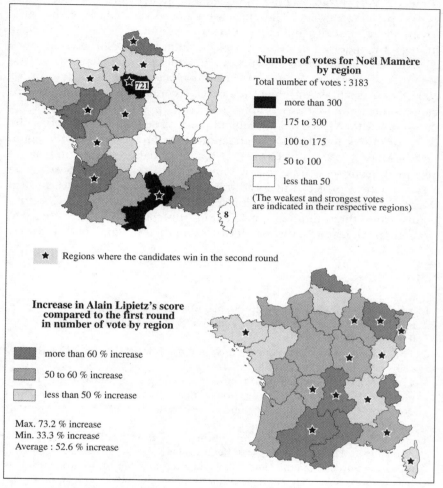

Source: Green Party official figures

and idealistic member of the party system, and had become an important partner within the *gauche plurielle*. However, this unprecedented situation should not be allowed to disguise two uncertainties. First, the Greens cannot claim the ecology vote for themselves alone as the 2002 elections showed once more.[22] Without any doubt, managing an independent left-wing ecology pole will become a major issue in the near future. The evaluation of their time in power is the second uncertainty: what have they gained from this systematic power-sharing with the PS? Unsurprisingly, internal debate over this has been rife.

For some Greens, such as the Autrement les Verts, Ecologie et Démo-cratie or Vert Ecolo factions, government policy was not sufficiently swayed by Green policy. They have denounced the failure of the 1997 Green–PS agreements, and in particular the continued pursuit of a nuclear strategy, the ignoring of thousands of illegal immigrants, the renaissance of road and motorway construction, insufficient consideration of the greenhouse effect, and the failure to introduce PR electoral reform for 2002. Some, such as Autrement les Verts, recommended leaving government; others would have simply preferred to clarify and consolidate the terms of the Green–PS agreement, and consequently to redefine the policy priorities and electoral negotiations – the line taken by Dynamiques Vertes, Maison Verte and Ouvert. Debate is equally as lively on what to take away from their time in government.[23] It is clear that constructing a new political project will force the Greens to look long and hard at their own agenda and organisation in order to ascertain the key positive points from their time in power, and subsequently to use these to strengthen the legitimacy which derives from their unique political stance.

Notes

1 All motions winning the required majority at the national level, once the regional scores are added, are considered passed and are therefore not debated at the FA.
2 The amount varies between regions, but the lowest amount is EURO 30, equivalent to the national allocation.
3 This cartographic depiction of membership can also be calculated using the number of members as a proportion of the departmental population. However, the raw figures illustrate more clearly the weight of certain regions within the national organisation.
4 The influence of Noel Mamère is clearly significant, but needs to be put into context. He became Mayor of Bègle and vice-president of the *communauté urbaine* of Bordeaux in the 1989 municipal elections, standing on the presidential majority ticket. He subsequently moved to GE, before returning to the Greens in 1997.
5 Aube and Cantal appear in white because the number of members is tiny; Réunion and Guadeloupe each have a local organisation.
6 Source: survey by Daniel Boy (CEVIPOF), Agnès Roche (Clermont-Ferrand University) and Bruno Villalba (CRAPS-Lille 2), 1998, with the cooperation of the Greens. The data can be downloaded at http://www.les-verts.org/documents/enquete.html
7 http://www.sofres.fr/etudes/pol/130700_references_n.html
8 Conversely, PCF bastions are often Green-electoral wastelands.
9 In 1995, 26 per cent of Voynet voters made their choice 'at the last moment', compared to an average of 11 per cent; 17 per cent made their choice 'in the last few days of the campaign', as against 10 per cent on average.

10 For instance, the major storm in December 1999, the sinking of the *Erika* and *Ievoli Sun* petrol-tankers off the Brittany coast in December 1999 and November 2000 respectively, and the flooding of the Somme in the successive winters of 2000–1 and 2001–2.

11 The 1974 election is distinct from the rest: for the first time the ecologists fielded a presidential candidate, René Dumont, an agronomist not previously known for his ecologist leanings. A political presence for ecology only began to develop in the municipal elections of 1977.

12 It should be noted that the electoral results, in terms of valid votes, are figures which take into account the size of the population, whereas the membership figures do not.

13 Especially in the Parisian district: 20.75 per cent in Yvelines and 20.44 per cent in Val d'Oise.

14 In Hautes-Alpes (9.94 per cent), Ariège (9.6 per cent), Corrèze (7.12 per cent), Creuse (8.7 per cent) Haute-Garonne (8.18 per cent), Gers (12.42 per cent), Haute-Loire (10.2 per cent), Haute-Marne (14.51 per cent), Nièvre (7.8 per cent), Hautes-Pyrénées (9.16 per cent), Haut-Rhin (14.6 per cent) Saône et Loire (9.01 per cent), Deux-Sèvres (10.68 per cent), Tarn (6.53 per cent), Territoire de Belfort (14.43 per cent).

15 See their website: www.novomundi.com/mei/.

16 Electorally, they have had extremely indifferent results – no candidate in the 1995 presidential election; 1.5 per cent in the 1999 European elections.

17 The following splinters were formed: 1992 – François Donzel's Alliance pour l'Ecologie et la Démocratie (AED); 1993 – Jean-François Caron's Ecologie Autrement (EA); 1994 – Noël Mamère's Convergence Ecologie Solidarité (CES), etc. Some were inclined towards the PS (AED) or negotiated agreements with the Greens (EA). Others, after some hesitation, finally joined the Greens (CES).

18 www.generation-ecologie.com/.

19 Representing that diverse group often labelled 'apolitical'.

20 Marie-Hélène Aubert, Yves Cochet, Guy Hascoët and D. Voynet (Greens); André Aschieri, Noël Mamère, and Jean-Michel Marchand (ecology deputies in Radical, Citoyen et Vert parliamentary group); and Michèle Rivasi (ecology deputy affiliated to PS parliamentary group).

21 Dynamiques vertes led by Guy Hascoët and Noël Mamère; Notre Maison Verte led by Marie-Christine Blandin; Ouverts led by Dominique Voynet; Autrement les Verts led by Martine Billard; Verts Ecolo led by Maryse Arditi and Etienne Tête; and Ecologie et Démocratie led by Françoise Duthu.

22 In these elections, of the 32 formations presenting at least 50 candidates nationally, 8 stood under an ecology banner.

23 See the CNIR debates of 23–24 June 2001, and the *EcoRev* dossiers (http://ecorev.org).

5
Managing the plural left: implications for the party system

David Hanley

Introduction

The plural left marks a new type of alignment within the French party system. Left parties had cooperated previously according to varying formulae. The type of majority known as *concentration républicaine* (Goguel, 1946) is arguably the first manifestation, followed by the hegemony of the *délégation des gauches* in the 1900s, which put through anti-clerical measures of 'republican defence'. The interwar period witnessed the *cartel des gauches* – tactical electoral alliances of Radicals, SFIO and selected 'left republicans' – invariably unstable and short-lived. Famously, the 1936 Popular Front, a formal alliance of the three main left parties plus smaller allies, managed to campaign on an agreed programme but, although a government was formed and enjoyed some success, this too fell apart under various pressures. After the Second World War, formulae for broad left cooperation ran from tripartism (SFIO and PCF without any Radicals, but including the new force of Christian Democracy) to the more restricted and temporary defensive arrangement of SFIO, Radicals and centre oddments in 'Republican Front' alliances excluding the by-now pariah PCF.

Under the Fifth Republic, the growing reality of bipolarisation drove the left's leaders to the inevitable – a pact between the PS (as it now was) and the PCF, resting on a detailed and ambitious programme to which the incoming coalition government would be committed. The break-up of the Common Programme alliance generated sufficient movement to bring about Mitterrand's 1981 win and, significantly, for him to feel obliged to involve the PCF in government for the first time in thirty-four years. PCF failure to use this opportunity intelligently soon led to further marginalisation, and by the mid-1980s the left-wing alliance consisted of a large PS with an undisputed leader of high status capable of winning a second presidency (and thus itself capable of winning a majority or nearly), trailing in its wake a small ally (the left Radicals),

76

and a shrinking PCF, not in total opposition to the PS and usually forced at election time to agree a deal. This unbalanced left duly won the presidency and a working majority in 1988. During this period a sizeable Green vote emerged in France. Yet this new but unfocused challenge was mostly ignored by the left parties (Boy, 1993).

All these cooperative attempts recall two underlying tendencies. First, the left parties have usually been involved in some kind of alliance. The winning of an outright majority by any one party has remained mostly an impossible dream, even after the PS flash in the pan of 1981, though this does not mean that *rapports de force* in a left alliance are necessarily equal. Second, these alliances have usually been fragile, tactical and short term. The object has been to win an election and govern as best one could, basing government on the *rapports de force* within the winning coalition. There has been nothing permanent about the pact; sometimes there has been no agreed programme or even clear understanding beyond *discipline républicaine*. Partners have felt free to drop out (PCF refusal to join government in 1936) or change partners in mid-term (the Radicals on numerous occasions between the wars, the SFIO after 1947) or even to vote with the right (the PCF against Rocard after 1988). No party leaders thought in terms of developing an ongoing alliance which respects the different identities and contributions of partners while demanding agreement and discipline on a number of policies and procedures. As a result, little long-term commitment could be given; partners might have to be changed. Hence it always suited the PS to keep alive the (increasingly unlikely) threat that it could revive the old type of Third Force deal with the Christian Democrats; or the PCF could threaten to withdraw into total opposition, e.g., by leaving candidates in at the second ballot (again an increasingly incredible scenario).

The seismic shock of the 1993 defeat shattered PS dreams of being a natural party of government. Rocard, now party leader – in itself a symbol of how low it had sunk – described the left as 'a field of ruins' and called for a 'big bang' to revive the PS, hinting that it might even have to merge with other left forces. Jospin's emergence as a credible leader after the European defeat of 1994 and Rocard's departure stemmed the decline and gave hope that the left could return to office. But Jospin had realised that this could only happen if a new type of relationship were established among its components. Thus was born a new concept of left unity in the shape of the plural left. Negotiations between the parties were direct and clearly focused, and carried out by a small team from each – the PCF, MdC, PRG, and, perhaps most significant of all, the Greens under Dominique Voynet (Amar and Chemin, 2002: 13–74). Each party retained its own electoral programme, but it was understood that all components would be in government if the plural left won.[1]

Such a strategy clearly has implications for the party system, both in terms of its individual components and of the dynamics between these which constitute the party system per se. First, we need to examine the motivations of the PS, principal mover in this strategy, but also to a lesser extent, those of its partners. We need then to examine what the plural left implies in terms of day-to-day relations between its components, especially in the light of recent government experience. These analyses may enable us to see how far the new experiment has actually transformed the party system, not just in terms of relationships within the left, but between the plural left and the rest of the system.

The PS and the plural left: strategy and motivation

As the motor force behind and principal beneficiary of the plural-left strategy was the PS, we need to understand its analysis of the party system and its motivations in pushing the plural left. Jospin's team began with the idea that the left–right polarity remains fundamental in French partisan life (Duhamel, 1997, Mossuz-Lavau, 1998, Cambadélis, 1999: 71–83). This is not just due to electoral bipolarisation, which may be as much a reflection as a cause; voters do still tend to split broadly along the left–right axis, as they have done since republican democracy became the norm (Charlot, 1993, Boy and Mayer, 2000). Obviously the values that underpin left and right identities evolve, as do the partisan forces that express them. But on election day, left-wing voters expect to find an adequate supply in party terms for their aspirations. This supply should normally confront a similar supply on the right in what was a moderately polarised system.

The state of this supply in 1993 was problematic, however. Previously, the PS thought of itself as embodying the only serious left. The PCF was shrinking; allies like the PRG had long been vassalised. Even the newly created MdC might not prove much of a nuisance, as Chevènement's followers might be more easily bought off from outside the party rather than cause trouble from within. From this viewpoint, then, the PS bossed the left and others fell in behind, with little input into policy and having to bargain for what they could in terms of seats, patronage, etc.

All this changed with the scale of the 1993 defeat, when the PS lost 217 deputies (282 to 65) and only took half of its 1988 vote, sliding back to the levels of the mid-1960s. Its allies, being smaller anyway, suffered proportionately less. The left faced a long haul to reconquer voters, but even if voters were to come back, there was no guarantee that they would all go to the PS, especially as the sour end of the Mitterrand presidency had degraded yet further the image of socialism. An alternative strategy therefore seemed attractive: why not build on the very diversity of the left, encouraging each of its components to draw in voters as widely as possible?

Clearly, this meant a downplaying of the hegemonic role which the PS had exercised since the late 1970s and a hard-headed assessment that it could probably never again achieve the scores of 1981 or 1988 nor hope to dominate in the same way. Obviously in any new left alliance the PS would be the biggest player and expect to lead in government; pluralism is a '*réalité hiérarchisée*' (Cambadélis, 1999: 136). But this position differs from the previous winner-take-all arrogance. The PS would have a more consultative, less domineering profile; it would also have to be more generous in sharing seats, posts and resources.

This was a bold step, and Jospin was the right man to take it. Inclined by temperament to a less personal style of leadership, he was also favoured by the institutional context; a plural-left win in 1997 would not be a presidential one (with all its implied legitimacy for one man and his programme). Rather it would be a parliamentary win, a win for parties; any government would have to be based on those parties, even if it was then to govern under cohabitation. The PS thus accepted a changed role for itself within the subsystem of the left. It did so as the best way to preserve its longer-term interests; better to be consensual leader of a broad-left coalition with some chance of gaining office than to be hugely dominant within a divided left with much less chance.

The plural-left strategy also reflected PS views about the left-party sub-system. It divided allies into three categories. The small parties (MdC and PRG) were seen essentially as *notable* movements with particular local strengths. MdC, with its vigorous republican nationalism, would refuse such a description, and certainly its ideological profile promised to cause problems. But in terms of putting together an alliance, these were small organisations with whom one could broker a deal. This meant a guarantee of a few seats for sitting deputies and a place in government, which the PS had indicated its willingness to provide. Previous republican alliances had done no differently.

In a different category was the PCF. Even in the 1980s the PS had arguably never pushed home its advantage, in terms of candidacies for seats or town halls, despite a clear drift of voters towards it away from the PCF. The hope was that the PCF would gradually prove redundant. Realistically, though, this would take a long time, as the party hung on in its last bastions. The PS thus resigned itself to the continuation of a sizeable number of PCF deputies, crucial to its majority, as well as Communist presence in government. This did not rule out hard bar-gaining at local level, but it did imply a willingness not to tread too hard on the PCF's toes. The PS also sought to influence the PCF's internal development. By incorporating it in a new majority, the PS could only increase the tension between modernisers who broadly supported Hue and who needed positive results (in terms of influencing policy) and the older, pure oppositionists (Hage, Auchedé, etc.) who wanted the PCF to immure itself in a ghetto of protest before the Trotskyists usurped its role in such arenas. The party's internal process remains problematical, and largely independent of PS intervention; but if the PCF were to 'social-democratise' itself yet further and lose some of its hard core, then the possibility of absorbing the social-democratic remnants back into the PS might arise (Cambadélis, 1999: 133ff.). The PCF itself did not believe that the PS's weakening in 1993 opened up any new space. As Lajoinie revealingly told Cambadélis, the only way forward for both parties was together (1999: 26).

The Greens were a case *sui generis*, and PS treatment of them is arguably the boldest and most system-modifying part of the plural-left strategy. Pro-Green sentiments continued to rise among voters, despite finding no successful partisan outlet (Boy, 1993). Several factors ensured this, including division among Green elites, the entry barriers imposed by the electoral system to all new parties and even sharp practice (for instance, Interior Minister Quilès allowing the registration of numerous doubtful ecology candidacies in 1993, thus scattering the Green offer confusingly). The Greens were even unable in 1994 to re-elect their MEPs from 1989. Undoubtedly their challenge could have been ignored by the plural left, which could easily have stopped them winning seats under the two-ballot system.

A bolder alternative was to recognise that the Greens' own ineptitude and the electoral system might not keep them out of Parliament forever, and certainly not without risk. Even if they could only mobilise a first-ballot electorate, it might not be deliverable to the plural left on the second. In other words, the Greens might have some blackmail potential. Taking them into coalition held problems; their demands were far-reaching, not just on environmental questions. But cold-shouldering them was just as risky an option.

The PS grasped this nettle resolutely, with an offer of seats and a place in government. It sought to decant the Green movement, to sort out those interested in political responsibility from those concerned with protest; it sought to distinguish politicians from ideologues, realists from moralisers. It did so with admirable succinctness; the main body of Greens followed Voynet into the plural left. This passage from periphery to centre stage was dramatic; no party can assume such a brusque change of status overnight. By decanting the Green movement and bringing its mainstream firmly into the plural left, the PS knowingly affected not just the internal functioning of the Greens but the workings of the whole party system. It also gambled that the Greens could be fitted successfully into the left, challenging the assumption that they represent a new cleavage (centred on the environment), unassimilable into the left–right matrix. As for the far left, by now capable of around 5 per cent of the vote, the plural left took the common-sense view that its voters are unlikely to support a reformist politics (at least on the first ballot). But since its representatives were unlikely to figure on the second, it could for coalitional purposes be ignored.

The anchoring of Greens and PCF has also blocked any evolution of the party system towards a two-tier variety. Before 1997, concern was regularly voiced at declining turnout and an increasing tendency to vote for 'protest parties' as opposed to potential government parties. Such worries about a crisis of representation depended on an ontological characterisation of certain parties as being mere protest vehicles, hence unfit for government. Such dubious assumptions fed anxieties; critics dwelt on the increasing share of the first-ballot vote won by such peripheral parties, as opposed to the core of serious parties.[2] Apart from the FN and Trotskyists (Pingaud, 2000), the main members of the peripheral crew were the PCF and Greens.

If one accepts the hypothesis of a core–periphery division within the party system, one must note that it was nullified at a stroke by Jospin's voluntarism. The plural-left pact tied the Greens and PCF into the responsible camp, leaving the protest to the Trotskyists (rising slowly) and an FN soon to be victim of gross self-mutilation. Suddenly the proportion of core party voters climbed by some 16.8 per cent, leaving only about 18 per cent voting for the peripherals and casting doubts on the extent of the crisis of representation. Seen thus, PS strategy seems not only a voluntaristic attempt to recast the party system but also a profoundly civic action, bringing back into the fold a large percentage of voters and reducing citizen alienation. Such happy coincidences of civic duty and one's own strategic interest are infrequent.

The PS triggered a voluntaristic recomposition of the party system. Within the historic left–right cleavage, it energetically re-organised the left pole. This strategy involved downgrading its own position somewhat, while continuing quasi-clientelistic relationships with small allies. But the dynamic counterpart to this was the challenge thrown out to Greens and Communists; they were offered measurable rewards in return for their cooperation. Yet acceptance of rewards put pressure on them as parties, highlighting their internal contradictions as they moved into a new role of responsibility as opposed to criticism. The PS pursued a calculated strategy of interference in the affairs of other parties, aiming to modifying their behaviour, the better to reshape the whole party system. The strategy sought to make the broad left viable again. It worked quicker than expected, but the experience of government opened a new chapter.

The plural left in government

The management of intra-left relationships is seen first in terms of distribution of rewards and second in the regulation of tension between partners. The basic reward for any party is places in government. Jospin's smallish government respected electoral weight in its shareout of posts but not to the extent of the proportionality used to compose Italian cabinets under *partitocrazia*; pluralism is indeed a hierarchised reality (see Table 5.1).

TABLE 5.1 Vote–position ratio in first Jospin government

	Ministers (N)	*Government posts* (%)	*Share of total Left vote* (%)
PS	19	70.4	50.0
PRG	3	11.1	3.1
PCF	3	11.1	21.8
MdC	1	3.7	2.4
Green	1	3.7	14.5
Other left	–	–	8.2
	27	100	100

The second Jospin government in 2000 was again based on PS supremacy, but added an extra dimension to the formula. It brought in the Fabius tendency, neutralising Jospin's only serious rival for leadership of the PS. Jospin also added Mélenchon and his *gauche socialiste*, main source of internal party criticism. After this internal rebalancing only the Poperenites, persistent old-left militants, remained outside the magic circle.[3] Thus groups within the PS became part of the balancing process alongside allies from outside the party. This new government also saw an extra junior post for the Greens, a deliberately belated recognition of their success in the 1999 Euroelections.

Jospin played the numbers game, but only on his terms. Ministers from smaller parties tended to be confined to specialist areas. Thus Voynet was given Environment and specifically denied Health; Hascoët's junior ministry was environmentally tagged. The Communists received social ministries, including Transport, where access to unions is still important. Even the placing of Chevènement at Interior showed that the most republican force in the government had its very specific place (but no other?).

If distribution of rewards was relatively mechanical, control of this delicate alliance was complex. Jospin was a hands-on prime minister, at the heart of policymaking and attending personally to relations with allies. He used formal and informal contacts, from traditional weekly breakfasts with senior PS 'elephants' to formal meetings with other party leaders,[4] as well as less visible social contacts with the latter. While a relatively high degree of public argument was tolerated, the PS was clearly leader of the coalition. Regular complaints about PS hegemony, by Voynet in particular but also Buffet, are one indication of this.[5] A more convincing one is the semi-public slapping down of allies for crossing a line in the sand. This happened to Voynet after she launched into Jospin's leadership style in a regional council of her party; she simply took the lesson on board and did not resign, suggesting that the Greens had to accept PS primacy in the last analysis.[6] Voynet's late departure from government was not a rejection of Green participation in a plural-left government but a career move to become mayor of Dôle – a failure, but she did become party leader (Amar and Chemin, 2002: 218–27).

More subtle techniques were also used by the PS to maintain its ascendancy, notably attempts to influence the internal workings of other parties, as described above. Jospin held contemptuous views about the chronic fissiparity of the Greens which he strove to increase.[7] Hascoët's appointment was a masterstroke, as he and Noël Mamère, the vocal Bordeaux deputy who criticised Voynet's failure to obtain more radical environmental policies, formed increasingly a pole of opposition to Voynet within the Greens. While differences between the factions may well be exaggerated, each was keen to secure the nomination as Green candidate for the 2002 presidentials, as Villalba and Vieillard-Coffre demonstrate in this volume (see Chapter 4). The more divided the Greens were, the less their first-ballot impact and the bigger Jospin's score, in theory. Thus putting both groups in government might have increased tension within the Green Party and weakened their electoral appeal. In party system terms, therefore, the PS sought to weaken competition within the left sub-system from the inside, by modifying the behaviour of one of its protagonists.

A major source of tension was clearly policy-making (Szarka, 1999). Examination of the policy process since 1997 requires a separate study, but several points can be made. First, the plural left generally found agreement easiest on libertarian matters like PACS or parity legislation. Second, PS partners continued to argue for their favourite radical policies (wealth tax for the PCF, regularisation of all *sans-papiers* and commitment to phase out civil nuclear energy for the Greens) while knowing that the PS would not accept them, at least in untrammelled form. Third, the junior partners had to swallow some bitter pills (adoption of the Euro for the PCF, burial of nuclear waste or reactivation of the *Phénix* nuclear reactor for the Greens). That said, however, many government bills were the product of horse-trading between the parties, a classic example being the hunting bill, which Voynet defended in Parliament although it was not fully to her liking. The last-minute withdrawal of PCF opposition to the social modernisation bill in June 2001 saw compromise stretched to the limits. The PCF accepted face-saving amendments to a bill which in the end removed protection from workers.[8] Tension was frequent, but a deal was usually struck.

The major clash was undoubtedly over Corsica. The special arrangements proposed by Jospin were denounced by Chevènement's MdC as
incompatible with republican principles. Jospin could not withdraw from
an arrangement whose impact might prove as spectacular (initially, at
least) as the Ulster Good Friday agreement, in order to appease a minor
ally. No public row occurred, and each side expressed its views; but
Chevènement resigned (Amar and Chemin, 2002: 204–17). He was
replaced by a Jospin loyalist Vaillant; but MdC did not get even a junior
post in compensation. This reflects the lack of talent in MdC, but also
the PS's calculation that it could tough this challenge out, as the blackmail
potential of MdC was small. This was a grave miscalculation. MdC's
blackmail potential would be seen on the evening of 21 April 2002 to
amount to some 1.5 million votes; the margin of Jospin's defeat, which
put him out of the second ballot, was only 190,000. Retrospectively,
MdC's exit was probably the moment when the plural left lost the 2002
elections. At the time, MdC made clear its continuing commitment to
the coalition, but the damage was done.

The Greens could muster more immediate blackmail potential, however, as they showed in a cantonal by-election in Ardèche by maintaining
their candidate on the second ballot and costing the PS the seat. This
was doubtless connected with the length of time it took to appoint
Hascoët, some nine months after the Greens had 'earned' the seat by
their European election performance. Jospin had also leaked it out that
he wanted the Greens to have a group in the next Parliament (even if
the threshold had to be reduced), which meant that he expected to offer
them some winnable seats. Clearly, *rapports de force* were perceived differently; the Greens were respected more than MdC because it was felt
that they could do more damage. This was despite PS annoyance at the
Greens' political style, notably their constant moralising about the low
standards of public life in France. This is a dossier the PS would rather
have buried, as it had its own Mutuelle Nationale des Etudiants Français
(MNEF) scandal to set alongside Tibéri and the Paris *mairie*. But it dared
not revenge itself too heavily on the Greens, because they could cost it
seats.

The PCF position was always going to need subtle handling both by
its leaders and the PS. The PCF could logically pose only as the radical
pole of the coalition, seeking to drag it further towards progressive
policies without being irresponsible, to criticise constructively without
being disloyal. It had to be a Janus, sending a populist message to its
constituents and a more consensual one to its partners. Generally it
managed this balancing act about as well as any could have. Initial
hostility to the euro never led the PCF to vote against this key measure
of the government, though it never abandoned its criticisms. Demonstrations planned against the second round of legislation on the

thirty-five-hour week in October 1999 seemed unacceptable for a governing party and led observers to ask whether this was the line in the sand. But Hue needed (and got) a big demonstration on an economic issue like this, to persuade his people that the PCF still counted and could mobilise people. The circle was squared by presenting the protest as directed not against government but against the Mouvement des Entreprises de France (MEDEF), which was trying to block measures in favour of workers. An indulgent PS under Hollande even pretended to endorse this strategy. Clearly the PS calculated that the PCF needed some visible protest in order to comfort its natural base and that this was a way of keeping the PCF at a certain strength, for the time being at least. Again it had too much blackmail potential to be alienated brutally, hence the protest could be accommodated. The resultant compromise suited both sides; lines in the sand have sometimes to be moveable.

By such devices was the balance maintained between coalition partners, albeit with a fairly visible degree of dissent; Szarka notes a 'pragmatic level of cohesion' (1999: 31). Problems as awkward as the Kosovo crisis or the launch of the euro were managed. Two major sets of elections (municipal and European) saw either joint lists or competition kept within amicable bounds. There was no major crisis of the type that plagued coalitions in previous republics, and no party voted down government bills. The plural left sustained a viable social-democratic government up to the 2002 elections.

These were traumatic for the plural left, though it remains to see how far they have rendered the concept invalid. All the component parties ran a presidential candidate, even the PRG whose black, female and overseas candidate, gifted most of her 500 signatures by the PS, seemed a living symbol of the diversity of the left today. Conventional wisdom has it that this plurality cost Jospin his place in the second round and let in Le Pen, but this is simplistic. The timidity of Jospin's campaign (downplaying all reference to socialism) and his late and unconvincing attempts to climb onto the law-and-order bandwagon were fatal. His inversion of the electoral calendar was absurd; why did a man running as leader of a governing *party* give first priority to a contest where personality and stature override partisan considerations? The argument about plural candidacies is also misleading. Every party must put up a candidate if it is to be taken seriously; previously, PCF, Greens had always done so, making their point in the first round before mostly supporting the Socialist in the decisive vote. A plural left should logically imply a plurality of candidates, but capable partners should be able to bargain enough to prevent plurality from degenerating into fragmentation.

The problem with this was Chevènement, whose candidacy sanctioned an ego trip in preparation for over thirty years. For all his talk of overcoming the irrelevance of the left–right cleavage (language already heard in the Third Republic), the ex-PS leader was really targeting left voters worried about law and order and the economic consequences of European integration. Like the Trotskyist candidates who took over 11 per cent and played, in different words, on similar fears, he bit deep and knowingly into Jospin's reserve of votes. He was quite entitled to point out that Jospin had lost 2.5 million votes after five years in government. But one can retort that without his candidacy Jospin would have easily made the second ballot, with a good chance of beating Chirac. Chevènement's motives, and his support, deserve painstaking investigation; but he dealt the plural left a body blow. The June parliamentary elections found it struggling against the tide. All the parties campaigned on their own platforms, but with enough residual unity, helped by fear of letting the FN onto the second ballot in numerous seats, to prompt a high degree of concerted candidacies. Thirty-four seats saw one joint candidate (14 PS, 12 PCF, 4 PRG and 4 Greens).

Variable geometry prevailed elsewhere: the PS made way for 31 PRG and carved up 130 seats with the Greens (70 PS, 60 Green) and 28 with the PCF (15 PS, 13 PCF); only one PS–PCF dogfight took place, in Marseilles.[9] The plural left turned on the MdC with some relish, running candidates in all its seats; only one incumbent survived out of eight, and angry voters sent Sarre and Chevènement to comprehensive defeat. This revenge was meagre consolation for an outcome which left the PS with 146 deputies (from 250), the PCF 21 (from 36), the PRG 7 and the Greens a bare 3; overall, the left went from 319 to 177 and faced a block of 399 right-wing deputies.

Dramatic developments had been occurring on the right since the first presidential ballot. Sensing the magnitude of his victory over Le Pen, Chirac seized the opportunity to pressure the right's parties into a merger. The measure, often adumbrated in the past, seemed feasible at last. In the new chamber, the President's embryonic new party UMP and its satellites boasted 363 seats; Bayrou's maintained UDF scraped 29. A special congress in autumn would officially launch the new party and consecrate the disappearance of the RPR and DL. Faced with what looked like a mass conservative party, solidly ensconced in office, the battered left had plenty of time to take stock. Despite the hurt of defeat, however, it is questionable how much has really changed in the situation of the party sub-system, which we term the plural left.

Consequences for the party system

The plural-left experiment has clearly had consequences for the party system, mostly for the left sub-system, though also for the system as a whole. The left sub-system has been reorganised voluntaristically, from above. What exists now is a semi-permanent constellation of parties around a hegemonic pole, the PS. To use neo-Weberian analysis (Gaxie, 1996, Offerlé, 1987), an entrepreneur, the PS, has cartellised the competition within its sector of the market, guaranteeing itself and its cartel allies a larger share. As this move came about after a huge loss of market share, we could even parody political-market language further and say that it had turned a reverse into an opportunity.

The PS gambit assumes that the left can normally enjoy at least half of the electoral market; it has to make sure that internecine competition does not stop it from realising its share. To identify its product to customers, the plural left branded itself firmly as such. Its discourse picks up classic left themes; in economics, it is Keynesian and regulatory, striving for full employment; in social affairs, it stands for 'cultural liberalism' and inclusion. Politically, it is republican and *laïc*. The gambit also assumes a certain division of labour, with each party picking up a distinct electorate (Giacometti, 1998); these can then be reconciled under the broad headings just described. Far-left voters are assumed to be of a distinct type and the hope is that many will support the plural left on the second.

The plural left has involved its components more closely than most previous arrangements of this type. There were joint declarations, if not a common programme, and joint lists (or failure to put up a rival candidate) seemed as frequent as traditional *désistements*. The work of Parliament seemed subject to the same process of *compromis majoritaire*, even if smaller allies complained that executive decisions were dominated by the leading party. One might agree with Cambadélis (1999) that the left parties are being changed by their participation in the plural left; they are becoming more used to a culture of compromise. This does not mean that they are will lose their identity or merge, but they seem likely to be increasingly attracted to coalitional logic. The plural left looks set to become a lasting feature of the political landscape, notwithstanding changes of nomenclature. The alliance produced electoral victory and workable government for five years; it then lost but not hugely. What does this suggest about the future of the plural left and of the party system generally?

First, relatively little has changed within the components or within the dynamics between them. To take the protagonists in turn, the PS still remains the biggest party. It faces a period of intense leadership struggle in the short term, but that will be resolved. It will continue to have difficulty in defining what socialism really means today. Its linguistic rigours and ideological traditions make this task harder than for some sister-parties, but that is a detail. The PS and all social-democratic parties are all struggling with the same problem, which Rosanvallon summarised neatly: finding out how to reconcile the increasing individualism of modern societies with that desire for security which the left saw as needing collective solutions.[10] There is no easy answer to this question, and failure to provide a ready-made one will not stop the PS or any similar party from winning elections again. When the left wins again, then the PS will be the major player in that victory.

Its partners in the plural left remain in its dependency. The PRG will never be more than a local satellite. The PCF continues to lose lifeblood but is far from dead. It saved its parliamentary group and it still runs 84 towns of over 10,000 and two *conseils généraux*. It lost money in the presidentials, as Hue took less than 5 per cent. It too will undergo a leadership struggle, linked to an identity crisis, as it oscillates between protest and the aspiration to be a government party.

The Greens are still stuck with the same contradictions. Mamère's pragmatic campaign rescued them from the electoral consequences of undiluted radicalism and saved their election expenses. But the tension between governmentalists and radicals remains, the more so as even Mamère began to cast doubt on whether the PS could be relied upon to deliver enough (with particular reference to the commitment to wind down the nuclear power programme). But the Greens' modest electoral appeal probably means that they can maintain a presence in a left alliance but not twist the arm of the leaders. Portelli wonders if the movement has fully accepted the logic of being a party as opposed to a social movement.[11]

All of the above was true when the plural left began life in the mid-1990s. So was the fact that one segment of the party system, the far left, remains hostile to the whole notion of a reformist left alliance. Its thus remains a potential threat, capable of biting indiscriminately into the left's electorate. What has really changed in the dynamics of the plural left is the role of the MdC. Chevènement's movement is at war with the plural left. It did fatal damage in the presidentials, but its parliamentary performance was poor. It remains to be seen whether, with considerable debts, the movement can go very far in its attempt to draw together *républicains des deux rives*, basically Jacobin nationalists of left and right. It could prove to be a mere club for intellectuals and politicians at the end of their career, but remains for the moment a residual threat for the left parties. This one minor exception does not, however, invalidate the concept of the plural left for the future.

One of the strongest consequences of the plural left was, perversely, its effect on the opposite side of the partisan spectrum. The plural left put itself into the driving seat of party politics in France with only 44 per cent of the vote in 1997. This had implications for the right. It had always hitherto understood the logic of bipolarisation better than the left. It usually managed to present voters with an agreed programme and arrange a highly sophisticated carve-up of constituencies and/or places in government, with measurable criteria (Hanley, 1999b). Logically it ought to have responded to the plural left with a display of tighter unity; but its recent history has been one of internal strife compounded by the rise of the FN. The European elections saw the right's offer fragmented into RPR, a UDF which had lost its liberals (now DL) and the sovereignist RPF, not to speak of the two branches of the ex-FN.

Strategists hypothesised about the creation of a plural right, which would take in RPR, RPF, DL and UDF in the hope of further marginalising the far right. France would then have a polarised two-bloc system, with a radical element (Trotskyists and FN) on either side. Given the small size of the radical elements, it would be a moot point whether such a system deserved to be called 'polarised pluralism'. That one could even envisage such a two-bloc system shows how far the party system has moved from the days of the *quadrille bipolaire* of the 1970s. Within the many-membered left bloc there is a clear dominant pole; within the right the RPR would have to claim a similar position of ascendancy. The plural left, by its successful take-off, put major pressure on the right sub-system.

However, there seemed little positive reaction by the right until the 'divine surprise' of Le Pen's presence on the second ballot of the 2002 presidentials. The presence of this bogeyman allowed Chirac to pressure the right parties towards a merger that shows every sign of being more workable and lasting than anything previously attempted, even if the maintaining of the UDF outside the UMP umbrella means that the 'French Tory party' is less than complete. Certainly the right sub-system appears to be in a process of radical and further-reaching reorganisation as a result of what has happened on the left. Within it, the RPR would appear to have played a dominant role similar to the PS on the left and the new party will be very much under its influence.

Faced with the dramatic movement towards unity on the right, some have expressed the wish that the left follow and create a broad-based party. This is unlikely. The smaller parties have distinct identities and ideological traditions, somewhat divergent electorates and above all apparatuses keen to preserve their prerogatives. Leaders such as Hollande seem perfectly aware of this and are not pushing for any sort of merger. Some PS leaders are counting on the demise of the PCF, but that will be some time in coming. In the meantime, a politics of alliance seems the only way forward, with separate identities, but regular electoral alliances and a broadly agreed programme of government. The parties will have to work more closely on a day-to-day basis and manage their unity without taking it for granted. In other words, they will have to carry on doing what they learned to do in 1997–2002. The French party system will not be suddenly bipolarised *à l'anglaise*. But a much more unified right will now confront a left whose success will depend on a constant ability to work out a creative tension between unity and difference.

One final point must be made. The success of the plural left brings out a constant of the French party system ever since it first became recognisable in the late nineteenth century (Hanley, 2002). This is the ability of party elites to collude when necessary in order to modify or restrict competition. Such a strategy has usually necessitated fine judgement and readiness to act boldly; the agents had to challenge the structures in which they operated in order to modify them. Looked at in long-term perspective, the plural left – and its imitators on the right – are simply repeating this pattern.

Notes

1 In competitive terms, PS and MdC agreed not to challenge each other's incumbents; PS also left the Greens a free run in 30 seats. PCF and MdC agreed 48 joint candidacies. PS and PCF signed a joint electoral declaration, focusing on demand stimulation and job creation, the thirty-five-hour week, tax reform, an end to ongoing privatisations and a new immigration law (Szarka, 1999, Buffotot and Hanley, 1998).
2 By this logic, in 1993 only 58.98 per cent (of a 70 per cent turnout) were voting for potential governing parties and two-fifths of voters were mere 'protesters' (Habert *et al.*, 1993: 300).
3 *La Croix*, 28 April 2000.
4 *Le Monde* 26 April 2000.
5 *La Croix* 2 June 2000.
6 Voynet claimed that there was no real collective strategy in government. Major decisions were taken in ministerial meetings dominated by the PS or during Tuesday morning breakfasts with PS 'elephants'; future measures were announced to PS summer schools, but not to ministerial colleagues; smaller alliance partners were simply used for dirty jobs – nuclear waste to herself, transport unions to the PCF's Gayssot (*Le Monde* 23 May 2000).
7 *Le Monde*, 23 May 2000.
8 *La Croix*, 14 June 2001.
9 *La Croix*, 7 June 2002.
10 *La Croix*, 3 July 2002.
11 *La Croix*, 15 November 2000.

6
Beyond the mainstream:
la gauche de la gauche

Jim Wolfreys

Introduction

In the summer of 1998 an article in *Le Monde* entitled 'Quand la France
s'amuse' compared the apparently beatific state of mind of the French
in the wake of the national team's World Cup victory with that evoked
by Pierre Viansson-Ponté in his celebrated essay 'Quand la France s'en-
nuie ... ' written on the eve of the May '68 events.[1] As with the original
article, such complacency proved at odds with a powerful undercurrent
in society which, from the mid-1990s, had seen a backlash against
neo-liberalism gather pace against a backdrop of growing social inequality.
The backlash took the form of a so-called 'social movement' encompassing
the revival of working-class militancy signalled by a major public sector
strike in November–December 1995, a wave of occupations and demonstrations by immigrants, the homeless and the unemployed, the rebirth
of the engaged intellectual, and unprecedented electoral success for the
revolutionary left, whose two presidential candidates, Lutte Ouvrière's
Arlette Laguiller, and the Ligue Communiste Révolutionnaire's Olivier
Besancenot, achieved in 2002 a combined score approaching three
million. The growing influence of *la gauche de la gauche* was accompanied
by the mushrooming of various militant groups and associations cam-
paigning against racism, unemployment, homelessness and homophobia,
boosted from the turn of the century by an emerging anti-capitalist
movement spearheaded by individuals like the sociologist Pierre Bourdieu
and the anti-globalisation campaigner José Bové, and by groups like the
Attac association against financial speculation.

The class conflict and political polarisation at the heart of the 1995
strikes appeared to confound orthodox analyses which saw late twen-
tieth-century France as a society of consensus and institutional stability
(Furet *et al.*, 1988). This polarisation, however, was expressed almost
exclusively outside the major political parties. Yet the political system

itself, despite the turbulence of intra-party relations, underlined by a series of splits from the RPR and UDF in the wake of the left's return to power in 1997, appeared relatively stable in the period following the strikes. In particular, Lionel Jospin appeared to have consolidated the revival signalled by his showing in the 1995 presidential poll through his management of the governmental plural-left coalition, not least in helping to nurture the PCF through its transformation into a mainstream social-democratic party, and in facilitating the integration of the notoriously indisciplined Greens into the party system. Indeed, the most dramatic split to occur, that of the FN, was interpreted by some, although not this author (Wolfreys, 1999), as a triumph for the absorptive capacity of the system, drawing former FN chairman Bruno Mégret into its orbit and leaving Le Pen severely weakened.[2] Since April 2002, however, the credibility of all claims about the system's capacity to neutralise anti-establishment forces must be questioned. When, as happened on the first round on the 2002 presidential election, fewer people choose to vote for all of France's mainstream parties combined than opt for the extreme right, the Trotskyist left, abstention or spoiling their ballots, the term 'crisis of representation' no longer seems excessive.

This chapter will argue that the phenomenon of the 'social movement' is the product of a process of social and political polarisation to which France's party system has been unable to respond, largely because of the broad consensus which now governs most areas of policy. We begin with an outline of the way in which fundamental ideological differences between the parties of the mainstream left and right are being eroded. The perception among grass-roots activists that the PS in particular is no longer either able or willing to provide solutions to long-term problems like unemployment, job insecurity and discrimination, is a major reason for the development of the social movement, or *gauche de gauche*, whose principal elements will be assessed below. The argument put forward in this chapter is that behind an atrophied party system, a culture of protest and dissent is developing which opposes neo-liberalism but has yet to put forward an alternative vision of society of its own. This lack of a clear ideological focus limits its ability to provide clear political solutions, contributing to a general political climate characterised by both stagnation and volatility.

Changes in the party system

Belated industrialisation, the Socialist–Communist split and longstanding ideological divisions have all been cited as factors delaying the formation of modern, disciplined party machines in France. Long into the twentieth century, the political system incubated numerous parties, most of them with weak structures and limited militant bases. Under the Fifth Republic, revision of the electoral system forced parties to combine in alliances. This, along with various other changes linked to economic modernisation, meant that the number of parties represented in the National Assembly was greatly reduced during the post-war period. The subsequent establishment of what is quaintly known as the *quadrille bipolaire*, a left–right polarisation dominated by the four main parties, was generally held to be a consequence of newfound constitutional stability which derived from a number of factors, notably the consensus over major policy issues after the Socialists' emergence as a party of government; the experience of cohabitation between a president and prime minister of opposing tendencies; and the decline of ideological factors linked to class and religion which accompanied the emergence of a post-industrial or post-materialist society. 'It took centuries to establish [the] ideological structures [of France]', wrote Emmanuel Todd in 1988, 'and only five years to liquidate them' (cited in Safran, 1998: 89). But no sooner had this model been established than it began to disintegrate. New parties, in the shape of the FN and then, to a lesser extent, the Greens, emerged as major players. Three authoritarian nationalists, the Gaullist Charles Pasqua, who broke from the RPR, the aristocratic Philippe de Villiers, who broke from the UDF, and the republican Jean-Pierre Chevènement, who broke from the Socialists, emerged as significant minor players. This fragmentation of the party system, although partly based on personal ambition and petty rivalries, was also a product of the dilution of three major ideological currents in post-war French politics; socialism, communism and Gaullism.

In the late 1980s a debate took place within the Socialist Party about whether its commitment to managing capitalism, confirmed by the abandonment of its reform programme and the adoption of austerity measures in the early 1980s, was robbing the party of its specific identity. By 1991, former Prime Minister Pierre Mauroy was redefining the party's role as that of a brake on the excesses of the market, while the Rocard government was responding to the crisis of Keynesianism in an era of globalisation by championing the 'reform of the infinitely small' (Moreau, 1998: 291–6). The dangers of this approach were signalled by Henri Emmanuelli in 1989, who warned that if the Socialist party were 'to limit itself to managerialism' by renouncing its vocation 'as an instrument of social transformation', it would lose its identity (cited in Moreau, 1998: 285–6).

Jacques Moreau has argued that the Socialists' hesitancy and loss of direction during Mitterrand's second *septennat* derived from an inability to come to terms with the retreat to austerity in the 1980s. Whereas in the past the left had concluded that failure to deliver on electoral promises required a redoubling of revolutionary ardour, allowing leadership and rank and file to be reconciled around an ostensibly class-based analysis of society, no such reconciliation took place after 1983. This was partly because the party's founding Epinay programme of 1971 was not rooted in any doctrine that would allow it to learn from failure and lay the basis for regeneration. But the 'presidentialisation' of the PS during the 1980s further prevented party activists from drawing lessons from the experience of office or even discussing party policy, a shift of authority underlined most dramatically by the imposition in 1988 of the *Letter to all the French*, written by Mitterrand and embodying a 'reformism without principles' (Moreau, 1998: 278). While in office the Socialists had in any case dismantled many of the tools that would have permitted state direction of the economy, through financial deregulation and integration into the European monetary system. Although most European social-democratic parties emerged from the 1980s with neither Marx nor Keynes as points of reference, the history and traditions of France's political culture made the abandonment of the rhetoric of radical change particularly proble- matic (Hincker, 1997: 123). In particular, greater French integration into the world economy called into question the French left's allegiance to republican nationalism. How could the defence of *service public* be recon- ciled with privatisation? How could the universalism of the social security and health system be defended in the face of moves to privatise pension schemes and health insurance? Such questions, as we shall see below, were to be taken up and thrown back at the Socialists by activists angry at their perceived abandonment of republican principles.

    Although the plural left was essentially an electoral alliance, it grew out of an initiative to re-establish links with ordinary activists and revive, 'more modestly than before', as Jospin once put it,[3] the notion that the Socialists could act as a brake on the market. Efforts at a recomposition of the left had begun with Michel Rocard's *Assises de la transformation sociale*, which brought together Socialists and various 'progressive' forces. Jospin and his allies continued to pursue the initiative long after others had forgotten it (Mercier and Jérôme, 1997: 144–7). Jospin's strategy of seeking alliances with the left, rather than the centre, along with his 1997 election platform, promising to fight unemployment and reduce the working week, sent out a message that the left would attempt to offer regulation and state intervention to ensure job creation and the preser- vation of public services. In 1981 it was Jospin who had wondered aloud whether there would be 'a clash or a compromise' between the government and French capital (Moreau 1998: 272–3). After his election in 1997, he famously attempted to provide his own answer to the question, claiming to want 'a market economy but not a market society'.[4] But having held out the prospect of a break with the neo-liberal orthodoxy, his government chose not to act when workers at Renault-Vilvorde, Michelin and Danone called on Jospin to make good his campaign promises to make it harder for companies to make mass redundancies.[5]

By 1999, he appeared resigned to the impotence of government before the market, announcing on national television that 'I do not think our role is to administer the economy'.[6] His attempts to emphasise that there remained a left–right divide were increasingly reduced to symbolic acts, provoking angry clashes with the opposition by calling for the rehabilitation of First World War mutineers and accusing the right of being on the wrong side in the Dreyfus affair. But the most symbolic of all the government's acts, Martine Aubry's long-awaited thirty-five-hour week, with all the evocations of the Popular Front government this brought to bear, failed to live up to expectations. Michel Rocard's references to Paul Lafargue's *Le Droit à la Paresse* during Jospin's 1995 presidential campaign seemed a far cry from the flexible working practices, proliferation of short-term contracts and increased job insecurity which the measure was to produce (Fondation Copernic, 2001).

When the 2002 campaign came around, Jospin appeared to have returned to the hesitancy of the early 1990s, initially denying that his programme was Socialist before re-emphasising his identification with the left as election day neared. Voters, three-quarters of whom claimed to be unable to tell the manifestos of Chirac and Jospin apart, were unforgiving, and Jospin's result was the worst of any Socialist presidential candidate since the party's formation. The PCF was hit even harder. Its leader, Robert Hue, in a typically gauche turn of phrase, had warned in 1998 that the left would fail if it did not 'have a symbiotic relationship with the social movement'.[7] But participation in government, not least that of PCF transport minister Jean-Claude Gayssot, who oversaw the 'partial' privatisation of Air France, undermined whatever relationship the party might have had with the movement in the first place. In 2002, Hue's electorate fell to a level which more or less approached parity with what the party had claimed in membership only twenty years previously.

Although economic growth and the introduction of the thirty-five-hour week had led to a fall in unemployment, Jospin's coalition left office with the problem of job insecurity unresolved. Despite the introduction of various youth employment schemes since the 1980s, in the 1990s only 20 per cent of the 17–24 age group entered the job market on indefinite full-time contracts (Mouriaux, 1998: 146). The practice of issuing part-time contracts for all workers continued until by 1998 they made up one fifth of all contracts issued. By the end of the decade almost one third of all workers felt that their jobs were in danger (Filoche, 1999: 127). The role of the Socialist party, then, in the absence of either a doctrine or a radical reform agenda, appears once more reduced to a predominantly systemic function, devoted to 'the organisation and legitimisation of the electoral process' (Yanai, 1999: 6–7). This view would seem to be supported by the changing social composition of the mainstream left's electorate. In the 2002 parliamentary election, as in 1997, the PS won the support of a greater proportion of senior managers (35 per cent) than either white-collar (30 per cent) or manual workers (33 per cent).[8] Studies have shown that the activist base of both the Socialist and Communist parties is now older and less working class than ever before. Only 5 per cent of Socialist Party members are under 30. The average age of Socialist party members (55), Communists (49) and even Greens (47) tells its own story.[9] All these factors, in a context of rising inequalities and scepticism about the Socialists' commitment to reform, help to explain what has given rise to the emergence of the autonomous groups and associations which make up the 'social movement', to which we now turn.

The 'social movement'

The literature on social movements generally stresses their emergence in two waves, the post-1968 liberation movements (gays, women, immigrant workers, ecologists) and the post-1981 movements typified by SOS Racisme. New social movements in general, the argument runs, are linked to the decline in traditional areas of conflict such as class or religion (Kriesi *et al.*, 1995). They espouse 'post-materialist' themes and use unconventional forms of participation (Dalton and Kuechler, 1990). While the orientation of the first, post-1968 wave centred on policy, with movements cultivating close links with political parties, the second wave has been characterised by a desire for autonomy from traditional institutions and shaped by motives which are held to be expressive and affective rather than instrumental.

Conflicting interpretations of this shift in emphasis have been offered. The most orthodox contends that political opportunity structures hold the key to understanding the interaction between state institutions and social actors. The Mitterrand election victory of 1981 recast relations between the state and civil society, giving rise to a new kind of social movement which, disaffected with the refusal of the Socialists to provide such groups with the political opportunities they sought, radicalised and followed a more autonomous path after 1988 (Fillieule, 1997). Others have argued that new social movement theory offers an inadequate framework for explaining the emergence of these grass-roots currents, which instead embody a new form of active citizenship (Waters, 1998). Where once new social movements operated within the political system, the second wave forms a 'civic front' in defence of specific groups all united by a desire to defend basic rights and freedoms. Their altruistic outlook, *ad hoc* structures and identification with 'civic humanism' represent a democratic revival (Duyvendak, 1994, Waters, 1998). Their new model of flexible *regroupements* based on medium-term engagements has also been cited as evidence of a new type of activism stripped of both the republican notion of individuals as citizens and the communitarian sociabilities which, despite everything, managed to insert themselves between the citizen and the nation to structure the work of voluntary groups (Ion, 1994: 36–7).

Clearly, during the 1980s the relationship between the mainstream left and social movements, once fairly close, changed significantly. Symptomatic of this change is the experience of SOS Racisme. By the end of Mitterrand's first term of office, it was suffering from widespread disillusionment with its image as a satellite of the Socialist Party. Cynicism about the Socialists' commitment to confronting racism in general and the FN in particular led to the adoption of a different strategy by rival anti-racist groups in the early 1990s. Where SOS had attempted, with some success, to mobilise a new generation of activists around the republican ideal of equality, new groups, such as Ras l'Front and the Manifeste contre le Front National were more focused on specific, immediate objectives, than the pursuit of equal rights for all (Fysh and Wolfreys, 1998).

At the same time, the apparent 'exclusion' of those at the bottom of society, brought home to many by the parliamentary debate on the *Revenu Minimum d'Insertion* and the growing proportion of long-term unemployed among the rising numbers of those without work, led to the development of a *crise de l'avenir* as the realisation spread that the continuous post-war rise in living standards was now being reversed. A number of protests took place in the early 1990s which appeared to contradict some of the assumptions made by social scientists during the 1980s about greater affluence leading to 'post-material' forms of protest. Those taking strike action and marching through the streets were now the professional classes, not usually associated with labour militancy: Air France pilots and bank workers, or those anxious about entering professional life like the school students who demonstrated in 1994 against the Balladur government's youth employment scheme (Castel, 1993: 717–18).

The tendency to seek autonomy from established institutions began to generalise. In the trade unions a movement had surfaced with the student protests and railway workers dispute of 1986, which were led not by the official bureaucracies, but by strike committees or coordinations (Futur antérieur, 1996). Rejecting negotiation and compromise by delegated officials in favour of a more militant approach, the coordinations set great store by the participation of rank-and-file activists in decision-making. Some of these structures became unions in their own right, activists expelled from the Confédération Française Démocratique du Travail (CFDT) setting up Coordonner, Rassembler, Construire (CRC) in the health service and the Fédération Solidaire, Unitaire, Démocratique des PTT (SUD–PTT) in the post office, both of which now form part of the Groupe des dix federation of independent trade unions. SUD, which recruits a high proportion of previously non-unionised workers and has won significant support in elections to post and telecommunications workplace committees, was to play a prominent role in the social movement which emerged in the mid-1990s (Coupé and Marchand, 1999: 244–5).

At the heart of this movement were the *sans* groups of 'those without'. The association of the homeless, Droit au Logement (DAL), formed in 1990, and the civil rights group, Droits devant!! (DD!!), formed in 1995, pushed the issue of homelessness up the political agenda with an occupation in the rue du Dragon in the Saint-Germain area of Paris during the 1995 presidential campaign. The most prominent of all these groups, the *sans papiers*, immigrants made 'illegal' by government legislation introduced in 1994, won broad public support when their occupation of the Saint Bernard church in Paris was broken up by riot police. In the winter of 1997–98, associations such as Agir ensemble contre le Chômage (AC!), formed by the left opposition within the CFDT, and the Communist-led Association pour l'Emploi, l'Information et la Solidarité (APEIS) organised a wave of protests demanding increased state aid for those out of work. Act Up, a dynamic and highly visible Aids-awareness group, was founded in 1989 as a the result of similar frustrations with the institutionalisation of associations and the shortcomings of the left. It used shock tactics (during one protest a giant condom was fitted over the obelisk at the Place de la Concorde) to advance its argument that the inadequacies of state action leave the most marginal and vulnerable disproportionately affected by Aids, making it a 'political disease'.

In *Le Nouvel Esprit du Capitalisme*, Boltanski and Chiapello (1999) offer an explanation for the emergence of these movements. The decline in influence of Marxism, they argue, both as a political force and an analytical tool, means that the concept of exploitation has given way to the notion of exclusion. When society is viewed in these terms, attention tends to focus not on the system of relations which produces economic inequalities but on those who suffer. But without a sense of where exclusion fits into the broader picture, it becomes harder to develop a vision of an alternative society. The consequences of this were twofold: on a practical level, political engagement shifted during the 1980s to humanitarian work and the defensive reflex to relieve suffering, while in theoretical terms macro-socio-historical critiques have given way to the micro-analysis of specific situations. In other words, with social criticism no longer able or willing propose alternative solutions, those who oppose social injustice are left with little recourse other than to express indignation in the face of suffering. The humanitarianism of the 1980s, represented by initiatives such as Coluche's Restaurants du cœur or Bernard Kouchner's Médécins sans frontières, operated outside the frame of reference of the labour movement, and tended to represent the dispossessed as victims. Hence the identification of the excluded as those without: the *sans parole/ domicile/papiers/travail/droits*, and so on (Boltanski and Chiapello, 1999: 416, 429). These groups combined aspects of 1980s humanitarianism, through their appeals to the rights of man and their high-profile direct action, and elements of 1970s activism, both via individual veterans of Maoist and Trotskyist groups and in their use of the '*geste transgressif*' designed to expose institutional bad faith (Boltanski and Chiapello, 1999: 434).

They have also demonstrated a capacity to unite over specific concerns for a limited period around a loose, 'fluid' concept of citizenship based on a minimal definition of rights rather than any ideologically charged notion of republicanism. For Boltanski and Chiapello, the historical significance of the new forms of protest resides in their 'morphological homology' with remodelled capitalism (1999: 434). Where the bureaucratic organisations of the traditional labour movement find their ability to effect change stalled, flexible groups uniting around precise issues are able to ask participants for specific commitments over a limited period. Delegation and action by proxy are replaced by the authenticity of direct engagement in protest activities.

Leaving aside the more contentious aspects of the 'network society' paradigm deployed in a series of recent influential studies (Boltanski and Chiapello, 1999, Hardt and Negri, 2000, Castells, 1998), specifically the notion that a fundamentally new social structure has taken shape, it is clear that some of the transformations they describe, in particular the simultaneous crises of global capitalism and the nation-state and the reconfiguring of their relations, have had a profound effect on parties and protest groups alike. For Hardt and Negri, social movements today represent a fundamental break with the past. Traditional distinctions between economics and politics are dissolving as conflicts take on a wider 'biopolitical' dimension and each struggle 'leaps to a global level' (Hardt and Negri, 2000, 56). Certainly, as we shall see below, it is true that groups setting out to address specific concerns are increasingly being drawn into wider struggles, while the decline of social democracy gives an intensely political dimension to the movement.

Anti-capitalism and the far left

We have seen how in the early 1990s a limited and sporadic revival of labour militancy took place alongside the mushrooming of autonomous associations. In the presidential election of 1995, a third important development occurred when the Trotskyist candidate Arlette Laguiller passed the 5 per cent barrier for the first time, indicating that a sizeable electoral constituency was emerging to the left of the established left.

The effect of the November–December 1995 strikes and their aftermath was to bring all these tendencies to the fore. The main trade union federations were forced to come to terms with the threat posed by the rank-and-file coordinations, which led to far greater democratic participation than in previous strike waves. There was also much greater unity between different unions and between different branches of industry. In some areas, such as the twentieth arrondissement of Paris, mass meetings were open to all and attended by teachers, postal workers, railway and metro workers, along with members of various associations. On demonstrations led by public sector workers, anti-nuclear protesters joined contingents from anti-racist groups, unemployed and homeless associations and Act-Up, indicating that the frequently made distinction between the 'old' labour movement and the 'new' social movements is in fact far less clear-cut.

After December a process of generalisation took place. This was partly due to the context of the demonstrations themselves, which reacted vociferously to the contrast between the Juppé plan and Chirac's 1995 populist campaign theme of the fracture sociale. Subsequent protests by the *sans* associations and by teachers, truckers, students and school students all made reference to this general context. The intervention of the sociologist Pierre Bourdieu also played an important part in ensuring that the strikes developed into a wider reaction against the neo-liberal consensus forged in the late 1980s by the mainstream parties and subsequently propagated via a range of publications and think tanks. Bourdieu consciously attempted to polarise the situation, linking the neo-liberal content of Juppé reforms to the broader question of corporate-led globalisation. In doing so, a shift in the intellectual climate took place. A famous quarrel flared up over a petition in the journal *Esprit*, when various leading academics backed the emollient stance towards the reforms taken by the CFDT leader Nicole Notat. Bourdieu condemned those behind the initiative, like the sociologist Alain Touraine, not just for signing it, but for putting their expertise at the service of the state which such movements were directed against, making them, as Bourdieu declared with some relish, 'lackeys of the establishment' (Wolfreys, 2000).

Bourdieu engaged in a series of initiatives which aimed both to broaden the scope of the movement and to politicise it, principally through the use of his publishing house, Liber/Raisons d'Agir, which produced accessible and polemical publications bringing some of his theoretical preoccupations to a wider audience. A Raisons d'Agir association was formed and provided the launch pad for Bourdieu's November 1996 call for an Estates General of the Social Movement, followed, in April 1998, by an article entitled 'For a left left' [10] in which he called on the various components of the social movement to oppose the neo-liberal policies of Europe's newly elected social-democratic governments in an 'international of resistance', a call which later formed the basis of an appeal issued at a European level.

The proposal for an Estates General of the European Social Movement argued that the inability of social democratic parties to offer an effective alternative to 'growing inequality, unemployment and casualisation' necessitated the development of an 'authentically critical counter-force' capable of bringing these issues 'constantly back onto the agenda'. The search for such a counter-force explains the phenomenal development of Attac, perhaps the most striking indication to date of the size of the audience for groups operating beyond the mainstream. Set up in 1998 by various trade unions, associations and radical journals following an influential article by the editor of the *Le Monde Diplomatique* entitled 'Disarm the markets', Attac's goal was the imposition of a so-called Tobin tax, or 'global solidarity tax', on financial transactions. The money raised would then be used to fight global inequality and fund sustainable development. According to Bernard Cassen, the association's first president, the call for a Tobin tax is symbolic of the desire to defend democracy against the threat posed by the freedom of capital to circulate. Attac's success – by the turn of the century it had formed well over 100 local committees in France with over 40,000 members, along with an international network covering around twenty countries – underlines the growing impact of the anti-capitalist current which first came to light internationally with the November 1999 protests in Seattle against the World Trade Organisation (WTO).

One of the most prominent symbols of this emerging movement is the unlikely figure of a middle-aged sheep farmer from Larzac, José Bové. In 2002, Bové was sent to prison for his part in the dismantling of a McDonalds in Millau in the Tarn by members of his Confédération Paysanne in protest against *la malbouffe*, mass-produced processed food and the economic and environmental threat which it poses. As with other initiatives of recent years, from the anti-FN protests at Strasbourg in March 1997 (organised by a Comité de Vigilance uniting dozens of organisations) to the wave of mobilisations that followed Le Pen's first round presidential success in 2002, Bové's trial in Millau brought together a range of groups from across the social movement, both in France and elsewhere, in a 50,000 strong demonstration in June 2000. His trial was an illustration of both the breadth of the movement and of the way in which it was generalising. Around the figurehead of Bové, then, groups which had started out occupying derelict buildings in Latin Quarter back-streets now found themselves making common cause with international protests against global capitalism sparked off by demonstrations against the WTO on the north-west coast of the United States.

Clearly this is a period of transition when old relationships are breaking down and the ideas and aspirations which shaped and coloured them are being recast. This raises an important point about autonomy. In 1998 a number of groups, including DD!!, SUD and the AC! unemployed association signed a declaration asserting the autonomy of the 'social movement' (Brochier and Delouche, 2000: 163–71). While the intention may have been to avoid recuperation by the mainstream left, the way in which the movement was developing showed that 'autonomy' did not really exist, neither in the sense of discrete groups working towards their own particular ends, nor in the sense that the movement could lay claim to a distinct and independent political standpoint of its own. But just as the shrinking ambitions of social democracy were creating an expanding space for these groups to occupy, so political questions previously debated within its institutions were being transposed onto the social movement. Groups like Attac therefore found themselves called upon to adopt positions on issues that went far beyond anything contained in the proposal for a Tobin tax, from the war on terror to the question of whether to vote for Chirac in the second round of the presidential poll. Such questions formed part of much bigger debates on broader points of strategy and principle, the most important being that of Attac's role. Was it essentially a radical anti-capitalist association based on grass-roots campaigns and direct action, or a lobbying group whose aim was win the support of political parties for a Tobin tax? Perhaps it was both?

Since such groups achieve unity on the basis of identification with a relatively narrow set of aims rather than a general political outlook, these debates tend to be dealt with either in a piecemeal fashion, responding to events as they occur, or by organisational manoeuvres, highlighted by Bernard Cassen's attempt to place his supporters in positions of responsibility when he stepped down from the presidency.[11] The absence of a general political platform is both the strength and the weakness of the social movement, providing on the one hand the basis for unity and the capacity to mobilise widely, but carrying with it the risk either of cooptation by political parties or of paralysis, as the ability to act decisively is sacrificed for the sake of unity (Sommier, 2001: 97–110).

The search for political alternatives beyond the mainstream is an important element in the electoral success of the far left. Since Arlette Laguiller won 1.6 million votes in the 1995 presidential poll, LO and the LCR have gone on to perform impressively in elections at local, national and European level, sending five deputies to the European Parliament in 1999 and winning more votes between them than the combined scores of Hue and the Green candidate Noël Mamère in 2002. The respective campaigns of Laguiller and Olivier Besancenot highlighted some of the differences between the two organisations. Laguiller drew large gatherings to her campaign meetings in towns affected by job cuts, such as Nancy, Caen and Reims. Her calls to prevent companies in the black from making redundancies, and to make public the details of the bank accounts of major firms and their directors, won her the support of 10 per cent of manual workers, compared to 3 per cent for Hue (www.ipsos.fr/CanalIpsos/poll/7549.asp).

Besancenot, meanwhile, a previously unknown postal worker, won over one million votes, his sensitivity to the social movement reflected in his post-election call for the unity of anti-capitalist forces. LO's rejection both of this proposal and the LCR's offer to stand joint lists in the June 2002 parliamentary election stemmed partly from the organisation's preoccupation with building its own organisation rather than engaging with other parties or movements. This has led it, outside of election campaigns, to focus its activities on the workplace, dismissing developments like the anti-WTO protests and the Attac associations as distractions which would serve no useful purpose.[12] Neither of the most explicitly political organisations associated with the new mood in French politics have as yet found a way of addressing the question of the political direction of the social movement. If the LCR's enthusiastic involvement in a range of groups linked to the social movement, notably Attac and SUD, leaves it vulnerable to the same weaknesses as the movement itself, then LO's defence of its independent political stance is at times so fierce as to risk alienating it from those outside its ranks. Despite the echo which Besancenot's proposal met, the thorny question of the relationship between the broad movement and whatever specific, organisational political form it might take will not be resolved overnight.

Conclusion

The progressive estrangement of French voters from the political process can be gauged from their response to recent elections. The 1999 European elections produced the lowest turnout for an election under the Fifth Republic, with 53 per cent of voters abstaining. Pollsters concluded that as much as 71 per cent of the population used the election to express dissatisfaction with political elites (Méchet, 2000: 21). In the September 2000 referendum on the reduction of the presidential term of office, even this figure was exceeded when nearly 70 per cent of voters abstained, while almost two million of those who actually went to the polls only did so to spoil their ballot papers. In the two elections held in 2002 the number of abstentions on each of the first round votes meant that France was to find itself with a president backed by under 15 per cent of the registered electorate and a parliamentary majority with the support of less than one quarter of those eligible to vote. Surveys have shown that the majority of the population neither believe that politicians are working for their benefit or feel represented by a political party.

Consensus, then, instead of bringing a more stable and ordered party system, has accentuated a crisis of representation, while post-materialist society, as we have seen, has proven a surprisingly fertile ground for protests over material issues. In the late 1980s Herbert Kitschelt argued that although France had a societal potential to generate left-libertarian parties, its concrete political opportunity structure remained unfavourable to the emergence of such organisations. The effect of neo-liberalism and attacks on the welfare state in most western democracies, moreover, meant that left-libertarian concerns such as feminism, ecology, energy and anti-nuclear issues would fade and give way to 'economic distributive' issues (Kitschelt, 1988). By the late 1990s, however, it was clear that such distinctions between 'new' and 'old' struggles were beginning to break down.

France has witnessed both the growth of parties and associations generally associated with left–libertarianism and the emergence of organisations and networks whose primary focus is on class issues. The slow dissipation of the ideological and organisational reserves of parties of both left and right is symptomatic of the growing divide between political parties and society. This in turn explains the attraction of the diverse components of the social movement. These currents are neither 'post-material' nor can they be described as simply a 'new citizenship movement'. What we are witnessing is a revival of collective protest at social inequality which is reconfiguring the relationship between a burgeoning associative network, the labour movement and the political left. But it remains a movement whose own lack of political and organisational focus has so far hampered its ability to mount a meaningful challenge from beyond the mainstream. That distinction belongs to Le Pen.

Notes

1 *Le Monde*, 8 August 1998.
2 *Le Monde*, 24 January 1999.
3 *Le Point*, 30 May 1987.
4 *Le Monde*, 25 July 1998.
5 *Le Monde*, 26 June 1996.
6 *Le Monde*, 15 September 1999.
7 *Le Monde*, 27 January 1998.
8 *Libération*, 11 June 2002.
9 *Le Monde*, 15 January 2002.
10 *Le Monde*, 8 April 1998.
11 *Le Monde*, 20 June 2002.
12 *Lutte de Classe*, December 2001.

II

THE RIGHT

7

The UDF in the 1990s: the break-up of a party confederation

Nicolas Sauger

Introduction

The principal dynamic of the French party system under the Fifth Republic has been that of the so-called 'bipolar quadrille'. By the end of the 1970s, four parties of approximately equal strength were monopolising over 90 per cent of the vote in their respective left and right blocs (Parodi, 1989). Nevertheless, this end-state had taken twenty years to produce, concluding in 1978 with the formation of the UDF. The UDF managed to create an unprecedented alliance between liberal, Christian democrat and radical currents,[1] taking its place as the second right-wing pole next to the Gaullist RPR. The UDF represented the desire to institutionalise the centrist coalition formed around Valéry Giscard d'Estaing, who had been elected president four years earlier. At the same time, however, none of the constituent parties of the new confederation had ever agreed to merge themselves into a single organisational entity.[2] It was only on 16 May 1998, by a single motion passed by its national congress, that DL ended twenty years of the 'moderate alliance' by withdrawing from the confederation.[3] DL represented the largest component of the UDF, accounting for around one-third of its members and elected representatives. Its separation allowed the creation of a significant new party, even if some of its members did not defect from the UDF. With a parliamentary group of 44 deputies in the National Assembly, together with 46 senators,[4] DL immediately asserted itself as an indispensable partner.

These events by no means marked the end of the UDF, but the secession did significantly alter its format. Lacking one-third of its former activists and a large chunk of its liberal wing, the balance of power noticeably shifted within the UDF. In particular, the descendants of the Christian democrat *courant* have become the dominant force. From this, a fusion of the remaining components into the New

107

UDF – although only partial – was announced at the Lille Congress in December 1998. At the same time, François Léotard, the former President of the Parti Républicain (PR) who was elected to the head of the UDF in 1996, resigned, to be replaced by the leader of Force Démocrate (FD), François Bayrou. In simultaneously giving birth to a new party actor and significantly weakening one of the main existing parties, the UDF split would seem to signal major changes within the party system. However, the bipolar quadrille had already been shattered by the emergence of the FN, a new actor excluded from coalition, and by the shifting equilibrium between the two partners in both blocs.

Since the initial pendulum swing of 1981, the RPR had established itself as the dominant partner on the right (Schonfeld, 1986). However, the results of the 2002 elections introduced a novelty, namely the appointment of Jean-Pierre Raffarin, a member of DL, as Prime Minister. This is the first time since 1981 that one of the two heads of the executive has been filled by a member of a party other than the RPR while the right is in government. But this novelty should not be exaggerated, reflecting less a new development in the right bloc and more a reward for loyalty to Chirac's 'clan'.

Indeed, the split in the UDF seems even less significant for the French party system when one realises that its direct consequences, beyond the formation of the new parliamentary group in 1998, are difficult to identify. Two reasons can be given for this. First, the split of the UDF was not accompanied by a challenge to the existing governmental coalitions, unlike cases where a split in one party leads to the collapse of an alliance or a change in the systemic status of such an alliance.[5] The new UDF, DL and the RPR still constitute the moderate-right coalition and all participate in the new governing coalition since the 2002 electoral victory. DL was not excluded, by dint of being a close partner of the RPR, a role from which it did not try to distance itself. Second, the organisation of the UDF itself has tempered the consequences of the split. For twenty years, the UDF had been considered a party living on borrowed time, such were the internal divisions within its ranks. The threat of defection had been one of the basic negotiating tools within the confederation. In this respect, the difference between a heavily factionalised party and a coalition is minimal.

However, the very presence of the threat of defection throughout the old UDF's twenty-year existence shows that its stability was at issue, and that its disappearance should therefore have some consequences. Within a weakly institutionalised organisation such as the UDF, it is difficult to argue routine behaviour as the source of stability. Such consequences can be seen in the shifting of these parties in political space, as well as in the modification of intra-bloc dynamics on the right.

The split and the modification of parties in political space

The logics of electoral coalition on the one hand and of demarcation between the different moderate-right parties on the other are obviously mirrored in the definition of ideologies within each organisation. The split occurred around reactivated latent cleavages and has broadly led to a relocation of the party positions in political space, consequently potentially affecting the general balance of the party system (Lane and Ersson, 1987).

Two main cleavages were key to the split. The first, social in nature, opposed two spiritual families, one descended from a liberal heritage, the other from a Christian democrat background. The second, more strategic, concerned the issue of relations with the extreme right. The split fundamentally separated the descendants of liberalism, regrouped in the DL splinter, from the Christian democrat successors, who now form the majority of New UDF. Each representing their specific spiritual family, despite the weakened contemporary nature of the cleavages, liberals and Christian democrats took different lines, especially on religious matters. Despite a lack of data on the subject, certain characteristics of this divide can be discerned through a survey of delegates to the PR (liberal) and CDS (Christian democrat) national party congresses (Ysmal, 1992).[6] All of the delegates were in agreement on most items pertaining to economic liberalism, but inheritance tax divided them – only 39 per cent of CDS delegates wanted its removal, as opposed to 65 per cent of the PR. In cultural-attitudinal terms, PR and CDS delegates shared some liberal positions (for instance, 21 per cent of CDS delegates and 20 per cent of PR delegates condemned homosexuality) but there was no consensus on the death penalty (almost 65 per cent of the PR wanted its re-establishment, as opposed to less than 40 per cent in the CDS) or abortion (45 per cent of CDS delegates against 34 per cent of PR delegates wanted to make it more difficult to obtain). The different components of the UDF were thus sensitive to different social issues. Finally, immigration preoccupied the PR more than it did the CDS.

In withdrawing from the UDF, DL finally confirmed its liberal identity,[7] starting with its change of name. Moreover, Alain Madelin announced the split in the name of liberalism:

> There are many French men and women who expect us to provide a future for their country and for their children which is different to the one the Socialists are proposing. This future can only be a liberal one. Throughout the world, people are rallying to those values and ideas which are our own. And so, my friends, we are not now going to fold up our flag, and dilute let alone dissolve our liberal heritage.[8]

For DL, the split was also the chance to present a manifesto inspired by liberalism. Beyond classic state reforms, the lowering of taxes and the simplification of legislation, DL's programme emphasised the promotion of intermediary associations and the value of autonomy for individuals, local organisations and public services, starting with the education sector.[9]

Even so, it is difficult to maintain that the UDF split has re-established a fundamental cleavage in French society. Christian democracy and liberalism are not bitterly opposed, after all, particularly since religion is no longer a central concern today. These two families are not to be found on opposing sides of a single cleavage (Seiler, 1984). Moreover, conflicts between Christian democracy and liberalism may be rooted in unarguable historical fact in France (Kalyvas, 1996), but today these conflicts have been superseded by fights between right and left. Third, New UDF does not play upon its Christian democrat heritage – indeed any such reference is completely absent – except in its belonging to the European Popular Party.[10] This absence of explicit ideological bench-marking is hardly surprising, given the extent to which the UDF is still a highly composite structure. Whether radical, liberal or even social democrat, the non-Christian democrat minority is still significant none-theless. More broadly, the collection of moderate-right formations plays host to a heterogeneous bunch within their organisations, despite their own fragmentation. The position of CDS and PR leaders mentioned above shows not only the differences between the different constituents of the UDF, but also no less significant internal oppositions between each constituent. On subjects as sensitive as abortion, the death penalty or the fortune tax, they tend to divide into one-third versus two-thirds, or sometimes 50–50. Similarly, the liberal credo vaunted by Madelin has caused difficulties within his own party in those areas touching upon society. His abstention in favour of the PACS, or his position on the decriminalisation of soft drugs on the one hand have not been followed, and on the other form part of his presidential campaign.

In sum, despite the apparent link to ideological streams which support the UDF split, no social cleavage has truly emerged or even re-emerged. Obviously, differences exists between New UDF and DL, but these are more a matter of nuance than of fundamental opposition, and revolve increasingly around the salience of certain issues such as European construction, in New UDF's case, or the defence of small traders and business owners, in the case of DL. Both find themselves in a politically conservative space, associated with economic liberalism. Despite the frag-mentation in organisational terms, the moderate right are undergoing a certain ideological homogenisation, questions about Europe, decen-tralisation or the role of the state no longer dividing them (Ysmal, 2000). This homogenisation has no doubt resulted from the general dissemi-nation of liberal ideas, which DL has helped to spread despite not reaping any significant reward from doing so. More fundamentally, however, it is the rise of the FN which has obliged this ideological tightening, providing as it has a point of negative identification for the moderate right. Furthermore, the FN has not only posed an ideological conundrum to the moderate right, but also a strategic one.

The split in the UDF resulted in part from an internal debate over the attitude to adopt towards the FN after the 1998 regional elections. In five French regions, these elections had led to a relative majority of the left where previously the right had dominated. The right, however, had the possibility of retaining control were it to have the support of the extreme-right councillors. Five former regional council presidents opted for this possibility in order to keep their title, against the advice of the national party headquarters. François Bayrou, then vice-president of the UDF, condemned anything which resembled an agreement with the extreme right, be it collusion or collaboration. Conversely, Alain Madelin asserted that the question of the FN could not be allowed to get in the way of the political programme, that to fight it one should fight its ideas. Without explicitly condemning the regional council presidents in question, and even supporting some of them, Madelin believed that to ask whether FN support was viable or not was to play the left's game. Many of his colleagues even drew parallels with the PS and PCF alliance in the 1970s.

This difference deeply divided the moderate-right camp. Its birth had direct consequences for party locations and thus for their coalition potential. In a position more to the right, DL was notably one of the groups where Millon's network in the shape of La Droite had more success.[11] Conversely, New UDF found itself in a centrist position, which allowed it to win the Rhône-Alpes regional presidency, thanks to Socialist support. Nevertheless, the FN split in 1999, which destroyed most of its coalition potential,[12] and Jacques Chirac's continued opposition to any alliance, prevented this new cleavage from becoming entrenched. On the other hand, New UDF itself became more entrenched in the centre in broadening its catchment area, while DL located itself more closely to its RPR partner.

The interplay between party demarcation and coalition integration should prevent the appearance of polemical debate on ideology between the different parties of the moderate right. Only strategic questions, such as the attitude towards the FN or the 2002 electoral calendar, cause real opposition. In the end, it is the articulation of different interests and party locations more generally which differentiate New UDF from DL. The UDF split did not engender polarisation, even within the moderate right. Certain cleavages may have appeared, but today they have dissipated. This evident proximity in ideological terms on the right betrays the clear divergence in organisational terms that has supported continued fragmentation within this bloc. Such differences have proved very bit as divisive as programmatic considerations.

The split and subsequent dynamics on the moderate right

The modification of the number of relevant parties in a system will modify the mechanics of inter-party relations therein (Sjöblom, 1968, Laver, 1989).[13] The formation of the UDF embodied this logic by reducing the number of independent actors in the game. In 1978, the UDF was initially created as a common electoral banner for the PR, CDS and Radical Party. The legislative elections of that year presented two dangers to Giscard d'Estaing. First, a left-wing victory could provide an electoral surge sufficient to secure François Mitterrand's election three years later in the presidential race; second, the Gaullists, under Jacques Chirac's leadership, had been engaged since 1976 in an internecine fight with the president from their position in the governing coalition. The re-grouping of the parties under the UDF banner was primarily designed to field common candidates at the first round of the two-ballot legislative elections. Without this, separate candidatures against the Gaullists risked seeing the latter reach the second round on their own, leading to the disappearance of the moderate camp from the legislature.[14] Since 1958, the moderate bloc had undergone a steady erosion in its parliamentary representation, from almost 200 deputies in 1958 to fewer than 100 in the 1970s. The 1978 elections in fact finished with the moderates victorious, achieving parity with the RPR.

This success ensured the permanence of the UDF by providing it with an organisational dimension above and beyond its cartel status. First and foremost, the UDF provided a stable arena for negotiation between its constituent parts, reinforcing the cohesion of a deeply divided coalition. In providing voters with a pole with which to identify, the UDF's existence strongly discouraged any strategy of defection to the left or right. Threats of secession may have been numerous, but none came to fruition until 1998 because their role was limited to that of a simple bargaining tool. The UDF can therefore be considered as a unitary actor throughout its twenty-year existence, even if the total was little more than the sum of its parts (Hanley, 1999b). Presidential and European elections are the important exceptions to this rule. For these elections, candidatures have rarely corresponded to narrow party delineations anyway, whether under a united right (such as the European elections of 1984 and 1994) or a divided UDF (European election of 1989 and the presidential elections of 1988 and 1995). Between 1981 and the split, the UDF had never presented itself as a united party at these elections.

Conversely, at the 1999 European elections, a single UDF list opposed a joint RPR-DL list.[15] Similarly, each of these three parties has fielded a candidate for the 2002 presidential elections – Jacques Chirac for the RPR, Alain Madelin for DL, and François Bayrou for New UDF. DL's return to independence, despite the component being formed before the formation of the UDF itself, can be considered the appearance of a new party. The split forced it to change arena, reintegrating directly into the party system, and no longer limiting its room for manoeuvre to the UDF's internal space.

The reappearance of DL on the right should not be seen as a preface to any major change. The third and dominated partner on the right, DL no longer seems to be an actor able to use the threat of coalition break-up. The political survival of DL relies from now on upon its continued participation in a moderate-right electoral alliance. Its own electoral pool, estimated at less than 5 per cent of the electorate,[16] is insufficient for a party which presents itself as 'office-seeking'. Its position on the right prevents it from any strategy involving overtures to the left. Its possible role as a pivot between the moderate and extreme right seems unlikely given the fragmentation of the extreme-right bloc [17] and Chirac's own opposition to it. Furthermore, Jean-Marie Le Pen's second place in the presidential race has definitively excluded him from future alliances. Conversely, New UDF's position is more flexible, due to its centrist location. A rejection of the current alliance in favour of the left at the moment seems unlikely, as much from the status of the PS, PCF and Green Alliance as much as from the internal opposition which such a strategy might provoke. However, this pivotal position can be used by the UDF under certain conditions, much in the same way as the CDS tried, albeit somewhat unsuccessfully, in 1988.[18] For instance, part of the UDF and the PS has already formed an alliance in the Rhône-Alpes region, to elect Anne-Marie Comparini (UDF) to the regional council presidency. This game played out between part of the right under Charles Millon's command, allied with the extreme right, [19] and a centrist pole, combining part of the UDF and the PS.

Nevertheless, these alliances are unstable and circumstantial. The split is thus unlikely to rearrange the structure of coalitions within the party system. Indeed, it seemed more likely to strengthen the RPR's domination. Paradoxically, if anyone seemed likely to derive benefit, it was the New UDF, and until the spring of 2002, this seemed to be the case. RPR, New UDF and DL fielded their own presidential candidates and simultaneously negotiated candidacies for the legislative elections. For twenty years, the single first-round candidate has become the rule for at least local and legislative elections.

Legislative and presidential elections nevertheless follow two separate logics. For the former, alliance is favoured inasmuch as the goal is the maximisation of elected candidates. For the latter, differentiation is key where only one position is at stake. The UDF may be an ineffective presidential machine,[20] but the post-split parties have included this election at the heart of their agenda. The presidential ambitions of François Bayrou and Alain Madelin were, moreover, considered to be key to the split. It should be noted that DL and the UDF obtain their best scores in opinion polls for the presidential election, their respective candidates receiving about twice as many voting intentions as their party in the legislative polls.[21] For the parties, the logic of differentiation and support of the leader is predominant. This has resulted in a frank discussion of the hegemony of the president over his own camp. The emergence of 'affairs' concerning Jacques Chirac or his entourage are subtly played upon, for instance. Cohabitation also reinforces this competition as far as the president is more or less directly involved in governmental business.

Conversely, because the French president and the RPR have a say in the selection of candidates for the next legislative elections, the majority of DL and New UDF deputies are in favour of a strategy based upon a single presidential candidate in the first round. A strategy too dependent upon differentiation could in the end threaten the legislative election alliance and therefore in turn threaten many deputies' re-election. Consequently, there is a growing dissociation within each organisation between their different manifestations. Notably, New UDF and DL are witnessing growing conflict between their party headquarters and parliamentary groups. In 2002, the legally fixed deadlines for the renewal of assembly and presidential mandates would have meant that the deputies had put themselves before the polls in advance of the President, a departure from Fifth Republic tradition. A bill put forward by Lionel Jospin's government proposed prolonging Parliament for a couple of weeks in order to return to the traditional order. The Communists and Greens, however, refused to support it, depriving the government of its majority – it was only thanks to one third of the UDF parliamentary group that the bill was finally passed. However, in the meantime, the Conseil National of the UDF had already unanimously adopted a proposal to support this bill strongly. The majority of the UDF parliamentary group, in disagreement with this, could thus have opposed a direct order from party HQ. The novelty of this situation is not so much the autonomy of the parliamentary group, but that it could take a clear line at all. The split in the UDF has thus served to fog the source of power, the parties seemingly more and more uncohesive.

This schism between DL and New UDF's parliamentary and party organisations gradually increased, peaking in the aftermath of the first-round presidential elections. Initially, the split of DL from the UDF produced a multiplication of apparatuses at the local and national level. The split of the party leadership into New UDF and DL was accompanied by similar splits among members and grass-roots organisations, but these latter were less problematic due to their already being largely separated out. However, these changes, particularly among groups of repre-sentatives, seem somewhat artificial. They may have come off at the national levels, with the National Assembly group separating into two – the Démocratie Libérale et Indépendants and the remaining UDF – but at the local level, such developments were far more limited: the old UDF partners continue to sit mostly in the a single group. Moreover, Jean-Pierre Raffarin created the Chiraquian club Dialogue et Initiative in 1998 with Jacques Barrot, Dominique Perben and Michel Barnier, in order to try to structure coordination and programmes on the moderate right. However, the main initiative in this respect was the creation in spring 2002 of Alternance 2002, an association formed in April 2000 by a group of RPR, DL and UDF deputies. Since its creation, two of its guiding principles make it a possible alternative to existing parties: individual membership, regardless of party status; and the creation of a common electoral banner for its members, effectively designed as a presidential majority banner. Nevertheless, this association did not emerge as a political party until its transformation after the second round of the 2002 presidential elections into the UMP.[22] At this point, the UMP stated four conditions for its supporting candidates. The UMP candidates had to provide a written undertaking to support the new government for the entirety of the first legislature; their candidacy must only be registered under the symbol of the UMP, and no other;[23] they must become a member of the UMP parliamentary grouping; and they must take part in the founding congress of the UMP. Thus, the UMP placed itself squarely in competition with the other political parties.

New UDF and DL's respective reactions to this challenge were different. François Bayrou opposed it utterly. Three-quarters of the UDF par-liamentary group requested UMP candidacies, but the remainder of New UDF decided to present its own candidates.[24] Conversely, Alain Madelin supported the UMP (given that his parliametary group joined the new party directly), dissolving DL in September 2002.[25] In general, however, the situation remains confused, given that none of the parties has excluded any of its members, with many members of the UMP remaining in executive positions within New UDF and DL.

The 2002 elections have resulted in a novel party sub-system on the right, characterised by two main changes from its recent past: the hegemony of the UMP, which holds 365 deputies in the National Assembly against only 29 for the New UDF; and the end of unique right-wing candidacies in the first round of legislative elections. In this sense, the moderate right has returned to its state in the 1960s or 1970s, but with a hegemonic Chiraquian party rather than a dominant Gaullist party. Furthermore, the similarities with the 1970s extend to the restrained level of competition between the moderate-right partners. The UDF only stood under its own symbol in 151 constituencies, in which the UMP only failed to field its own candidate in 19 cases. Thus, competition between the UMP and UDF only occurred in less than one-quarter of constituencies. However, even in these cases, true competition was rare, with one or other of the candidates having no chance of winning, either due to the strength of the incumbent or due to a failure to engage in a productive campaign.[26] To this extent, the 2002 legislative elections perpetuated the principal of 'fair share' put forward by Hanley (1999b) if we ignore the UMP umbrella label. Even today, the RPR receives around one-half of the candidatures, the DL one-fifth, and the CDS one-seventh,[27] with the rest distributed among the other coalition members.

Nevertheless, between 1978 and 2002, a clear tendency towards a shift in balance between the two main components of the UDF occurred (see Tables 7.1 and 7.2). In 1997, FD managed to get more of its candidates elected as deputies than the PR. The 2002 elections also confirmed this tendency inasmuch as DL lost some more common candidacies to New UDF, despite the latter only being partially integrated into the UMP. This sheds a new light on DL's fortunes after the schism. The double logic of the UDF alliance within a right-wing alliance lost it the status of second principal component of the French right,[28] without any equivalent shift in electoral support. This development in the relative positions of the different components within the UDF can mainly be explained by the mechanism of candidate selection.[29] The management of these compromises were carried out almost systematically against the interests of the dominant partner, leading to an overrepresentation of the second-placed party. Moreover, the figures concerning RPR-UDF shares give similar results, with the RPR losing out despite its own electorate growing relative to that of the UDF.[30] However, the split did not allow DL to become the second-placed partner of the right. In the end, the split did not allow it to cancel out this unfavourable dynamic.

The party landscape on the right appears uncertain subsequent to the 2002 elections. On the one hand, political supply has not been fundamentally changed by the UDF splinter by the creation of the UMP. The principal of incumbent support has not changed, and the few occasions where this has not pertained means that change is slow. Changes in party name have been apparent, but their effects are also uncertain. The creation of a UMP group in the National Assembly seems only to confirm the general unity of moderate-right deputies which has been implicit for a long time. Conversely, it will not present certain problems linked to parties where group discipline is not the rule. The main change has been the nomination of Jean-Pierre Raffarin as Prime Minister, albeit under the close scrutiny of the Elysée.

On the other hand, if the UMP turns out to be a long-term stable

TABLE 7.1 Party affiliation of single candidates fielded by the moderate right (per cent)

	1978	1981	1986	1988	1993	1997	2002
RPR	55	53	51	51	50	52	51
DL/PR	18	22	18	19	20	17	15
New UDF/FD	8	12	13	13	11	14	23

TABLE 7.2 Party affiliation of moderate-right deputies (per cent)

	1978	1981	1986	1988	1993	1997	2002
RPR	53	59	55	50	54	55	52
DL/PR	24	21	21	22	23	15	15
New UDF/CDS	12	13	14	19	13	19	25

organisation, presenting an alternative to New UDF, the change will be significant in that it will confirm the implantation of an essentially biparty system, substituing bipolarised multipartism. Deprived of their parliamentary presence, New UDF can no longer rely upon strong organisational or popular support to ensure their survival against the UMP. The UDF split may not have had direct consequences, but it did provide the first stage in French party system change due to the weakening of one of the poles of the bipolar quadrille. Without the split, the UDF might have been able to oppose the formation of a Chiraquian movement not only because of its electoral strength but also because the UDF appears a posteriori more coherent than its other manifestations.

Conclusion

The UDF split may seem to have had little impact on the French party system, but it nevertheless represents the beginning of changes which might represent a substantial change in the French party system, creating a single dominant moderate-right party in the shape of the UMP or one of its successor. In essence, the split has opened up more possibilities rather than exercised direct effects. One of its unwanted and paradoxical effects would be the initiation of a period of unification via a fragmenting dynamic. The dilemma between differentiation and integration would thus have been resolved in favour of the latter as a result of the legislative elections' dynamic, rather than the presidentials. The French political system thus still conforms to its semi-presidential model where winning a coherent parliamentary majority is indispensable to the president.

Although voters on the right have largely supported a single right-wing organisation since the 1990s, the parties themselves have gone in the opposite direction until 2002. The parties of the right have thus contributed to their own delegitimation, giving the appearance of private clubs run according to individual whims. New UDF and DL are consequently skeletal in their corpus, with less than 50,000 member, putting themselves at risk of being overtaken by some new initiative, such as Millon's which managed to garner 30,000 members in the space of a few months. Can the creation of the UMP thus be interpreted as a reconciliation of the right and French society? So far, the organisation has not gone down this road. Above all a parliamentary body with no real membership, the UMP elite appears to have little legitimacy given their lack of democratic mandate to their hegemony. The birth of the UMP has thus only been the first stage in a more generalised refoundation which should follow. The success of this will determine the long-term chances of the UMP. Too much prevarication might otherwise give New UDF a chance to rise from its ashes. With a parliamentary group and an electoral label, François Bayrou has not yet given up hope.

Notes

1 The three founding parties of the UDF in 1978 were the PR, from the liberal stream; the CDS, successor to the Christian democratic movements; and the Radical Party.
2 There were five components to the UDF on the eve of its break-up: DL, the new label for the PR since the election of Alain Madelin as its president in 1997; FD, the fusion of the CDS and the Parti Social Démocrate (which included Socialists who had rejected the Communist alliance in the 1970s); the Radical Party; the Parti Populaire pour la Démocratie Française, a splinter from the PR; and lastly direct UDF members.
3 The 'moderate' label is a practical label for UDF members in the tradition of the 'independent' *notables*. Political moderation is a negative definition, more defined by its opposition to the left, the extremes and Gaullism than by its own content. Above all, it evokes a political culture more than a position, being closer to centrism than to the centre (Hazan, 1997).
4 The *Républicain et Indépendants* group in the Senate is part of the liberal family along with DL. Despite DL's numerical domination, the Républicains Indépendants (RI) group includes a broader spectrum of parties, including several members of the UDF. It contains 46 senators and is thus the fourth largest group in the Senate.
5 The UDF had already undergone a split in 1994, when Philippe de Villiers' MPF was created for the European elections. The MPF diverged sufficiently to be excluded by the moderate right, and failed to make any alliances at the local level.
6 DL is directly descended from the PR, and New UDF mainly from members

of the former CDS. Unfortunately, no data exist since the SOFRES–*Le Monde* survey of 1990.

7 DL corresponds closely to the 'challenger' party identified by Lucardie (2000).

8 Alain Madelin, speech to the DL party conference (16 May 1998).

9 See the DL programme (*Dix Choix Forts* – Ten Strong Choices) at www.dem-lib.com

10 Since 1999, however, it should be noted that both RPR and DL MEPs sit in the European Popular Party.

11 La Droite is a political organisation started by Charles Millon in 1998 to garner support no matter what its party affiliation. In 2000, La Droite was transformed into a party, and renamed La Droite Libérale et Chrétienne.

12 The FN split may not have significantly damaged its electoral potential, but Bruno Mégret's failure to win away part of the FN's support has hampered any possibility of allying with the moderate right.

13 The crux of the argument lies in the fact that, as the number of parties increases, so the number of possible coalitions rises exponentially. If we take the UDF split as indicating a rise in the French party system from six to seven relevant parties, the number of possible coalitions rises from 63 to 127.

14 Schlesinger and Schlesinger (2000) have shown that if the UDF managed to improve its performance over the RPR at the second round, it would have much the better performance at the first round. Coordinating candidacies was thus indispensable for the moderate right to ensure qualification for the second round.

15 The situation in 1999 is thus similar to that of 1989 when the PR joined the RPR in a single list led by Valéry Giscard d'Estaing while the CDS ran its own list under Simone Veil.

16 Vote intentions for DL candidates vary between 3 and 5 per cent, according to the polling institute. The indicator has its weaknesses, not least because of the electoral coalition, but shows DL's tight margins. The party proximity indicator gives similar results, with 2 to 4 per cent of the sample naming DL.

17 The political space between the moderate and extreme right has been heavily contested by such actors as the MPF, the CNI and the Droite Libérale et Chrétienne. DL, at the moment of the break-up, could also have been situated among these, given that its position on the regional presidency affair was more tolerant.

18 In 1998, a parliamentary group – the Union du Centre – had been created by members of the CDS positioning themselves as a pivot to negotiate with Michel Rocard's minority Socialist government. However, these attempts failed, particularly because of the left, and support was limited to yes votes on a number of pieces of legislation.

19 The possibility of an overt alliance between Charles Millon and the extreme right was much debated. Relations between Millon and the FN are hazy, but there has certainly been an agreement between Mégret's FN splinter, the MNR and Millon.

20 Since 1981 and until 2002, the UDF has not managed to field its own candidate. It more or less endorsed Raymond Barre and Edouard Balladur in 1995, but both were beaten.

21 The results of the 2002 presidential elections gave François Bayrou 6.94 per cent and 3.96 per cent Alain Madelin. In the first round of the legislative elections, separate UDF candidates won 4.19 per cent with DL winning no significant share of the vote.

22 Alternance 2002 had already changed its name once before, becoming a *mouvement* rather than a *union*. The UMP will adopt a new symbol after its founding congress in the autumn of 2002.

23 See www.u-m-p.org; this condition is crucial, given the terms of state financing of political parties.

24 In some cases, separate UDF candidates stood against former UDF candidates who had decamped to the UMP.

25 Around twenty candidates stood under the DL symbol.

26 The decision to present separate candidates was only taken one month before the elections, and so a number of candidates were only fielded at the eleventh hour. Indeed, in some cases UDF candidates were in fact members of DL.

27 The growth of New UDF in 2002 (Tables 7.1 and 7.2) derive principally from other components of the UDF which remained within New UDF.

28 In 1958, during the first legislative elections of the Fifth Republic, the Independents of the CNI – the precursors to the PR – won 118 seats and became the second largest group in the National Assembly. General de Gaulle's UNR nevertheless won more than 200 seats.

29 Three key principles govern the selection of candidates within the confederation: automatic reselection of incumbents and most previous candidates who wish to stand again; a nationally negotiated distribution of constituencies among the member parties; and the individual choice of candidates according to their chances of victory (Sauger, 1998).

30 The electoral potential of the UDF and RPR is difficult to estimate precisely because of their alliance. Using party proximity as an indicator, 19 per cent of voters declared themselves close to the UDF in 1978 but only 10 per cent did so in 1997. For the RPR, the proportions move from 17 per cent to 18.5 per cent during the same period (CEVIPOF national surveys, 1978 and 1997). During this time, the RPR group in the National Assembly lost 14 deputies, whereas the UDF only lost 10.

8
From the Gaullist movement to the president's party

Andrew Knapp

Introduction

Most major European countries are content with just one major party of the centre-right: Britain's Conservatives, Spain's PPE, Germany's CDU–CSU. France has always had at least two. The electoral cycle of April–June 2002, however, held out the prospect of change by transforming the fortunes of France's centre-right in two ways. A double victory at the presidential and parliamentary elections kept Jacques Chirac in the Elysée and put a large centre-right majority into the National Assembly. Second, most of the hitherto dispersed centre-right family merged into a single formation, the UMP.

Why did this merger happen in 2002, and not sooner? The first part of this chapter will consider what kept the mainstream right *apart* before 2002. The second section will show why the parties had less reason to stay apart by 2002 than they had had five, ten or twenty years earlier. The third will show how a more favourable context was used to advance a concrete merger project, in the approach to and aftermath of the 2002 elections. The conclusion will assess both the UMP's longer-term prospects, and its more general impact on the French party system.

France's divided right

For most of the Fifth Republic, three things have divided the French right: real differences of ideology and policy; opposed organisational cultures; and the logic of presidential competition. On the other hand, although the right-wing electorate is far from homogeneous, divisions among voters had rather little impact on divisions between the parties – and voter demand was eventually to be important in the genesis of a merged party. René Rémond's classic study divided the contemporary

121

French right into three *familles spirituelles* which he related to the nine-teenth-century claimants to the French throne: legitimists, who rejected *en bloc* the values of the French Revolution (the far right); Bonapartists, standing for strong national plebiscitary leadership, and a 'social' inter-ventionist state (the Gaullists); and Orleanists – Anglophiles who stood for a moderate, socially and economically liberal monarchy supported by local *notables* (the *giscardiens*) (Rémond, 1982).

Despite the imperfections of such an essentialist view of the right's divisions, its proponents would have found empirical support in the policy differences between the Gaullists and the non-Gaullist moderate right in the first two decades of the Fifth Republic. These include, for example, the bitter disputes of the 1960s over French institutions and European integration between Gaullists (and the small group of their *giscardien* allies) on the one hand and the so-called 'centrists' (including Christian democrats and a significant part of the non-Gaullist conservative right) on the other. The Pompidolian succession in 1969 drew some of the passion from these debates. However, fairly clear distinctions within the French right survived into and after the 1970s. Jacques Chirac's relaunched RPR was generally more Eurosceptical, more *dirigiste*, and more authoritarian; the Christian democrat and non-Gaullist right um-brella UDF was altogether less jacobin, more Eurofriendly, and (usually) more 'liberal' on both economic and societal issues; each disputed the centre-right ground with the other (Colombani, 1984). The two sides still, to a degree, marched to different tunes.

Second, minimal party organisation is a tradition on the French right. France is the land, above all, of Duverger's cadre party, the loose, undisciplined, grouping of local *notables* of more or less the same sensibility (Duverger, 1951). For the Gaullists, on the other hand, the strong leader and the chain of command have been operating prin-ciples since the Resistance. These principles have, it is true, been imperfectly realised in practice. The first Gaullist party of any substance, the Rassemblement du Peuple Français, was wrecked in 1952 by the incorrigible independence of its *notables*. The Gaullist party of the early Fifth Republic, despite its nationwide organisation and membership, was materially far more dependent on its positions within the state than its leaders cared to admit. Chirac's relaunch of the party as the RPR in 1976 failed to re-establish it as a truly 'mass' party (Schonfeld, 1981).

Nevertheless, there were clear organisational contrasts between the Gaullists' quasi-military structures and nationwide membership and the much looser organisation of the non-Gaullist moderate right – local *notables* for the conservatives, local *notables* plus Catholic associative net-works for the Christian democrats. For Gaullists, 'we're a real party, with real activists', as one member said; 'the UDF is a country club'.[1]

UDF *notables*, on the other hand, described the Gaullists' *modus operandi* as *fascisante* (Frémontier, 1984: 180–1).

Lastly, the right was also predictably divided by presidential rivalries under the two-ballot electoral system. First-ballot competition need not damage the chances of second-ballot victory, provided the losing candidate in each camp endorses his better-placed rival for the run-off (which has always happened, though with varying degrees of conviction). The first five presidential elections of the Fifth Republic offered right-wing voters a choice between two credible candidates at the first ballot (Table 8.1). Although the presidential election is in principle a confrontation between individual candidates (rather than parties) and the electorate, candidates need the backing of parties to be successful. A party merger will therefore threaten the interests of any potential candidate who lacks an overwhelming lead within his own camp. This had been the major stumbling block to the first real attempt to confederate the RPR and the UDF, in 1990, in an alliance called the UPF. The organisation of presidential 'primaries' within the UPF, promised for 1995, never materialised because no candidate was prepared to surrender his chances of a first-ballot run (though in the event, the UDF failed to run its own candidate in 1995).

TABLE 8.1 The moderate right: presidential candidacies and share of votes cast (1965–2002)

		Gaullists		*Non-Gaullist moderate right*		
Year	*Candidate*	*First-ballot vote (%)*	*Second-ballot vote (%)*	*Candidate*	*First-ballot vote (%)*	*Second-ballot vote (%)*
1965	De Gaulle	44.7	55.2	Lecanuet	15.6	–
1969	Pompidou	44.5	58.2	Poher	23.3	41.8
1974	Chaban-Delmas	15.1	–	Giscard d'Estaing	32.6	50.8
1981	Chirac	18.0	–	Giscard d'Estaing	28.3	48.2
1988	Chirac	19.9	46.0	Barre	16.5	–
1995	Chirac	20.8	52.6	Balladur*	18.6	–
2002	Chirac	19.9	82.2	Bayrou	6.8	–
				Madelin	3.9	–

* Balladur: Gaullist anti-Chirac candidate supported by most of the UDF
Sources: Lancelot (1998) (for 1965–95), *Le Monde* (for 2002)

It should be noted, however, that while they have always been in competition for the presidency, of its nature a post which only one partner can win, Gaullists and the non-Gaullist moderate right have always been ready to negotiate common candidacies at other levels, and notably for municipal and legislative elections. Here, candidacies supported by both major components of the moderate right were the exception rather than the rule. Thus in 1973, the Gaullists and the parties making up the UDF presented 522 candidates between them for the 473 seats available in metropolitan France, or 1.1 candidates per seat; in 1978, a year of unusually intense competition between the parties, the figure rose to 1.84 candidates per seat; it fell back, however, to 1.28 in 1981, 1.05 in 1988, 1.13 in 1993, and 1.01 in 1997 (Lancelot, 1998). True, the *total* number of moderate right-wing candidacies was higher than this (2 per seat in 1993, for example) because of the number of right-wing candidates who stood without an official right-wing label – and some of these had the more or less official blessing of the two major right-wing groupings.

But in most seats and at most parliamentary elections, the RPR and the UDF, usually after fierce negotiations at leadership level, joined forces from the first ballot. Similarly, they ran joint lists at municipal elections in some 210 of France's 225 towns of over 30,000 in 1983, 1989 and 1995 as well as 2001 (Martin, 2001: 114, 130, 148, *Le Monde*, 19 January 2001). This was possible because few right-wing voters were very choosy about which right-wing party they supported. Even in the parliamentary elections of 1978, where they had a choice in four out of five constituencies, only 55 per cent of RPR and UDF sympathisers voted in full accordance with their party preference, with between a third and a quarter opting instead for the rival right-wing formation on the basis of candidate preference (Capdevielle *et al.*, 1981: 239).

The parties of France's moderate right were thus separated by their ideological roots, their policy preferences, and their different organisa-tional cultures, as well as by the ambitions of their *présidentiables*. At the same time, the institutional framework, plus the fact that their voters were less partisan than activists or elites, allowed the deployment of different strategies for different types of election: open competition in presidential races, maximum cooperation at parliamentary and municipal contests, as well a mixture of the two for European and regional elections, held on proportional representation. And of course every right-wing government was a coalition of Gaullists and their non-Gaullist partners and rivals.

France's convergent right

The electoral defeat of 1981 opened a slow and discontinuous process of convergence between the policies and, to some extent, the organisa-tional patterns of the Gaullist and non-Gaullist centre-right. Convergence would not, however, have produced a party merger without the trans-formation of the conditions of presidential rivalry that took place at the end of the 1990s.

Convergence: ideology and policy

Policy convergence on France's centre-right after 1981 involved the broad alignment of Gaullist positions on those of non-Gaullist moderate right. To a significant degree, it was the work of Jacques Chirac. But it resulted less from an ideological conversion, or from a grand strategy, than from the instrumental, opportunistic, attitude to policy issues characteristic of the man (Rémond, 1988). In particular, Chirac has sought to minimise policy friction so as to maximise the support of the non-Gaullist right at second ballots of presidential elections. Three episodes highlight this.

In the first place, within three years of 1981, the RPR abandoned much of the *dirigisme* characteristic of Gaullism of the 1960s, as well as the Euroscepticism. Instead, it adopted a panoply of neo-liberal policies (privatisation, deregulation and tax cuts) and agreed to a joint list with the UDF parliamentarian Simone Veil for the 1984 European elections. The common platform signed by the RPR and the UDF in February 1986 confirmed this pro-European neo-liberal shift. Moreover, when the right won the parliamentary elections the following month, Chirac flew in the face of orthodox Gaullist views about presidential primacy by accepting the post of Prime Minister from President Mitterrand – and thus the very un-Gaullist principle of *cohabitation* that went with it.

Second, Chirac contributed to the 1980s relaunch of European integration by accepting the two key treaties that it embodied. It was the Chirac government that piloted the ratification of the Single European Act through Parliament in December 1986, thus ensuring, against the preferences of Gaullist die-hards, a breach in the national veto for which de Gaulle had opened the 'empty chair' crisis twenty-one years earlier (Favier and Martin-Roland, 1991: 556). It was Chirac himself who, after much hesitation and against the preferences of his own party, chose to support the Maastricht Treaty, and in doing so probably saved its passage at the 1992 referendum, thus ending the link between currency and national sovereignty which de Gaulle had seen as essential (de Gaulle, 1970: 399–400).

The final episode was the 1995 presidential election and its aftermath. The untidy line-up of support behind candidates in 1995 itself signified a blurring of party differences: Chirac was backed by most of the RPR and a minority of the UDF, Balladur by most of the non-Gaullist moderate right and a number of the RPR's national and local elected officials. Chirac's 1995 campaign was a sort of last hurrah for traditional Gaullist values: he beat Balladur to the second ballot by promising to place an absolute priority on reducing joblessness, regardless of the pressures of the global economy and of France's European commitments. But in October 1995 Chirac abandoned his election rhetoric and recommitted France to deficit reduction in line with the Maastricht convergence criteria.

By effectively adopting Balladur's programme, Chirac brought policy convergence to its culmination. Policy convergence on the moderate right did not mean uniformity. Even in the 1990s, there remained substantive policy differences among the elites of the RPR and the UDF over the state and the market, over European integration, over societal questions (sexuality, drugs, policing, or immigration), and on the strategic issue of relations with the FN (Habert, 1991, Ysmal, 1992).

But these differences no longer corresponded very well to party divisions between the Gaullists and the non-Gaullist moderate right. Free market, pro-European right-wingers like Alain Madelin, leader of Démocratie Libérale and Nicolas Sarkozy, his RPR partner at the head of the right-wing list for the 1999 European elections, had more in common with each other than with a jacobin Gaullist like Philippe Séguin or with a centrist Christian democrat like François Bayrou. Nor were these differences very much greater than those that agitate a unified conservative party. This was all the truer after the departure of leading Eurosceptics from both parties: Charles Pasqua, Chirac's former loyal lieutenant, left the RPR to run a competing 'sovereignist' list for the 1999 European elections with Philippe de Villiers, who had himself quit the UDF in 1993. They did well in 1999, beating the Sarkozy-Madelin list by 13.1 per cent of the vote to 12.7, but their attempt to found a new Eurosceptic party, the RPF, was a failure.

The crucial element of policy convergence was the effective disappearance, as a package of policies, of Gaullism, the French right's most distinctive element for the previous half-century. Thus Serge Berstein closed his history of Gaullism in 2001 with the assertion that 'Gaullism now belongs to history, and the party that is its last manifestation is nothing but a fraction of the French right, into which it is doubtless destined to merge' (Berstein, 2001: 519).

Organisational convergence

The organisations of the RPR and the non-Gaullist moderate right converged rather less obviously than their policies. Nevertheless, the contrast of the 1980s between the creaky UDF federation and the well-oiled RPR machine, dedicated to getting Chirac into the Elysée, was far less clear ten years later. The main changes occurred, again, within the RPR. They opened with Chirac's severe defeat at the hands of president Mitterrand by 54 per cent to 46 at the presidential election of 1988. That provoked criticism of the party's authoritarian leadership style, and thence a reform of party statutes which allowed, for the first time, policy differences to be expressed through organised currents. A more or less open challenge to the leadership from Pasqua and Séguin followed at the 1990 Le Bourget congress.

The Maastricht treaty offered a further occasion for dissent: Chirac's decision to support a Yes vote at the 1992 referendum was personal and he made no attempt to bring his party behind it. Two years later, many of the RPR's elected officials, including 126 deputies or senators, withheld their support for their party leader's presidential candidacy, preferring Balladur. It was only the support of Alain Juppé, Chirac's second-in-command in the RPR, that brought the bulk of the party's cadres behind his candidacy, and probably only Chirac's backers in the UDF such as Alain Madelin or Hervé de Charette that gave Chirac his crucial 700,000-vote first-ballot lead against Balladur.

The pre-1988 symbiosis between Chirac and his party had therefore been badly damaged by 1995. Nor did Chirac's presidential victory put the clock back; quite the contrary. Heads of state and government tend in any case to try and reduce their dependence on party and to appeal to a wider electorate. This tendency is reinforced in France, where one of the founding myths of the Fifth Republic is of the president 'above parties' (Bell, 2000: 7). It was further accentuated by the division between *chiraquiens* and *balladuriens* which continued, thanks in part to Chirac's own miscalculations, to poison the RPR well after May 1995 (Ottenheimer, 1996: 137–8). But if 1995 had left durable traces, the split between Chirac and the RPR was consummated by the trauma of the right's defeat at the 1997 parliamentary elections, which the President himself had provoked by an ill-judged snap dissolution of the National Assembly (Knapp, 1999). The 1997 defeat almost lost Chirac control of his party: the loyal Juppé, who had combined the posts of Prime Minister and RPR President since 1995, was removed from the former post by the voters and from the latter by an unholy alliance of Sarkozy and Séguin, which left Séguin as effective party leader.

Chirac was never, it is true, without some supporters in the RPR. One of them, Jean-Louis Debré, was elected to the key post of parliamentary group president in September 1997; and a message from Chirac received a twelve-minute standing ovation at the February 1998 party congress, much to Séguin's embarrassment (Hecht and Mandonnet, 1998: 40–9). And the RPR still differed from the UDF in having a more or less nationwide organisation. But as an instrument for the reconquest of power, the RPR was infinitely less reliable for Chirac than it had been a decade earlier. It was of uncertain loyalty; it was divided; it was unpopular, with negative poll ratings outnumbering positive ones by roughly 2:1, thanks in part to an association of the RPR with corruption for which Chirac's own performance as mayor of Paris before 1995 had been very largely responsible;[2] it was organisationally weakened (membership fell from over 142,000 in the late 1980s to under 100,000 by 1999, and activism had much diminished in intensity).

In short, the RPR had converged, though only partially, onto the ramshackle UDF model. Chirac could do little to reinforce it; on the contrary, he was obliged to undermine Séguin even if it meant weakening the RPR – a task completed by April 1999, when a series of provocations led the ever-susceptible Séguin to resign his party posts (Séguin's successor, Michèle Alliot-Marie, elected party president in December 1999, was not Chirac's first choice, but nor was she an open threat). With the RPR an inadequate base for the reconquest of power, the only alternative was to draw *chiraquiens* from both the RPR and the non-Gaullist moderate right into a cross-party network. That network would become the UMP.

The changed dynamics of presidential competition

The French voter has been kind to presidents who have suffered reverses in parliamentary elections. François Mitterrand's standing with the public recovered briskly when he appointed right-wing governments of cohabitation after the elections of 1986 and 1993. Chirac, too, was quickly forgiven. Having plumbed the depths of unpopularity, in tandem with his prime minister Juppé, throughout the year 1996, he was already enjoying a modest rehabilitation by December 1997, just six months after the election defeat. A year later, assisted no doubt by his skilful use of the role of genial host at the 1998 World Cup, which France won, his ratings had returned, more or less, to a positive balance. The French found him warm, competent, tolerant and energetic, even if neither sincere nor modest (Witkowski, 2001). Though not enough to guarantee Chirac a second term, the recovery did restore the position as a credible contender which he had temporarily lost with the fiasco of the 1997 dissolution.

What transformed Chirac's limited recovery into a dominant position on the right was the break-up of the UDF federation, as recounted in Chapter 7 of this volume. Lacking strong presidential rivals from this quarter, Chirac had established himself by 2000 as the only right-wing candidate capable of a presidential victory; not since 1965 had the right been so dominated by a single presidential candidate (see Table 8.1). Moreover, after April 2001, when Parliament voted to hold the presidential election first and the legislative elections second (ironically, against the President's opposition), it was clear that the former would condition the latter, and thus that a right-wing presidential victory, which could only be a Chirac victory, would materially assist a right-wing parliamentary win. For that reason, Chirac would henceforth find a critical mass of parliamentarians, not just in the RPR but also on the non-Gaullist moderate right, ready to support him from the first ballot. In other words, the newly asymmetrical terms of presidential competition on the right removed a crucial obstacle to a party merger.

Party convergence and voters

The Maastricht referendum of September 1992 was perhaps the last occasion when a major distinction was discernible between electorates of

FIGURE 8.1 Votes for Gaullists and for all moderate right-wing parties at parliamentary elections (1958–2002)

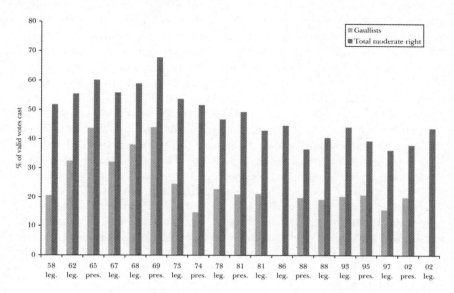

Sources: Calculated from Lancelot, 1998 (for 1958–97), and *Le Monde* (for 2002)
Note: figures for Gaullists are not available for 1986, an election held in proportional representation at which RPR and UDF ran joint lists for most seats, and for 2002, when RPR candidates ran under the UMP label (UMP 34.2 per cent, UDF 4.2 per cent, other right 4.45 per cent)

the Gaullist and the non-Gaullist moderate right: RPR supporters voted by 2:1 against the treaty, while UDF supporters backed it by 3:2 (Duhamel and Grunberg, 1992). By the decade's end, though differences between supporters of the two parties had not disappeared altogether, they were slight (Ysmal, 2000: 152–3). And, in any case, most moderate right-wing voters had long since decided that their differences did not justify continued party division: as early as 1989, a SOFRES poll indicated that 71 per cent of both RPR and UDF sympathisers wanted 'a single right-wing party with several currents' (Bourlanges, 1990: 49). They readily saw the moderate right's divisions as having contributed to the long-term drop in its share of the vote after the mid-1970s (Figure 8.1), and especially to the defeats of 1981 and 1988; the third defeat, in 1997, would give the Socialists a further five years in government, bringing their total to 15 of the 21 years after 1981, compared with the right's 6 and further exasperating the right-wing electorate.

By the turn of the century, existing party labels actually put off many right-wing voters. The monthly SOFRES polls showed negative opinions of the RPR and the UDF outnumbering positive ones by about 3 to 2 between 2000 and 2002. And moderate right-wing voters were increasingly attracted to 'various right' candidates with no specific party label. Thus in the 970 cantons where they ran in the cantonal elections of 1994 and 2001, 'various right' candidates led right-wing party candidates by 27.6 per cent against 21.5 per cent in 1994, and by 32.3 per cent against 15.3 per cent in 2001 (Chiche and Reynié, 2002). Again, in cantonal by-elections during 2001, the official right-wing parties actually lost 15 out of the 56 seats at stake to 'various right' candidates. In other words, even in a year when the right as a whole was regaining public confidence, the *parties* of the right remained unpopular. Similarly, the right's provincial gains at the municipal elections of 2001, in Roanne, Toulon, Chartres or Tarbes, Rouen, La Seyne, Drancy or Blois, were primarily achieved by candidates who stressed their closeness to *le terrain*, not their party label.

Thus few of the reasons that had kept the RPR and the non-Gaullist moderate right apart still applied at the turn of the century. The ideological and policy gap had been bridged; the organisational contrast had narrowed; presidential competition was no longer a real obstacle; and the voters were receptive. But the existing parties did not melt away. The president's party was the fruit of a project undertaken outside of, even against, the leaders of all three established parties of the moderate right.

The genesis of the president's party

The projects of a united right-wing party and that of a *chiraquien* grouping were not necessarily identical. A *chiraquien* grouping, Bernard Pons's Association des Amis de Jacques Chirac, had existed since 1995. Its role was to create a network of support for Chirac's eventual re-election outside party structures, comparable to the association which had initially managed de Gaulle's 1965 campaign. With the loss of a solid party base for President Chirac after the defeat of 1997, Pons's association, and its anniversary banquets in celebration of Chirac's election, acquired renewed importance as a *chiraquien* rallying-point. But Pons, a Gaullist of the older generation and former RPR secretary-general, never saw the association as a vehicle for dissolving the RPR into a larger right-wing grouping. On the other hand, a project of a united right-wing confederation, called the Alliance, launched in May 1998 by Séguin and Léotard, was still-born because it was obviously non- or even anti-*chiraquien*. The President had not been consulted about it, and so opposed it, albeit discreetly; the loyal Debré, at the head of the RPR deputies, would have nothing to do with it; the Alliance had died by the year's end.

The first sketch of a united right-wing party that was also *chiraquien* was set out in a note to Chirac from a young UDF Deputy, Renaud Dutreil, in May 1999. Dutreil had supported the idea of a merged party even before winning election to his Aisne constituency in 1994 (Dutreil, 1993). His memorandum recommended that the Association des Amis de Jacques Chirac should provide a meeting-point for those who 'within each party of the right, sought to head off inopportune adventures' (in other words, to sabotage competing presidential candidacies). Further, Dutreil argued that an essential second stage would be 'the concentration of opposition Deputies into a single movement, depriving the other parties of financial means and of a parliamentary platform'.[3] The novelty was in this focus on the material organisation of a new party. Half of all state funding for French parties is allocated on the basis of the number of their parliamentarians, which in turn depends on the ticket on which they choose to run for election. Within the National Assembly, debating time and committee places are allocated on the basis of parliamentary groups. Dutreil argued that if only a critical mass of parliamentary candidates could be persuaded to accept a single right-wing ticket and join a single group, then these institutional arrangements would ensure the discipline needed to create a new party; and, crucially, that the new party would not be a vague federation of existing ones, but would entail their dissolution or asphyxiation.

Chirac took over a year to react, approvingly but privately, to the Dutreil memo. In the meantime, his own interventions with the right-wing parties were hopelessly counter-productive. Chirac had sought a single right-wing list for the 1999 European elections; instead there were three, and they attracted just 35 per cent of the vote between them. He promoted the candidacy of Jean-Pierre Delevoye for the presidency of the RPR, and was rewarded, in December 1999, with the election of Michèle Alliot-Marie. Thereafter Chirac's interventions in the structures of the right passed through the discreet intermediary of Jérôme Monod, who joined the Elysée staff in June 2000.

Monod, who had known Chirac since 1963 and had run his *cabinet* at Matignon from 1975 to 1976 and the RPR (as secretary-general) from 1976 to 1978, had then spent nearly a quarter-century at the head of Lyonnaise des Eaux-Dumez. Monod's mission was to renew contacts with the right-wing elite at all levels. He could do this more readily than Chirac himself, or than other Elysée advisers, because he was both familiar with the parties of the right (from his past, and also possibly because Lyonnaise-Dumez had provided extensive legal and illegal funding to parties) and remote from recent party conflicts. With rank-and-file parliamentarians of all three parties of the moderate right, Monod embarked on a gruelling round of lunches aimed at clinching first-ballot support for Chirac in 2002. At a higher level, he brought together a cross-party group of four former ministers to consider themes for the future Chirac campaign: they were Dominique Perben (RPR) deputy-mayor of Chalon-sur-Saône; the European Commissioner Michel Barnier (RPR); Jean-Pierre Raffarin, the DL president of the Poitou-Charentes regional council, and Jacques Barrot, the UDF deputy and president of the Haute-Loire *département* council. Other former ministers, such as Antoine Rufenacht, mayor of Le Havre, and François Fillon, the *séguiniste* president of the Pays de la Loire regional council, joined the group from the summer of 2001.

At the same, time Monod established relations with Dutreil, who, with two other young deputies, Dominique Bussereau (UDF) and Hervé Gaymard (RPR), produced an initial text for a joint 'Alternance 2002' grouping in January 2001. Finally, Monod renewed his links with Juppé (whom he had brought into the Matignon staff in 1976). The mayor of Bordeaux and former premier, only half-rehabilitated within the RPR after the debacle of 1997 but still enjoying the President's support, became a strong supporter of Alternance 2002 as well as a frequent presidential visitor. These preliminaries over, Alternance 2002 was relaunched as the Union en Mouvement (with Dutreil as president, Busserau as treasurer, and Gaymard as secretary-general) on 4 April 2001, at the Paris Mutualité before 1,500 national and local elected officials of the right. The timing was auspicious: the right had just done unexpectedly well at the municipal elections. And the UEM appeared to respond to four requirements: the wishes of right-wing voters, the growing impatience of many right-wing deputies with existing party structures, the need for a loose structure to accommodate *chiraquiens* from the UDF and DL, and the need for a base for Juppé's return to national politics (Cathala and Prédall, 2002: 167–8).

At the same time, the clear threat that the UEM posed to the three parties of the moderate right, the RPR, the UDF and DL, as well as its early identification as a Juppé vehicle, provoked resistance not only from outside the Gaullist ranks – Madelin was dismissive, Bayrou solidly opposed – but from most of the RPR leadership too. Balladur, Séguin and the RPR president of the Senate, Christian Poncelet, stayed away from the Mutualité. Debré and Sarkozy turned up, but chiefly in order to voice their misgivings. As late as December 2001, at the RPR's silver jubilee celebrations, not just Séguin but most of the RPR leadership, including Michèle Alliot-Marie and even habitual Chirac loyalists like Debré, Pons or François Baroin, queued up to declaim variations on the theme that 'the RPR does not want to die'.[4]

The RPR jubilee, however, was the last open act of Gaullist resistance; in the new year, Chirac's continued ascendancy in the polls, and the approach of the presidential elections, secured silence from Alliot-Marie and her colleagues. Sarkozy became a cautious supporter of the project; Douste-Blazy, meanwhile, was instrumental in securing the goodwill of many UDF parliamentarians. Madelin never attempted to impose a line on his DL deputies, almost all of whom rallied to the UEM project. Thus by the time of the second launch of the UEM, at Toulouse in February 2002, the only clear voice of opposition came from François Bayrou. Delegates were invited to support the right-wing candidate of their choice at the first round, so long as they rallied to Chirac for the run-off – entailing a clear (and realistic) assumption that the first round would eliminate Bayrou and Madelin.

If pressing for the creation of a fully-fledged party before the presidential elections would have been premature, the results of the first ballot of the presidential election might have been calculated to hasten the birth of the president's party. That it was Le Pen, not Jospin, who reached the run-off practically ensured Chirac's re-election. At the same time Le Pen's high first-round score (16.9 per cent) indicated both to the press and to Chirac's campaign team that at the parliamentary elections, the far right could be the arbiter of the second-round contest in over 300 constituencies, with the clear potential to lose the election for the right through three-cornered second-round races.[5] That calculation, however false – it exaggerated the far right's second-ballot presence by a factor of ten – alarmed most sitting right-wing deputies sufficiently for them to seek protection under the UEM's broad cross-party umbrella. The price of that protection was spelled out when the UEM was relaunched, again, as the UMP on 23 April 2002, two days after the first ballot – a single UMP candidate, a single National Assembly group and participation in the eventual founding congress.

For Gaullist candidates, the UMP ticket entailed a further constraint: for the first time in the history of the Fifth Republic, they fought a parliamentary election behind a non-Gaullist campaign leader, Raffarin, whom Chirac had made premier on 6 May and who figured prominently on all UMP campaign material. But discipline brought its rewards: the June elections gave the UMP over one-third of the first-ballot votes and 369 out of 577 Deputies, compared to just 4.2 per cent and 22 seats for the rump of Bayrou's UDF, the only organised part of the right to stay out of the new grouping. The first stage in the construction of the president's party had succeeded beyond all expectations.

Conclusion: prospects for the presidential party

Juppé's ambition, to make the UMP 'a modern party, expressing different currents of thought, open to society', like the CDU–CSU, or the PPE, or Britain's Conservatives, or even France's Socialists in their heyday, benefited from an exceptionally favourable context in June 2002. The UMP's assets in the aftermath of the June 2002 parliamentary election victory were fivefold. First, it possessed a merged party leadership: a single parliamentary group chaired by Jacques Barrot of the UDF; a 50-member Founders' Council dating from the UEM period, which had elected a president (Juppé), a vice-president (Jean-Claude Gaudin, the DL mayor of Marseilles), a secretary-general (Douste-Blazy); and a carefully balanced executive committee of 31 members, of whom 15 came from the RPR, 9 from the UDF, and 7 from DL (15 of the 31 were also members of the government).

Second, the June elections had won the UMP an undeniable legitimacy as France's majority party; it was only the third party in the history of the Fifth Republic to commanded an overall National Assembly majority. Third, it responded to voter demand; the UMP on its own won as good a share of the vote in 2002 as the RPR and UDF had won together in 1997. The UMP electorate, though somewhat skewed to conservative categories (with 46 per cent of the farmers' vote and 50 per cent of the over–70-year-olds) was not outrageously so: its support among blue-collar workers was 26 per cent, among white-collar staff 30 per cent (higher than the Socialists), among the under–25-year-olds 23 per cent. And it attracted 16 per cent of Le Pen's voters from 21 April, as well as 26 per cent of Jean-Pierre Chevènement's and between 12 and 14 per cent of voters who had supported the Trotskyist candidates Laguiller and Besancenot.[6]

Fourth, the UMP had the President's full backing; there was now no question of Chirac attempting to distance himself from the party he had helped call into being weeks before. Finally, having survived the parliamentary campaign period on a shoestring, with activists and money borrowed from component parties, the UMP could now look forward to an annual income from the state of nearly EURO 30 m. or some 45 per cent of all public funding distributed to parties, over the 2002–7 legislature, plus inherited assets from the RPR and PR. To the extent that finance was the key to success, as Dutreil had argued, this was a political as well as a merely material advantage.

At the same time, four elements helped to cast doubt on the UMP's prospects. First, despite the June victory, the moderate right's electoral support was merely at the upper end of its post-1978 trend (Figure 8.1). It was less than half a percentage point above the level at which the right had crashed to defeat in the 1981 parliamentary elections, and fully ten points lower than the worst pre-1974 result. Second, despite the merged leadership, and the opening of the UMP to new membership applications, the UMP was not yet a party. Its founding congress – a fourth launch – was scheduled for October 2002. Moreover, the fusion of two quite dissimilar organisations presented real difficulties, especially at local level. If the RPR's superior activist base were given its full weight in the new party, it ran the risk of being perceived as an 'RPR mark 2', with attendant consequences for its image. However, to downplay the asset represented by the Gaullists' nationwide organisation would demobilise their activists and turn the UMP into something close to a cadre party, reinforcing the original sin of the French right. A third danger was that the old party divisions would fossilise within the UMP, turning it into a holding company rather than a real party and preventing the emergence of currents based more on real policy issues rather than on superseded party loyalties. The careful dosage of leaders from different parties in the UMP's provisional organisation indicated the continuing force of such party loyalties among the UMP's elites in this initial period. Closely linked to this issue of party 'currents' was that of party cultures: the culture of intra-party policy debate, essential to Juppé's ideal for the UMP's development, was largely alien to the Gaullists who still provided the UMP's big battalions.

Finally, the conditions of presidential competition, which had favoured the UMP's emergence, changed on the night of Chirac's election because presidential competition henceforth focuses on the succession to Chirac, who will be 74 in April 2007. The UMP contains three *présidentiables*, at least on their own estimation: Raffarin, Juppé and Sarkozy; Bayrou is a rival on the outside. One challenge for the new party, therefore, will be to canalise and control these rivalries, possibly establishing an intra-party primary process. That, however, would run directly against the Gaullist myth of the president, a man above parties who presents himself directly to the nation.

The UMP's possible impact on the party system can be considered at three levels. In the first place, it is unlikely to make a radical difference to the choices available to right-wing voters. The broad pattern established in the 1980s and 1990s of untidy right-wing unity, with the RPR and the UDF running joint candidates most, but not all of the time, and facing dissidents here and there, is likely to be perpetuated. The 2004 European elections, for example, could readily see a UMP list competing with a Bayrou list. Second, however, the UMP's success could be expected to reinforce existing tendencies towards bipolarity. The party system of Fifth Republic France has been characterised by a fine balance between the dynamics of fragmentation and bipolarity (Knapp and Wright, 2001: 264–5), and the electoral cycle of 2002 was an excellent illustration of this. Fragmentation was expressed in a presidential first round that saw sixteen candidates competing, extremes of right and left picking up a third of the vote, and the candidate of the far right beating the Socialist to the run-off.

The June parliamentary elections, on the other hand, were fundamentally bipolar with, crucially, each mainstream coalition dominated by a single partner, the Socialists on the left and the UMP on the right. The UMP's success would perpetuate this single-party dominance in each camp. A final dimension to the UMP's impact depends on its ability to fulfil Juppé's ambition and resolve the difficulties outlined above. A party of the moderate right that is capable of managing the inevitable competition between its *présidentiables*, and of canalising intra-party conflict into useful policy debate, would gain considerably in credibility by comparison with the right's record in the recent past. It could even contribute to reducing the widespread disenchantment with politics among French voters. Probably the UMP's leaders would settle for a less grandiose goal, but one that has become the unattainable Holy Grail of French party politics since 1981: the re-election of an incumbent governing coalition.

Notes

1 RPR activists quoted in *Le Quotidien de Paris*, 2 December 1986.
2 The figures were worse than those for the Communists: the monthly SOFRES poll in the *Figaro*-Magazine (7 November 1998) showed that a mere 27 per cent of respondents had a 'good opinion' of the UDF and 31 per cent for the RPR, compared with 37 per cent for the PCF. Poor opinions ran at 60 per cent (UDF), 58 per cent (RPR), against 50 per cent (PCF).
3 *Le Canard Enchaîné*, 20 February 2002.
4 *Le Monde*, 30 November and 15 December 2001.
5 *Le Monde*, 24 April 2002.
6 IPSOS-*France2* survey, www.ipsos.fr/CanalIpsos/poll/7571.asp.

9

The FN split: party system change and electoral prospects

Gilles Ivaldi

Introduction

The question of electoral change in France has received a great deal of attention in the past fifteen years, as evidenced by the volume of literature on French parties and elections. The rise of the FN and its ability to establish itself as a serious competitor against mainstream parties of the moderate right are clearly central to this question. The success of the extreme right has largely contributed to altering the balance of forces within the party system: while electorally irrelevant throughout the 1970s and the beginning of the 1980s,[1] Le Pen's party has enjoyed high levels of electoral support over the past decade with an average 15 per cent of the national vote cast in the successive elections of 1995, 1997 and 1998 (see Table 9.1).

TABLE 9.1 The FN in national elections (1984–2002)

Year	Election	%	Note
1984	European	11.4	10 MEPs elected
1986	Legislative	9.8	35 deputies
1988	Presidential	14.4	First round, Le Pen
1988	Legislative	9.7	One deputy, Yann Piat
1989	European	11.7	10 MEPs
1993	Legislative	12.4	No deputies
1994	European	10.5	11 MEPs
1995	Presidential	15.0	First round, Le Pen
1997	Legislative	15.1	FN + other minor extreme right candidates
1999	European	9.1	FN = 5.8%; MNR = 3.3%
2002	Presidential	19.2	First round, Le Pen = 16.9%; Mégret = 2.3%
		–	Second round, Le Pen = 17.8%
2002	Legislative	12.4	First round, FN = 11.1%; MNR = 1.1%
			No deputies

Source: Ministry of Interior

In contrast to the interest aroused by the electoral dynamics of the extreme right, there have been fewer attempts to formalise the various dimensions of party system change at a time of growing electoral volatility and increasing level of fragmentation within the system. The extent to which the French party system has moved away from the long-lasting dual format as a consequence of extreme-right success, particularly with regard to the resilience of the traditional cleavage structure of French politics, remains a debated issue (Cole, 1998, Hanley, 1999a, Guyomarch, 1995).

This chapter will first look back at the pre-1999 period to assess the role played by the FN in challenging the traditional bipolar format of French politics. It will then move on to analyse the historical and political factors underlying the split, the electoral performances of the two parties that emerged from this critical breakdown and the key features of party ideology within the extreme, right pole. Third, it will address the electoral prospects of the FN and MNR in the light of their results in the presidential and legislative elections of spring 2002.

Extreme-right politics and party system change in the mid-1990s

A glance at the results of elections over the past fifteen years reveals the amplitude of changes which have been taken place in the balance of power between the main competitors in the French polity, and the crucial role played by the rise of the FN in the weakening of traditionally two-bloc politics.

Over the 1988–98 period, one key feature of mass mobilisation on the extreme right has been the FN's ability to secure its electoral support between elections. Voting for the FN became more permanent and less volatile. In the 1986 and 1988 legislative elections, the FN achieved political relevance in about 90 per cent of the 555 metropolitan constituencies and gained around 10 per cent of the vote on both occasions. The 1990s were to witness the growth and stabilisation of the far-right electorate. In 1993, the extreme right attracted 12.4 per cent of the legislative vote but failed to gain parliamentary representation. In the first round of the 1997 general election, the FN candidates surpassed the 10 per cent threshold in over 80 per cent of the constituencies with a total vote cast of 15 per cent. No fewer than 132 FN candidates went forward to the second round to confront candidates of the left and the moderate right. In the 1998 local election, the FN won 275 seats in the regional councils under the proportional electoral rule and achieved 15 per cent in nearly half of the 96 metropolitan departments.[2]

With regard to party organisation, the strengths of the FN were well in evidence by the end of the 1990s (Birenbaum, 1992, Ivaldi, 1998a).

Individual membership rose from an estimated 15,000 in 1986 to 40,000. The decade witnessed the development of the basic structures and reinforcement of the entire party apparatus at both local and national levels. This internal development was associated with the founding of a large number of flanking organisations, newspapers and clubs, whose main purpose was political lobbying within specific fields of concern or particular social and professional sectors (Buzzi, 1994, Ivaldi, 2001).

Like other right-wing populist parties in Austria, Belgium or Norway, the social basis of the FN's electorate has become less heterogeneous over the years and, by the mid-1990s, developed a predominantly male, blue-collar worker and petty-bourgeoisie support, with low education (Betz and Immerfall, 1998, Kitschelt, 1995). In addition, anti-partyism, criticism of the 'political class' and recurrent attacks on both the left and moderate-right coalition have enabled Le Pen's party to generate increasing support from young voters less socially and politically integrated in mainstream politics (see Table 9.2).

TABLE 9.2 Change in the socio-demographic structure of the FN electorate (1984–97) in percentages

	Eur. 1984	Leg. 1986	Pres. 1988	Leg. 1988	Euro. 1989	Leg. 1993	Euro. 1994	Pres. 1995	Legi. 1997
Gender									
Male	14	11	18	12	14	14	12	19	18
Female	8	9	11	7	10	13	9	12	12
Age									
18–24 years	10	14	15	16	9	18	10	18	16
25–34 years	11	10	17	9	18	10	15	18	19
35–49 years	12	11	17	8	12	13	10	15	15
50–64 years	12	9	11	10	15	13	12	17	15
65 years+	10	6	12	10	12	13	7	9	12
Occupation									
Farmer, fisherman	10	17	13	3	3	13	4	16	4
Shopkeeper, craftsman	17	16	27	6	18	15	12	14	26
Professional/Manager	14	6	19	10	11	6	6	7	4
Routine non-manual	15	11	13	8	9	13	9	16	14
Routine manual	8	11	19	19	15	18	21	30	24
Not working*	9	8	12	9	13	12	9	11	15
Education									
No education/Primary	8	8	15	7	13	13	7	14	17
Secondary school	12	15	13	12	14	16	16	17	14
Technical	17	12	18	12	11	14	16	21	19
University	11	7	12	10	9	8	5	9	10
All	11	10	14.5	10	12	13	10.5	15.5	15

* 'Not working' refers to retired people, students and housewives who have never worked outside of the home
Source: Perrineau (1997: 102)

Particularly striking was the ability of the unitary FN to set foot on working-class soil and bring together two sectors of the working population – namely blue-collar workers and owners of small businesses – which were traditionally opposed on the left–right continuum in France. Changes in the FN social structure were discernible as early as 1988: in the first round of the presidential election, Le Pen won 19 per cent of the working-class vote and secured 27 per cent among shopkeepers, traders and craftsmen, a group traditionally inclined to support the extreme right. By 1995, the comparable figures were 30 and 14 per cent. Looking more closely at the class structure of the FN in the general election of spring 1997 shows the importance of the contribution by both the lower-class and petty-bourgeoisie voters to the electoral dynamics of the extreme right: together the latter groups accounted for nearly half (46 per cent) of the whole FN electorate in 1997.[3] On that occasion, the FN candidates received 26 and 18 per cent of the vote among unskilled and skilled manual workers respectively.[4] In the subsequent 1998 regional election, the lists presented by the extreme right won 17 per cent of the vote cast among small business owners and 27 per cent among blue collar workers.[5]

By attracting significant shares of the vote among secular blue-collar workers and the traditional Catholic conservative petty bourgeoisie, the party has managed to broaden its electoral appeal to disillusioned voters characteristic of the two sides of the political spectrum (Perrineau, 1995, Mayer, 1999, Evans, 2000a). The increase in electoral support from the working class has led to a significant shift in party ideology in the aftermath of the 1995 presidential election, with the FN clearly placing more emphasis on securing social benefits for the lower social strata and protecting France from the threat embodied by economic globalisation. While stressing the need for economic intervention on the part of the state, the party has continued to seek electoral support from the petty-bourgeois component of the conservative right by rejecting state collectivism and promoting liberal policies that would include tax reduction for small business owners. Another important explanation for the party's ability to step over the traditional ideological boundaries of French politics lies in the development among extreme-right supporters of a set of ethnocentrist, authoritarian and anti-system values which echoes the hard stance taken by the FN on social issues such as law and order or immigration, and tends to differentiate the extreme-right electorate from those of both the left and the UDF–RPR.[6]

In terms of party system dynamics, however, there is a need for considering another two important dimensions correlative to the established change in the social support for the extreme right in French elections. Looking first at changes in patterns of party cooperation and competition, and the tactical manoeuvring which was developed as a response to the alteration in the balance of power between the moderate right and their new challenger, it is true to say that the early 1990s witnessed the end of the 'conciliatory' phase: the development of formal links between the mainstream right and the FN became much less likely, as it was evident from electoral outcomes that Le Pen's party was the only beneficiary of such a strategy. It would be difficult to argue that contacts between the UDF–RPR alliance and the FN have never taken place subsequently, but overall it was clearly stated that the construction of a right-wing pole would not embrace the extreme right.

After a period of uncertainty and flirtation with the UDF–RPR in the late 1980s, the FN was pushed back towards the extreme-right fringe of the political spectrum and condemned to political isolation. In the face of this strong commitment from the ruling parties of the right, the FN shifted its own position during the mid-1990s from one which favoured a broader right-wing alternative to the existing UDF–RPR coalition to one of fierce hostility towards the mainstream parties of the right and President Chirac.[7]

Second, if we are to address the evolution of the party system which took shape during the pre-1999 period, it is essential to outline the impact of the institutional setting on the dynamics of French politics. The emphasis is on the tension between proportionalist voting behaviour in the electorate on the one hand,[8] and constraints inherent in the two-ballot system on the other. Pressures for change coming from parties outside the mainstream have met with strong resistance from the majoritarian dynamics of the system (Ysmal, 1998). In France, the number of parliamentary parties is largely influenced by the mechanical process of translating votes into seats (Charlot, 1993).

Analysis of vote transfers between the two rounds of legislative elections points out the substantial effect of the bipolar constraints imposed by the second ballot, the impossibility of minor parties gaining sufficient support to win parliamentary representation, and the tendency for the electoral system to manufacture parliamentary majorities for parties that have not necessarily received majority support from the voters. The analysis of seats–votes ratios shows how the electoral system benefits well-entrenched parties by cancelling the effects of party fragmentation at parliamentary level.[9]

The constraints of the majoritarian rule have significantly limited the reshaping of the party system particularly when taking account of the FN's inability to gain parliamentary representation despite polling substantial shares of the vote in successive elections. Under the department-list system that was introduced in the 1986 legislative election (highest- average formula with a 5 per cent threshold), the FN first-ballot score in the first round of the 1997 election would have brought the party large gains in the Assembly and an estimated total of 77 legislative seats. With an expected number of only 223 deputies, the mainstream right would not have secured enough seats to form a government on its own.[10]

To summarise: that the state of the French party system between 1993 and 1998 was one of transition and instability is beyond doubt. In many ways the combination of electoral realignment, party fragmentation and party aggregation around electoral poles is a good indicator of the waning of the traditional bipolar party system which became apparent in the mid-1990s and gained momentum in the period thereafter. In terms of electoral dynamics, by 1997–98 party competition was tripolar with the FN being the third competitive actor isolated as a distinctive pole of French politics and capable of affecting the outcome of both the legislative and the regional contests (Jaffré, 1997).

And yet, however significant changes in patterns of electoral mobilisation were, they did not produce a truly tripolar system, particularly if the shape of the party system is to be assessed at parliamentary level. One first reason, as mentioned above, is the absence of a clear structural group underlying the support for the third bloc represented by the FN and the necessity of taking into account the protest, issue-oriented and political disenchantment components of voting for the extreme right. Another important reason for this is of course to be found in the distorting effect of the majoritarian system and the constraints it placed on the overall process of electoral dealignment in France.

The 1999 split of the FN: intra-party conflict, party ideology and electoral competition

Despite electoral success, the FN has suffered severely from the factionalism endemic on the extreme right since the end of the Second World War. Together with more than half of the top-level party elites and a sizeable segment of grass-roots members, Bruno Mégret, general delegate of the party, left the FN in January 1999 to form a rival group, the Mouvement National, subsequently renamed Mouvement National Républicain (MNR).

This organisational schism was largely determined by historical, tactical and personality factors. Since its foundation in the early 1970s, the FN has been weakened by internal fights between factions and relatively unsuccessful in its attempt to bring together various opposing strains of the French extreme-right family. In 1999 the quarrel between Le Pen and Mégret was mostly about party strategy and whether the FN should begin a process of seeking electoral alliances with the mainstream right at both the local and national level. While Le Pen strongly favoured the continuation of the 'neither left nor right' strategy initiated during the 1995 presidential campaign by the youth section and old guard within the party, Mégret and his followers advocated a more flexible approach supportive of cooperation with the RPR–UDF–DL electoral pole (Ivaldi, 1999a).

To a large extent, the parties that emerged from the 1999 split are identical to the two major groups of power-holders which traditionally competed for influence within the former FN. Most of Le Pen's companions in today's renewed FN belong to a well-identified faction, namely the old orthodox guard composed of the historical 'founding fathers' of the party, the neo-fascist activists who joined the FN in the late 1970s, the traditionalist Catholics led by Bernard Antony, and some 'pure at heart' drawn from among the ranks of the youth organisation (FNJ), such as Carl Lang and Samuel Maréchal, who rose to prominence within the national staff through a long process of internal promotion.

The group of elites that left the party with Mégret represents another very specific strand of opinion. Most of the group came to the FN in the mid-1980s following Le Pen's attempt to integrate the party into the moderate-right's political space by establishing links with the national-conservative fringe of the New Right. The MNR leadership consists predominantly of those who, like Bruno Mégret, Yvan Blot, François Bachelot and Jean-Yves Le Gallou, joined the party in 1985–86 in anticipation of the general election. In 1999, the endeavour of the former general delegate of the FN was also supported by some of the cadres of the new generation (Philippe Colombani, Franck Timmermans, Philippe Olivier, Damien Bariller) who were eager to challenge the uncompromising party line and autocratic hegemony of Le Pen.

By 1997, important changes occurred in the balance of power within the FN national leadership. In the face of its political isolation, many in the party perceived the dangers of the hard-line imposed by Le Pen. At grass-roots level, an increasing number of federation secretaries and local party representatives joined Mégret in his plea for an electoral cartel with the mainstream right in the forthcoming general and regional elections. By winning a significant share of the votes to the Central Committee, the *mégrétistes* emerged as an extremely influential grouping at the 10th party congress in Strasbourg in April 1997. Mégret and Le Gallou came first and second respectively ahead of Bruno Gollnisch, a result which was soon to represent a major threat to Le Pen's uncontested power.[11] The FN departmental conferences that took place in January 1999 largely confirmed the predominance of Mégret and his followers within the party apparatus, with a total of 58 federal secretaries and 141 regional councillors supporting the delegate general in his attempt to convene a party congress. The *mégrétistes* were also found in the majority in 14 out of the 22 regional councils.

As suggested above, the dispute between Le Pen and Mégret was not a fight over the ideological stance of the movement, the FN being indeed largely indebted to the contribution made by Mégret and the previous members of the conservative New Right for some of the most popular themes of the FN political agenda. As evidenced by the MNR manifesto *La Charte des Valeurs* ('The Values Charter') publicised at the constitutive congress of the party in Marignane in January 1999, the schism had no clear implications for the ideological direction of the two resultant parties. Nor did the subsequent party literature published in 2000–01 by Mégret's movement differ significantly from the 1997 electoral platform *Le grand changement* ('The Great Change') of the former Front National (Ivaldi and Swyngedouw, 2001).

Electorally, the split on the extreme right resulted in fierce competition between the remaining FN and the newly formed MNR in the 1999 European election fought at a national level under proportional representation. Mégret's party performed badly: by polling a mere 3.3 per cent of the vote, the MNR notably failed to pass the 5 per cent threshold of representation for the European Parliament. The FN won 5.8 per cent of the total vote and five seats.[12] The whole of the extreme right was clearly weakened by its internal division but had also to compete at the time with the anti-European list headed by the very popular conservative leader of the 1992 anti-Maastricht cartel and former Minister of Interior, Charles Pasqua. The latter received 13.05 per cent and captured 13 seats in the election attracting a significant proportion of previous FN and RPR voters.[13]

In March 2001, the FN and MNR fielded candidates in the joint municipal and cantonal ballots which were seen as key elections for both parties of the extreme right. In the preceding local elections, the unitary FN had managed to establish a solid electoral base in most parts of France through a significant number of well-entrenched party activists and elected representatives in municipal and regional councils. In 1995, the FN had presented lists in 48 per cent of all metropolitan communes with more than 5,000 inhabitants; in 2001, the far right as a whole stood in less than one-third (31 per cent) of those municipalities and the two parties competed against each other in 77 cities. Both parties were heavily handicapped both by the difficulty inherent in finding the requisite number of participants to build lists in a large number of municipalities, and also by the additional constraints imposed by the new legislation on parity, which for the first time required political parties to put forward an equal proportion of men and women on their lists.

In 1995, the former FN had received 14.2 per cent of the vote in the first round of the municipal election compared with 11.3 and 12.2 per cent for the MNR and new Front National respectively in the 2001 ballot. On the latter occasion, the two parties kept control of three out of the four cities they had won six years before in the southern part of France – Orange (FN), Marignane and Vitrolles. More importantly, they also managed to secure most of the extreme-right electoral support in the concomitant cantonal election by winning a total of 10.2 per cent of the vote (FN 7.1 per cent; MNR 3.1 per cent) as opposed to 10.3 per cent for the FN in the previous election of March 1994. Of particular note is that the FN succeeded in presenting its own candidates in nearly all of the 1,900 cantons up for renewal in 2001, while the MNR only had a national coverage of about 78 per cent in this respect.

There is little doubt, however, that divisions within the extreme-right camp have had a major impact on the parties' ability to weigh significantly on the electoral outcome, and particularly in municipal contests. In most cases the FN and the MNR were not able to overcome the institutional hurdle to stand in the second round of the city council elections. In 1995 the FN had fielded candidates in 108 of the largest urban areas in France (those with more than 30,000 inhabitants); by 2001 the comparable figure for the whole of the extreme right dropped to 41 with an average loss of 2.2 per cent between the two rounds. In a significant number of municipalities, the electoral decline of the FN and MNR clearly benefited the mainstream right, as was the case in cities such as Blois, Chartres, Evreux, Nîmes, Strasbourg and Toulon for instance.

Electoral strength of the extreme right and party system continuation after 2002

With respect to the electoral strength of the far right and the format of the French party system, the 2002 elections have displayed similar trends to those observed in the preceding electoral cycle of 1995–98. Despite the relative decrease in electoral support for the FN at the legislative ballot, the 2002 elections have been a testament to the electoral health of the extreme-right camp in France. In the first round of the presidential election, the FN has reached its electoral apex by polling 16.9 per cent of the total vote, which allowed its leader to stand in the second round against the outgoing President Jacques Chirac. Together with Mégret's score of 2.3 per cent, the combined total for the far right added up to 19.2 per cent.

In 35 of the 96 metropolitan departments, Le Pen came ahead of the candidates of the mainstream left and right, and achieved a 20 per cent threshold in over 28 per cent of the 555 metropolitan constituencies. In the second round of the presidential ballot, Le Pen secured 17.8 per cent of the vote (around 5.5 million votes), far less than the 30 per cent he predicted for himself in the aftermath of the 21 April political earthquake but still a significant score in the context of popular mobilisation against the extreme right. On 5 May 2002, the FN's candidate attracted more than 20 per cent of the valid vote cast in over one-third (37 per cent) of the constituencies in metropolitan France.

The legislative elections of June indicated some limits to the influence of the FN and a substantial drop in the electoral support for Le Pen's party when compared with the outcome of the 1997 election. In the first round, the FN candidates won only 11.12 per cent of the vote (as opposed to 14.9 per cent in 1997), the MNR polling a mere 1.1 per cent. Unlike 1997, the FN could only progress to the second round in 37 metropolitan constituencies (against 132 in 1997) and captured no seats. Of the top-level party elite, only five national leaders were in a position to stand in the second round: Marine Le Pen, Marie-France Stirbois, Jean-Claude Martinez, Bruno Gollnisch and Jacques Bompard. With a total of 42.4 per cent of the vote, the Mayor of Orange achieved the best result of all FN candidates in the June legislative election yet failed to translate this performance into the only potential parliamentary seat for the party.

There were of course a variety of short-term factors that could account for the ebb and flow of the extreme right at the 2002 elections, the discussion of which is beyond the scope of this chapter. In terms of the party system dimension, however, four main aspects are noteworthy: these relate to party ideology, patterns of issue-voting, the socio-demographic structure of the extreme right electorate, and patterns of party cooperation.

Party ideology

Ideologically, the electoral platform of the FN and MNR in the 2002 elections was very similar to the programme published by the FN at the 1997 ballot or the party manifesto launched at the founding congress of Mégret's movement in early 1999. Both parties have continued to use anti-immigrant feeling as a campaign issue, this xenophobic line being linked with strong authoritarian views on criminality and insecurity, and associated with the traditional anti-system component. Consistent with the ideological shift of 1995–97, the FN placed an even greater emphasis on its socio-economic message to promote the synthesis of the traditional neo-liberal and anti-tax elements of the 1980s with renewed projectionist welfare state strategies and the populist claim to represent *les petites gens* ('the common people').

Patterns of issue-voting

Looking at the main issues for the FN electorate reveals a triptych very similar to that recurrently at stake in the history of the extreme right at the polls since the breakthrough of the 1984 European election. In 2002, Le Pen's first-round voters expressed once again worries about insecurity (74 per cent), immigration (60 per cent) and unemployment (31 per cent) as motivating factors for their vote. Essential to the understanding of the electoral dynamics of the FN in the presidential ballot is that the 'criminality' issue topped the political, public and media agenda, with nearly six out of ten voters (58 per cent) ranking 'insecurity' first on their personal scale of concern, far ahead of 'unemployment' (38 per cent) and 'poverty' (31 per cent).[14]

The analysis of vote transfers indicates a high degree of stability since 1995, and indicates that the party still possesses a stable core of voters: in 2002, the FN managed to retain the support of the vast majority of its electorate. At the first round of the 2002 presidential election, no less than 90 per cent of Le Pen's 1995 electorate voted either for him again or, in a much smaller proportion, for Bruno Mégret.[15]

Socio-demographic structure of the extreme-right electorate

The socio-demographic structure of the 2002 extreme-right electorate shows a lesser degree of heterogeneity and a sociological pattern similar to that observed since the 1988 presidential election. The FN's electorate remains predominantly male, younger and of low education. Looking at occupation in terms of social class, it is important to note the electoral dynamics of the FN and its continuing ability to draw growing support from working-class voters, reinforcing the more traditional petty-bourgeois element of the extreme-right electorate. Again, in 2002, the FN has managed to gather together these two socially and economically opposed groupings: in the first round of the presidential election, Le Pen won 19 per cent of the vote among shopkeepers, craftsmen and small entrepreneurs, together with 30 per cent of the working-class vote. In the second round, the FN leader secured 31 per cent of the valid vote cast among workers and 29 per cent in the self-employed.[16]

Patterns of party cooperation

Lastly, looking at patterns of party system competition, it was evident from the 2002 elections that both the FN and MNR continued to suffer from their lack of coalition potential and political isolation within the system. Despite efforts to establish links with the moderate right at the local level – which in the case of Le Pen's party unarguably represented a U-turn from the anti-right strategy initiated in 1995 – neither the FN nor the MNR really managed to escape from the fringe of the system and remained, as far as inter-party cooperation is concerned, as a third distinctive political bloc separate from both the left and the mainstream parties of the right.

The new balance of power between the FN and MNR

The balance of power between the two main competitors of the extreme right has undergone considerable change. A first nationwide test for

Mégret's party, the 2002 electoral contests demonstrated the lack of political opportunity for a French equivalent to the process of transformation of the Italian post-Fascist MSI into a mainstream conservative right-wing party by Gianfranco Fini. While it was fairly obvious that the personality factor would favour predominantly Le Pen in the first round of the presidential election, there were outstanding questions concerning the MNR's ability to benefit electorally from its entrenchment at the local level.

The presidential and legislative contests both illustrated the bitter setback of the MNR in challenging Le Pen's monopoly over far-right politics in France. The share of the extreme-right vote secured by the MNR in the presidential and legislative election represented only 11.9 and 8.9 per cent of the total vote for the far right respectively, as opposed to 36.2 per cent in the June 1999 European election. At the 2002 presidential ballot, Mégret secured his best scores almost exclusively in his three departmental strongholds of Bouches-du-Rhône, Bas-Rhin and Haut-Rhin, where he won over 4 per cent of the vote. Only in Vitrolles did the MNR leader surpass the 10 per cent threshold (with 11.5 per cent of the valid vote cast in the XII constituency of Bouches-du-Rhône) without being able, however, to move forward to the second round.

Faced with fierce competition on both its 'left' and right flanks by the newly formed UMP and the FN, the MNR experienced difficulties in making itself heard during the legislative campaign and suffered from the absence of a specific political space between the radical anti-system stance of the FN and the hard-line on criminality taken by the mainstream right and the newly appointed Minister of the Interior, Nicolas Sarkozy. A similar picture emerged from the legislative election: the party's best results were concentrated in a tiny number of constituencies, with only 14 cases of MNR candidates polling over 4 per cent of the vote. The figureheads of the party failed to progress to the second round: Jean-Yves Le Gallou received only 4.1 per cent of the vote in Gennevilliers, Damien Bariller won less than 4 per cent in Gardanne and Bruno Mégret attracted a mere 18.6 per cent of the vote in Vitrolles (as opposed to 35.5 per cent in the first round of the 1997 legislative election).

The severe electoral setback of the MNR at the 2002 elections raises doubts about the future of *mégrétisme* as a distinctive political current within the party system, located somewhere between the mainstream right and a more radical option embodied by the FN. Not only does the MNR suffer from the dramatic drop in its electoral support and the likelihood of a proportion of its members and sympathisers returning to a more successful FN but also the party has to take the financial consequences of its electoral failure and the cost of two expensive national campaigns in the absence of future state funding.

Conclusion: prospects for the extreme right

The 2002 elections have illustrated the continuance of electoral support for the extreme right in France, with a range varying from a minimum of 12 per cent (legislative) up to a maximum of nearly 20 per cent of the vote (presidential). It is true to say that the trauma caused by Le Pen in the second round of the presidential ballot and the spectacular demonstration against the FN by all political parties of the left, associations, Churches and trade unions have temporarily set some limits to the potential for electoral progress by the far right. These limits were well in evidence in the outcome of the legislative contest. However, there is little doubt that there will continue to be a political space for the FN within the French party system.

One first reason for this is to be found in the capacity of Le Pen's ideology to resonate with the beliefs of a significant proportion of the French voters. A trend analysis of opinion polls over the 1984–2002 period of time shows a fairly stable public support for the FN's themes and ideas, between 20 to 25 per cent of the whole population.[17] Opinions never translate mechanically into effective votes on the day of the election, yet there remains a 'reservoir' of potential voters for the extreme right, which goes beyond its actual electoral strength.

In terms of party organisation and intra-bloc competition, two additional factors must be taken into account. The dispute between the two main factions led by Le Pen and Mégret, and the consequent split of the FN in early 1999, had weakened the whole extreme right and reduced its ability to weigh significantly on the outcome of elections. In 2002, the FN has provided proof of its ability to take over the whole far-right camp at the expense of the MNR, and should be in a position to benefit from this situation of political hegemony in the near future. With Mégret and his followers departing from the FN in early 1999, Le Pen's party had also significantly reduced intra-party factionalism and ensured a greater level of homogeneity among top-level elites. One interesting observation in 2002 was the public announcement of Gollnisch's appointment at the head of the FN in the event of Le Pen retiring from the presidency, together with the key role played by Marine Le Pen in the legislative campaign and the media.

Lastly, the forthcoming electoral cycle of 2004 will be more propitious to the extreme right, with a set of two successive 'second-order' elections (regional, European) to be fought under proportional representation and traditionally providing a great incentive to protest voting by those dissatisfied with the incumbent government. In the 2002 legislative ballot, the logics of the majoritarian system and the electoral dynamics initiated by the unified moderate right seem to have discouraged a greater proportion of voters from 'wasting' their vote on the FN candidates. The landslide victory of the UMP has raised high expectations, particularly with regards to tax cuts and a tough stance on crime – both proprietary issues of the extreme right. Should the new government fail to meet those expectations, then it is clear that Le Pen's party would be the main beneficiary of a new wave of popular discontent.

Notes

1 Although founded as early as 1972, the FN remained electorally irrelevant until the mid-1980s. The impact of the party on French politics was negligible until its first success in the 1983 municipal by-election in Dreux where the extreme-right list headed by Jean-Pierre Stirbois won 16.7 per cent of the vote. This performance at the local level was followed by the impressive national breakthrough of the extreme right in the subsequent 1984 European election, with Le Pen's party polling over 11 per cent of the votes.
2 For a detailed analysis of the electoral evolution of the FN, see Perrineau (1997) and more generally Le Gall (1998).
3 Social class is measured here by the commonly used class schema based on occupation and divided in four main categories: professionals and managers, petty-bourgeoisie, clerical and routine non-manual workers, and manual skilled and unskilled workers.
4 SOFRES post-election survey, CEVIPOF–CIDSP–CRAPS, 26–31 May 1997, N = 3,010. Our calculation.
5 SOFRES post-election survey, 25 March–23 April 1998, N = 2,000.
6 However, according to recent research by Andersen and Evans in response to Grunberg and Schweisguth's *tripartition* argument, there is insufficient evidence to sustain the hypothesis of the emergence of the extreme right as a third distinctive political bloc *sui generis* (Grunberg and Schweisguth, 1997, Andersen and Evans, Chapter 11 of this volume).
7 In the second ballot of the 1997 election, the FN candidates stood in 76 three-way contests in which they were opposed to the UDF–RPR. In 1998, the FN presented its own lists in all metropolitan departments. Although the FN managed to use its blackmail potential in four regional council elections, Le Pen's party notably failed to dislodge and reshape the right-wing pole entirely by forming right/far-right coalitions at regional level. On this, see Ivaldi (1998b).
8 See Parodi (1997) on this dynamic.
9 Calculating an index of disproportionality for each of the legislative elections which took place in France since 1978 illustrates the distorting effect of the electoral system. Deviations between the percentages of seats and the percentages of votes received by the different parties, as registered by the Lsq index, were much larger in 1993 and 1997 with respective levels of disproportionality of 23.4 and 17.5 per cent as opposed to 7.3 per cent in the 1978 election.
10 It is worth noting that, assuming that many voters perceive distortions caused

by the electoral system, the prevailing logic of the two-ballot majority system did not discourage a significant group of voters from defecting to FN candidates with poor chances of gaining parliamentary representation over the 1993–97 period.

11 On that occasion, Mégret received 3,758 votes, Jean-Yves Le Gallou 3,439, Bruno Gollnisch 3,398, Roger Holleindre 3,381, Franck Timmermans 3,362, Jacques Bompard 3,328, Yvan Blot 3,316, Marie-France Stirbois 3,288, Carl Lang 3,287 and Damien Bariller 3,166.

12 Elected MEPs were Charles de Gaulle, Bruno Gollnisch, Carl Lang, Jean-Marie Le Pen and Jean-Claude Martinez.

13 According to various surveys conducted on the day of the election, the list led by Pasqua attracted between 10 per cent (CSA) and 17 per cent (IFOP) of those who had voted for FN candidates in the first round of the 1997 general election – see Ivaldi (1999b).

14 IPSOS–Vizzavi–*Le Figaro–France 2* survey, 12 April 2002.

15 IPSOS–Vizzavi–*Le Figaro–France 2*, 12 April 2002.

16 IPSOS–Vizzavi–*Le Figaro–France 2*, 21 April and 5 May 2002.

17 SOFRES–*Le Monde*–RTL, 23–24 May 2002.

III

SYSTEM CONTEXT

10
Europe and the French party system

Jocelyn A. J. Evans

Introduction

Since the advent of European Community/European Union politics and the growing influence the supranational arena has over domestic affairs, the potential for the European domain to impinge upon all aspects of national polities has grown. On the face of it, there has been no reason to suspect that European politics would not affect the party systems of these polities in the same way that it has affected, say, policy-making, judicial review and pressure groups. However, the effect to date has been perceived as minimal, even after the introduction of direct elections in 1979. At the comparative level, direct effects on party systems have been low: one author has commented that, '[T]o the simple question of whether Europe has had a direct impact on the format of national party systems, the equally simple answer must be an unequivocal "no"' (Mair, 2000: 31).

Other authors concur with this: for instance Kitschelt consecrates little time to it in his study of evolving European party systems, and indeed argues that in particular France provides little scope for mobilisation along a European dimension (1997: 148). Similarly, Ross emphasises the encroachment of the European Union on the French domestic arena, but beyond noting the growing incapacity of governments to respond unilaterally to areas of European policy dominance and the possible explosion of mass antipathy to Europe, little time is spent on electoral competition effects (Ross, 2000).

A number of contextual reasons can be given for the lack of change: the low education of the electorate on European matters; the lack of interest in European politics; the democratic deficit that puts the bulk of European policy beyond the electoral arena, and so on. More specifically, the format of the existing party systems is often consonant with a European dimension in their ideological, if not social, format. Parties which oppose Europe are often in opposition to other aspects of the national political systems – anti-system or protest parties – and thus simply add Europe to the litany of complaints against the system (Taggart,

1998). Leaving aside the anti-system or protest elements, other anti- or indeed pro-European stances are based precisely upon the same elements which form the foundation for domestic ideology and thus as of themselves form no basis for a shift in party system format (Evans, 2000b).

A potential source of party system change, however, derives from intra-party disagreements over Europe (Mair, 2000: 36). Parties which by necessity are often broad churches aggregating different ideological streams have been split over the European question both in terms of working within it and reaction to it. Some parties are unified in their opposition to Europe, and the French system contains examples of these. Given that for three of these parties – LO/LCR on the left, and the FN and MNR on the right – the clear anti-European stance largely mirrors their radical anti-system role in other policy domains, we will not spend much time on this for the reasons given above: such positions do not generally engender party system change.[1] More importantly, the French case provides ample evidence of previously cohesive party blocs divided by the issue and, moreover, parties split – sometimes physically – by disagreements over the European agenda. In particular, the Communist Party betrays an ambivalent position to Europe, as does the moderate right. Despite their recent decline, we will devote some time to examining the MPF and RPF which were formed from splinters from the UDF and RPR respectively and which, when united in the past, threatened to become a relevant force on the right.[2]

However, these schisms which presented themselves in particular in 1999 have apparently disappeared in the wake of the 2002 elections. The ability of French elites to collude and to put ideological differences to one side where it is strategic to do so applies to the European issue as it does to the rest of the political arena (Hanley, 2002). However, whether or not such latent divisions prove disruptive to individual parties and to the system itself depends not just upon the ideological and pragmatic considerations of the party elites themselves, but also upon the institutional context of the system itself. Consequently, this chapter will first consider the areas of divergence within parties and party blocs, the threat they posed to cohesion and the reasons for their recent disappearance. Second, it will consider the array of institutional factors which have contributed to keeping the European issue latent within the party system, and the extent to which possible changes to the institutional structure may in future promote party system change.

Partisan and intra-partisan Euroscepticism: sources and effects

A clear indication of the divisions within blocs and parties on Europe is to be found in elite voting on the two key expansions of the European

TABLE 10.1 Assembly votes on amendment of Article 88–2 and ratification of Amsterdam Treaty by parliamentary group

Assembly vote no. 149 – amendment of article 88–2				Assembly vote no. 160 – ratification of Amsterdam Treaty			
Group (N)	For	Against	Abst.	Group (N)	For	Against	Abst.
PS (250)	228	6	*1*	PS (250)	213	4	3 + *1*
RPR (137)	109	19	4	RPR (138)	113	18	5
UDF (69)	63	1		UDF (70)	63	2	1
DLI* (43)	42			DLI* (43)	38	1	
PCF (36)	28		1	PCF (35)	33		
RCV** (33)	23	10		RCV** (35)	16	16	1
No affiliation (9)	4	2		No affiliation (5)	4	1	

Source: Assemblée Nationale website (www.assemblée-nationale.fr)
Notes: Votes do not sum to parliamentary group sizes (N) due to absence. Changes in parliamentary group sizes due to shifts in affiliation/by-elections. Italicised PS abstention refers to Laurent Fabius, non-voting due to holding Presidency.
* Démocratie Libérale et Indépendants
** Radicaux–Citoyens–Verts

remit, namely the Maastricht and Amsterdam Treaties (Table 10.1). The Maastricht referendum of 1992 was the first time that pro- and anti-European positions cross-cut the principal axis of competition, 'uniting' extreme-left and right parties in opposition, ruling factions of moderate-left and right parties in support, and separating out the anti-European factions either in separate campaigns or in separate movements. Although held to be in part a pro- and anti-Mitterrand vote, this is the first explicit instance of the European project bringing Jean-Pierre Chevènement and his MdC, Philippe Séguin and Charles Pasqua with a separate 'no' campaign, and former PR/UDF deputy Philippe de Villiers out of the *souverainiste* woodwork. Within the National Assembly, the Communists were the only group against ratification in the majority. The three main party groupings – PS, RPR and UDF – were all pro-European, although in the first two a minority were against. The two former UDF *adhérents* Charles Millon and Philippe de Villiers within the non-affiliated group voted for and against respectively, as expected. Finally, the RCV group were split about 2:1 in favour.

Here, intra-party disparities appear in a number of ways. First, the principal left party was almost completely homogeneous – less than 3 per cent of its members voted against – together with the centre-right party of the UDF, a party which, despite at the time being neither in government nor the presidential party, was even more cohesively in favour. Conversely, the right wing was split, with almost 14 per cent against the wishes of its presidential doyen.[3] It is fairly clear that such opposition would have come from the nationalist *étatiste* wing of the party. Yet the party was clearly divided, and indeed such divisions were evident in the internal party wranglings and replacement of Séguin after his resignation from the head of the 1999 European list and as general secretary of the party.

Of greater interest, however, is the major split in the *gauche plurielle*. As has been noted, the Communists were adamant in their rejection of Amsterdam, and there is a fundamental divide in the RCV grouping. Jean-Pierre Chevènement's MdC expressed dismay at the relinquishing of economic sovereignty, and was firmly opposed to the removal of national sovereignty in foreign and military affairs, despite the joint list with the PS and the strongly pro-European left radicals in the 1999 European elections. More appropriate, perhaps, was his resignation from the *gauche plurielle* government over issues of sovereignty, and his separate *pôle républicain* candidacy for the presidency, renouncing the Europhile intentions of the main candidates.

Given the Green Party's campaign for a 'no' vote on the Amsterdam Treaty, it is fairly clear that the Green components of the alliance also opposed ratification.

> Nous rejetons ce traité qui ne fait avancer ni la démocratie ni les droits de l'homme, ni le progrès social, ni la défense de l'environnement en Europe, et qui interdit pratiquement l'élargissement.[4]

However, they voted in favour of the earlier amendment of Articles 88–2 and 88–4 on 1 December 1998. Indeed, looking at Table 10.1, the changes in the RCV parliamentary group are the only substantial changes between the two votes, and these are accounted for almost entirely by the shift by the six Green deputies. We would argue that, though the Greens are 'pro' Europe inasmuch as they support the supranational arena above those defined by national boundaries, they also betray elements of Euroscepticism because they oppose the rules of the game as currently defined, support of constitutional amendments permitting. For instance, opposition to the stability pact limiting budget deficits to 3 per cent 'privent [Les Quinze] des moyens budgétaires d'impulser une véritable politique de l'emploi à l'échelle européenne'.[5] Similarly, the lack of democratic checks on the European Central Bank raises fears of excessive monetarism on the part of European economic policies.

This again demonstrates the need to differentiate between bases to Euroscepticism, and certainly this is not limited just to the Greens. In the case of the PCF, for instance, shifting positions on Europe demonstrate a nuancing of the party's approach to the domain. How, then, have these differences over Europe manifested themselves in the case of the main parties, and to what extent have they been resolved in the recent elections?

PCF: from anti-system to system?

Historically, the PCF provides perhaps the greatest shift in party system role and European stance. The anti-system party *par excellence* since its inception and for most of its lifetime, since 1997 it found itself well established in a governing coalition with the Socialists, and in terms of Europe, as Lazar notes, '... dorénavant le PCF se veut euroconstructif' (1999: 695) ('... from now on the PCF wants to see itself as constructively European'). For the party which opposed Europe as a capitalist construct which opened workers to the perils of free market liberalism, such a change has occurred in a relatively short space of time. Under Georges Marchais, such a volte-face would have been unthinkable, yet under the reformist Hue the inevitable march of integration, and the disappearance of the alternative supranational agenda provided by the Workers' International, has – at least at the elite level – moved the PCF into a position remarkably similar to the Greens: anti-Maastricht, as Table 10.1 shows, but seeing in Europe an arena where egalitarian social policy can potentially be pursued.

> La promotion sans discrimination des hommes et des femmes; la démocratie et la citoyenneté; les droits de la personne et particulièrement l'antiracisme; le respect des équilibres naturels et le développement durable; des relations internationales pacifiques équitables et solidaires ... sont autant de valeurs montantes, dans nos pays, notamment parmi les jeunes.[6]

Notable by its absence is an overt call for economic *dirigisme*. Free market liberalism is held to be in crisis – 'Le mythe du capitalisme triomphant se dissipe' – but no alternative is provided, beyond vague references to a renewed role for the EU in international economic relationships.

Consequently, the emphasis of Bouge l'Europe! – the Communist-led list in the 1999 European elections – on social rather than economic factors, the famous double-parity list combining a non-Communist for every Communist, and its particular targeting of younger, socially aware voters brings it firmly into the moderate camp, most of these items being no more radical than the declared aims of European Social Democratic parties. Certain existing aspects of the EU institutions are challenged – for instance, the Schengen Agreement is seen as pernicious, particularly for the economically less anchored Mediterranean member states, and thus the protection of national borders is called for in rather more traditional Communist style – but it would be difficult to promote the PCF agenda as any more radical than the Green agenda.

In systemic terms, then, should the PCF now been seen as avowedly pro-European? We would answer 'not yet'. Three factors determine this response. First, the results of the European elections showed an essentially stagnant result, dropping –0.12 per cent from 1994, and at the national level the failures in the 2002 elections have emphasised this trend. The new Euroconstructive slant has hardly proved its worth in pulling in new electoral pools. As Bell surmises in his consideration of the strategic options now open to the PCF, this does not mean that it will immediately renounce such an agenda and return to dogmatic opposition (see Chapter 2 of this volume). However, two particular electoral dynamics which contributed to this unmoving electoral score in 1999 underline that the PCF must make some effort to regain its hard-line, anti-European voters.

First, Dolez notes that a number of Pasqua voters of 1999 came from Hue's 1995 presidential electorate (1999: 665); and Lazar notes that the PCF was beaten by its extreme Trotskyist rivals LO–LCR in many big towns, and in former bastions, such as Seine–Saint–Denis and Pas-de-Calais, the Communist lead over the Trotskyists has been eaten into (1999: 703–4). Undoubtedly, the Pasqua voters, although few in number, are evidence of former PCF voters disenchanted with the new soft touch on Europe; similarly, the Trotskyist defectors are disenchanted by the abandoning of a hard-line agenda more generally. A similar centrifugal dynamic pertained in the 2000 presidential elections, although clearly Hue's losses could not be accounted for by moves to Pasqua or de Villiers, neither of whom stood in the elections.

Such shifts are not a surprise, and the second factor to note: in 1997, the PCF electorate remained very strongly anti-European, with almost 60 per cent declaring that they would be relieved by the collapse of the EU (Evans 2000b: 550). Such centrifugal electoral dynamics are occurring at the expense of electoral support which was replaced in the 1999 elections by a number of former non-PCF voters in zones of previous weakness (Lazar, 1999: 704).[7] The success of appealing to the younger socially aware elements was clearly undercut by Daniel Cohn-Bendit's stronger appeal to this pool. As such, the PCF has to decide whether to continue to try to recruit this electorate – younger, new voters appealed to by the other, more traditionally libertarian parties of *la gauche plurielle* and even by a more socially liberal UDF – or whether to stick with the tried and tested – older, established voters with only abstention and the minority appeal of LO-LCR as alternatives.

Third, at the elite level there is evidence that the new pro-European line is not yet firmly established. The clearest evidence of this was during the Kosovan crisis when many of Bouge l'Europe!'s candidates supported European intervention in NATO, including Geneviève Fraisse, who held the number-two slot on the list, and Philippe Herzog the *rénovateur*. The Communist Party, however, opposed it. Undoubtedly, much of the opposition derived from US involvement and perennial concerns of imperial hegemony. However, as part of the EU's common foreign policy, such opposition together with other European Communist parties does not bode well either for Communist support of and participation in the European project or for future collaborations in double parity lists.

To refer to Chapter 2 again, the position of the party's ideology depends very much upon the role it decides to (try and) play within the system and consequently the extent to which it distinguishes itself from the dominant partner. The fault lines between the MdC, the Greens and the PS within the government demonstrated the extent to which left homogeneity is far from being a given. Moreover, as Andersen and Evans demonstrate in the following chapter, there is no evidence of growing homogeneity among the left electorate either. The possibility of future PCF antagonism can still not be ruled out. As such, the Communists may still be potential incumbents in the anti-system camp. However, the PS's need for a partner on the left and the Communists' desire to retain the possibility of future governmental participation means that the more 'obvious' strategic option is to try to contribute to a rebuilt *gauche plurielle* and rein in its criticisms on Europe and elsewhere, rather than return to the extreme fold where competition is now much stronger but less rewarding.

Pasqua – de Villiers and the MPF/RPF

Prior to de Villiers's departure from the RPF, it would have been impossible to conceive of the formation of this movement without the existence of a European dimension. From de Villiers's decampment from the pro-Maastricht UDF in 1992 to lead his own Combat pour les Valeurs and subsequently MPF, the internal divisions between pro- and anti-European members of both the RPR and the UDF became increasingly prominent, to the extent that the Pasqua–Séguin tandem who campaigned for a 'no' vote in the Maastricht referendum of 1992, had both departed by the European elections of June 1999, Pasqua to present a joint list with de Villiers, Séguin simply to resign both list and party leadership.

While the intra-party splits in the UDF and RPR are themselves of interest, and considered in the following section, the formation of an ultra-conservative *droite souverainiste* manifests a separate dynamic on the right. As Ivaldi notes in his assessment of the performance of the Rassemblement pour la France et l'Indépendance de l'Europe (RPFIE) in the 1999 elections (1999b: 651) the party and its electorate in the domestic arena are undoubtedly legitimist and represent the traditional bastions of conservative right-wing support in France. Older, male, petty bourgeois and agriculturally based, the electorate does not differ substantially from the traditional core support of the RPR (Ivaldi, 1999b: 643). Its score of 13.1 per cent represented the dual positive effect of the proportional electoral system combined with the importance of charismatic heads of the national-constituency lists. However, the elections also represented the first time since the onset of the third period of cohabitation that the Eurosceptic right-wing electorate was able to demonstrate its discontent at the national level, the need for a homogenised right vote in 1995 and 1997 being of perhaps a higher priority, and indeed the issue being kept off the agenda by the mainstream parties precisely because of its divisive nature. Undoubtedly, Séguin's resignation due to interference from an increasingly Europhile president and his RPR minions sealed the mass electoral defection to the Pasqua–de Villiers movement.

The French partisan pathology of leadership rivalry has seen de Villiers's subsequent departure, and Pasqua's greater desire for cooperation with the moderate right-wing neighbours may seem to indicate a return to at least allied unity, if not a united conservative right. The latter's withdrawal from the presidential race, ostensibly over doubts as to whether he could collect the requisite five hundred signatures for his candidacy, cost the RPF dear as did de Villiers's absence for the MPF. The parties' reliance upon leadership prominence and their relatively short existence meant that the absence of both of the *droite souverainiste* candidates from the presidential slate deprived them of vital campaign exposure. Moreover, an effective separate presence in the 2002 elections was hampered by the inability to present a national slate of candidates.

Thus, in second-order European list elections, the party can mount a serious bid to winning seats, but at the elections which count, a return to marginality is almost inevitable. This is not helped by the presence of two such parties, although the ageing Pasqua must soon leave the path open to de Villiers alone. A combination of party split, an absence of positive leadership coverage (Charles Pasqua featuring mostly in the 'arms to Angola' affair), the focused nature of regional support allowing de Villiers's election as deputy but winning only 0.8 per cent of the nation vote, and the omnipresent strictures of the institutional framework have seen the two parties almost vanish from the political map in the space of two years.

On the basis that Pasqua's political career is effectively over, only de Villiers can hope to re-establish his party, and, given the growing salience of the European issue, a likely strategy would be to use this to criticise pro-European governments either of the left or of the right. Much depends on the fortunes of the RPF's neighbours, the FN and the UMP. Looking first to the extremes before considering the moderate right, the schism in 1998 certainly provided added support for the RPFIE in the 1999 European elections. Le Pen's success in 2002 and the relatively small decline of the FN vote in the legislative election provides a less auspicious context for either the MPF or RPF to pick up disenchanted support from its right. Indeed, the lack of deputies for the FN seems likely to consolidate protest support in this party given the 'injustice' of the system which fails to allocate any seats to a party with 12 per cent of the vote. However, the age of Le Pen and the threat of fresh internecine rivalry, this time between his daughter Marine and the party number two Bruno Gollnisch, could leave the FN unable to hold onto much of its support. In a context of anti-European support, the MPF could provide an alternative representative. Similarly, a pro-European presidential party could lose Eurosceptic support in the same direction.

A widening gulf between UDF and UMP?

In many ways, the split over Europe which occurred in presenting separate lists in the 1999 elections simply highlighted one of the remaining ideological divisions between the two moderate-right parties.[8] The UDF being more socially liberal on its CDS wing, more economically liberal on its PR side, the RPR's cooperation with their federal neighbour was an example of intra-bloc strategy par excellence in the French institutional setting. Since the mid-1980s, there has been an element of ideological convergence of the two organisations – the PR was heartened by the RPR's conversion to market economics, even if it was half-hearted; similarly, the CDS wing saw greater proximity with the same party's conversion to Europhilia, even if this were even less well-founded for many Gaullists (Machin, 1989: 65).

However, the half-heartedness of such changes merely reflected divisions within the UDF itself, with the eventual split of Alain Madelin's DL – a more successful partner for the RPR in recent times – and the unification of the UDF into a single party after the CDS's conversion to FD by François Bayrou. Until this point, however, the party's prominent role in European matters within the moderate-right bloc had given it a purpose which the loss of its role as presidential party for Giscard d'Estaing had denied it. In the early years of integration, it provided the head of the moderate-right lists in 1984, 1989 and in 1994, the first election subsequent to the 1992 Maastricht acceleration of the European project, and the consequent departure of de Villiers from the UDF.

Similarly, the RPR's internal ideological splits had remained muted or channelled via internal struggles of *notables* until the manifestation of divisions over Maastricht. By the time Amsterdam and subsequently the European elections had arrived, precisely the proximate point to the RPR within the UDF – DL – had already split off. Even with Séguin's resignation, Bayrou and his party felt unable to join in a combined list, perhaps out of a certain resentment towards the UDF's Senate betrayal in the RPR successfully fielding Christian Poncelet for the presidency against their incumbent Monory, certainly against the RPR's chaotic response to the regional presidency debacle of 1998, but primarily over the UDF's demands for an EU endowed with a range of sovereign, legitimised institutions which could not have stood the test of proximity with the RPR's divided views (Bréchon, 1999: 654).

The European dimension has also played two roles in electoral competition terms. First, as we have seen, it has acted to sap both principal
members of the moderate-right bloc, both parties losing support to the
RPF in 1999 (Bréchon, 1999: 659). Second, the stability of intra-bloc
voting has been challenged further, with the RPR losing its centrist
electorate to the UDF – an electorate which furthermore had shown its
affinity with the UDF in their common support of Balladur in 1995, and
regionally in its clear approval of Maastricht. With the split between the
parties entrenched in part on the European dimension, some commentators saw this as a means for the UDF to challenge the Gaullist hegemony
within the moderate-right bloc (Dolez, 1999: 663). Given the unification
of RPR, DL and the bulk of the UDF into the UMP, however, such a
challenge to hegemony in the short term is untenable. But the UDF still
has an incentive to emphasise the differences between it and its hegemonic
neighbour if only to underline its right to a separate existence. Clearly,
the European dimension is one area for such delineation.

In terms of Europe, the UDF is certainly closer to its moderate-left
neighbours than to the Gaullists (Dolez, 1999: 671–2). If the UMP
continues to fail to produce a stronger line with less anti-European
sniping, this may produce one factor reallocating support from the UMP
to the UDF. Furthermore, prodigal UDF deputies who decamped to the
UMP in the elections may well find their way back to Bayrou's party
without threatening the overall stability of the moderate-right government. In economic terms, the departure of DL had already lessened the
divide between the UDF and the PS as well – acceptance of the market
and monetarist rigour to stay within EMU bounds are both examples of
policies espoused by both parties. The likelihood of a broaching of the
centre is minimal – Bayrou's desire for an autonomous centre-right for
strategic reasons renders the possibility of any such alliance at the national
level impossible in the short term, and the electoral consequences of
abandoning the traditional bloc would in all likelihood be disastrous.
However, the proximity does mean that the UDF is ideally placed to
compete with the PS for centrally located voters. A PS hampered in a
gauche plurielle opposition in providing a clear line on Europe, for
example, could see a critical but governing UDF pick up pro-European
support at a later date.

As we have seen, one of the principal reasons that the European
dimension has not had a greater effect on the party system is that its
proponents have been thwarted by the institutional rules of the game.
The two-bloc majoritarian straitjacket reduces the effectiveness of alternative agendas as a means of attracting electoral support either to bolster
flagging scores or to encourage new formations – the principal left-right
axis of competition remains the only game in town, and the European
dimension only wins support when it mirrors the traditional axis. An

implication of this is that changes to the institutional structure could allow a greater saliency to the European dimension at the national level. We turn now to the possible institutional changes in the French context and their likely effects.

Institutional context

We would posit three institutional factors as providing the framework determining the effect of the European dimension: the different levels of election; the electoral system at the presidential and legislative levels; and the presidential mandate and its recent emendation. To date, these have ensured continuity in the party system. However, changes in these increasingly threaten such stability.

Electoral levels and the 'electoral accordion'

As most voters would attest, France has a bewildering array of elections, including three at the national level – presidential, legislative and European – as well as a series of sub-national ballots. Many commentators have noted that, in recent years, the party system at the sub-national level has displaced itself from the national pattern. A number of factors have been responsible for this: the 'personality' politics at the local level; the lower stakes of a sub-national ballot; the electoral system using proportionality rather than a majoritarian system. Perhaps the most explicit example of this was the UDF regional presidents relying upon FN support to retain their presidency, thus forging de facto coalitions, if not outright alliances. Such legitimation has been fought against at the national level not for reasons of ideology or political correctness, but due to the increased electoral threat this poses to the moderate-right parties. At the local level, such desperate measures by Millon *et al.* are illustrative of the importance of the local power base over broader long-term considerations for the party. The internal wranglings in the UDF over this affair was in no small part responsible for the subsequent break-up with DL leaving the party after a less than condemnatory attitude towards the matter, and a more critical FD remaining within the newly unitary UDF.[9]

Such disparity between party system dynamics at different electoral levels is also present at the European level. Again on the right, the Séguin-led Eurosceptic RPR list was anathema to the UDF's pro-European equivalent. As we noted in the introduction, such divergence under Parodi's 'electoral accordion' (Parodi, 1997), which expands under PR systems to allow greater fragmentation, and contracts for the two-ballot systems, cannot go without certain osmosis between the levels. Parties which compete at other levels must find it increasingly difficult to reconcile differences they have emphasised to form alliances later on. The first ballot allows a certain level of fragmentation, but at the second, can competing parties which have previously differentiated themselves credibly support their difficult neighbours, or from another perspective, safely rely upon their support? The resolution of conflict between UDF and RPR derived not from any ideological shifts but by the simple expedient of a massive electoral imbalance in 2002.

In the past, 'better them than the other side' has been a powerful logic. Yet, under the apparent convergence which all European systems are undergoing, 'the other side' no longer constitutes the Communist or reactionary threat that it once did. In a system increasingly enmeshed with the European level, can parties which oppose each other vehemently on the nature of this arena forge unconvincing alliances, when, to their opposite side, a party with greater consonance on these and other matters is present? This logic is especially important for the UDF *sans* DL and the PS. Rocard's openings to the CDS may have failed in the early 1990s, but the mere fact of trying demonstrates its potential. When institutional incentives change, new dynamics can appear from parties who dare – and both the first-order electoral system and the bipolar presidential logic seem set to change in the future.

Post two-ballot majoritarianism?

While ever the two-ballot majoritarian system pertains for both legislative and presidential elections, the overriding logic will be for competing parties to try to form blocs, which, although riddled with internal divisions and personality rivalries, can at least command 50 per cent +1 at the second round. While triangular ballots have become more common, the two-candidate run-off for legislatives is still by far the norm, and for presidentials the rule. To this extent, many authors have been right to characterise the party system as being sustained in its traditional format. However, we believe that the existing tensions highlighted above are at least as important in demonstrating the potentially fragile state of the party system which in the late 1990s seemed *only* supported by its institutional structure. The 2002 outcome may have reduced fragmentation and re-emphasised the logic of bipolar alternation, but the plethora of presidential and legislative candidates and the radical stances of many of these cannot be ignored. Under different electoral rules, their influence can become more difficult to contain.

Threats to presidential power come from the *quinquennat* (see below). The main threat to the legislative elections comes from the left, where the Greens among others are pushing for a level of proportionality to be introduced into the electoral system. As Villalba and Vieillard have shown in Chapter 4 of this volume, Green factions such as Autrement les Verts and Ecologie et Démocratie have been highly critical of the national leadership for not pressuring the Socialists for electoral reform by 2002. Granted, such electoral reform was unlikely in the very short term under the Socialists and seems similarly unlikely under the UMP, despite declarations to the contrary. In terms of promoting democracy, the right has followed the left's lead in putting decentralisation at the top of the agenda.

However, in any reconstruction of the *gauche plurielle*, one of the key elements which the Greens will undoubtedly push for, if they are to join in a new common programme, will precisely be electoral reform to include a dose of proportionality in the legislative elections. If this occurred, the rebalancing of seats among the parties would give greater influence within the policy-making arena to precisely those parties which take a Eurosceptic line but which at the moment are marginalised or absent from the legislature.

Presidential shifts

The third aspect to be considered – and, despite being an actuality, still an unknown quantity – is the shortening of the presidential mandate to five years. Again, we would emphasise that this amendment alone will not inexorably lead to a change in the party system. Indeed, many of the arguments in favour of the *quinquennat* imply precisely the opposite. Following Olivier Duhamel's arguments,[10] for example, the shortening of the mandate will reinforce presidential efficacy by making cohabitation less likely and thus providing concurrent five-year terms for president and presidential party alike. The relevant factor to note here is the effect that the *quinquennat* will have on the reserved presidential domain. In terms of Europe, the arena – as opposed to the issues – has remained to date very much within the presidential domain first, and then under governmental remit where a president feels fit. Granted, under cohabitation, prime ministers have attempted to impose themselves on the European stage, Lionel Jospin perhaps enjoying the greatest success in international relations more generally, but the reserved domain and the independent mandate have ensured that the president's primacy has not been challenged. If Duhamel is correct, and the 'president + government' governing team is held accountable once every five years, then it is difficult to see how the former can prolong the pretence of his/her role as the neutral arbiter above party politics.

If this is the case, then the president's current unique role in foreign affairs must be questionable. Whatever Duhamel's constitutionalist arguments for the greater accountability of the president, it cannot follow that the president will be able to withdraw from the domestic arena in the way that Mitterrand managed, and thus the two domains will be inevitably brought closer. It takes little insight to see that with the ever closer European arena mentioned above, these domains will be even more closely linked. With 'foreign' affairs increasingly impinging on domestic affairs, the separation of domains will become increasingly untenable and unwanted. As such, presidential candidates within parties will have less opportunity to use these latter as their electoral support groups at one moment, and then ostracise them the next, any more than a prime minister is able to do this in a parliamentary system.

For the moment, Chirac's honeymoon period is allowing him to manipulate domestic policy, and fairly explicitly – the name of the new right-wing party emphasises that the governmental majority is a presidential one, as if this needed emphasising. However, the longer-term implications of such a tightening of the two branches of the executive must demand a revisiting of the head-of-state role which itself demands a veneer of neutrality. Whether the republican electorate which renewed Chirac's lease on the Elysée for another five years will support such political domination of foreign affairs remains to be seen.

Conclusion

The elements of continuity in the French party system, to which we will return shortly in the conclusion to this book, are deceptively powerful. In the 1999 European elections, the fragmenting forces at work on the right and the intra-coalition bickering on the left seemed to place the system on the edge of a fundamental crisis. Granted, not all of these divisions were based upon the European issue, but this issue did seem to be increasingly dividing a governing and opposition elite both from extremist elements and from factions within the mainstream itself. Moreover, a majority of votes in the presidential first round were won by Eurosceptic candidates. By 2002, such divisions seem to have returned to obscurity almost entirely. But the elements mentioned above emphasise that the latent support for Eurosceptic feeling against the predominance of pro-European incumbents remains and that, in the correct context, it can reveal itself as a powerful force within the French system.

Though we can at best speculate as to the future changes in the institutional context, the presidential *quinquennat* is one aspect which must inevitably change the executive relations with Europe and thus may well affect presidential candidate – party relations and by extension the party system. If nothing else, an unpopular president trying to assert the monopoly of a European role characteristic of the *septennat* may precisely find vituperative Eurosceptic opposition decrying the railroading of France into ever deeper integration. However, it seems likely that some *toilettage institutionnel* will take place (Le Gall, 2002: 43) and to the extent that many of the fundamental changes to date have responded to the European arena, so it is likely that future changes will follow the same pattern.

Indeed, this gives a clue to the steadfast inability of the European 'issue' to assert itself in party competition and within the national party system. The nature of Europe as an arena means that its effects are seen more through the processing of other issues in terms of policies, treaty ratification and the like than as a separate issue by itself. Despite increasingly encroaching upon the national arena, the saliency of Europe can be seen more in its effect on the traditional elements rather than in the introduction of a new element per se. In terms of the party system, then, the parties are increasingly functioning within an arena defined by Europe, rather than competing in a system on the issue of Europe. Only when adjustments to this arena are made, for instance in terms of the Maastricht and Amsterdam Treaties, does Europe become an issue in the common sense of the word. However, the examples we have given in this chapter demonstrate that, when such an issue does raise its head, the latent oppositions within and between parties on this question are sufficiently entrenched to provide for potential change. That such change to date has not occurred illustrates the strong currents of continuity within the system itself rather than the irrelevance of Europe.

Notes

1 For an account of FN opposition to Europe, see Benoît (1997, Ch. 2), Evans (2000b).
2 Saint-Josse's Chasse Pêche Nature Traditions is another party of the right which has limited first-order electoral support, despite winning 6.8 per cent of the vote at the 1999 European elections (all European election figures in this chapter are taken from the special feature on the European elections in *ECPR News*, autumn 1999). As an effectively irrelevant party at the national level, we will not spend any time on it. Similarly, the decline in the MdC of Jean-Pierre Chevènement has effectively ended this group's influence in the system.
3 Interestingly, Philippe Séguin, one of the principal antagonists in the 1999 right-bloc split, voted 'yes' to the Amsterdam Treaty.
4 *Les Verts*, communiqué de presse, 2 January 1998; 'We reject this treaty which makes no advances in democracy, in the rights of man, in social progress or in the defence of the environment in Europe, and which effectively rules out expression'.
5 *Les Verts*, communiqué de presse, 17 June 1997; 'deprives the fifteen member states of the budgetary instruments required to drive an effective employment policy at the European level'.
6 'Appel commun pour une nouvelle voie de la construction européenne', European Communist Parties, June 1999. Taken from PCF website (www.pcf.fr/europe/une.html); 'The promotion of men and women without discrimination; democracy and citizenship, the rights of an individual, and particularly anti-racism; the respect of nature's balance and sustainable

development; peaceful and fair international relations based on solidarity ...
these are the kind of values which today are spreading across the country,
particularly among its young people'.

7 Indeed Lazar notes that these dynamics are also affecting the PS in some
areas (1999: 705).

8 As Knapp and Sauger note, perhaps organisational differences between the
two parties are one of the fundamental reasons for separation of the components, militating against the desire for a single moderate-right actor among
many of its electorate (Sauger, Chapter 7, this volume, Knapp, 1999: 117
and Chapter 8, this volume).

9 See Sauger, in Chapter 7, this volume on this point.

10 Taken from the PS website (http://www.parti-socialiste.fr).

11
Contemporary developments in political space in France

Robert Andersen
and
Jocelyn A. J. Evans

Introduction

The emphasis of the book thus far has been on individual parties and coalitions. Nonetheless, the demand side of the equation also provides an important context to party success because it helps define the political space in which parties must compete for voters. In this chapter, then, we focus on French political space over the last fifteen years as defined by the socio-demographic and attitudinal profiles of the voters. We build upon findings from the two major studies of French voters in the last ten years, namely *L'électeur français en questions* (Boy and Mayer, 1990)[1] and *L'électeur a ses raisons* (Boy and Mayer, 1997).

The first of these studies was based upon SOFRES data from the 1988 presidential post-election survey and depicted the French electorate as occupying a bidimensional space defined by economic liberalism – state intervention versus laissez-faire – and cultural liberalism – libertarian versus authoritarian – axes. The latter used the 1995 presidential survey to update the analysis and presented a new model of political space at the electoral level – a *tripartition* into left, moderate-right and extreme-right political blocs – representing a radical departure from the traditional *quadrille bipolaire*, and exploding the bidimensional account into a series of cultural subdimensions. Employing these two datasets, together with the CEVIPOF legislative post-election survey from 1997 to update the analysis, we consider changes in the social and attitudinal determinants of political space since 1988. Our analysis takes into account the two principal partisan developments during this period – the growth and implantation of the FN and the more recent establishment of the *gauche plurielle* governing coalition – to assess the extent to which change took place during this period.

Traditional political space in France

Until recently, most research has found the left–right political spectrum and its underlying social bases to provide an enduring and simple map of political space in France. The French political landscape had been firmly implanted along the dual cleavages of social class and religion since the nineteenth century, producing strong left–right polarisation. In keeping with the general pattern found in predominantly Catholic countries, left voting had traditionally been broader than just the working-class, encompassing a secular and often overtly anti-clerical component composed of public sector employees and educators. Thus, the French left had always played host to a middle-class voter with a socially liberal value system focused upon individual equality and enlightened rationalism, as well as to the lower-class voter concerned more with economic equality and state-controlled protectionism.

For its part, the right bloc had traditionally been dominated by the Catholic conservative middle class composed of the traditional petty bourgeoisie (i.e., farmers, craftsmen, traders, owners of small businesses), professionals, and the upper salariat. Supporters of the right bloc could be further divided into those who were economically liberal and socially conservative, and those who were economically liberal but less socially conservative. The former characterised the petty bourgeoisie who shunned leftist collectivism and upheld the Catholic conservative value-system that promoted hierarchy and order (Mayer, 1983). The petty bourgeoisie also favoured economically liberal policies that provided tax incentives for small businesses and prevent excessive market regulation. Professionals and the upper salariat constituted the other group, typically being more socially liberal and owing as much to the liberal tradition characteristic of Northern Europe as to any Catholic doctrine.

Few challenged this basic designation of the French political landscape along social and religious cleavages. Sometimes mediated by the institutional framework or anti-system cleavages – for instance the pragmatic alliance of the centre characteristic of the Third and Fourth Republics or the anti-Gaullist cleavage of the early Fifth Republic – the left–right dichotomy and its economic and cultural subdimensions truly emerged as the effective predictor of voting choice by the 1980s (Capdevielle *et al.*, 1981, Bartolini 1984). Nuances of *patrimoine* and religious practice and the recently more complicated class structure aside, even the basic working class and Catholic labels remained largely synonymous with left and right bloc belonging respectively.

Although the extent of its predictive power has somewhat declined in recent years, left-right ideology still remains of paramount importance. The post-industrial shifts in the 1970s and 1980s which threatened the status quo with radical re/dealignment has in fact settled into a more nuanced but structurally similar competitive framework.[2] Even new issues, such as post-materialism, have easily been absorbed in France as elsewhere into the bidimensional economic and cultural liberalism foundations to left–right orientation (Kitschelt and Hellemans, 1990, Grunberg and Schweisguth, 1993, Knutsen, 1995). Moreover, parties mobilising around these issues, such as the Greens, have been integrated into the principal left–right axis of competition.

As Ivaldi has already alluded to, in recent years the extreme right of Jean-Marie Le Pen and the FN has posed a challenge to the effectiveness of this traditional map. Although conventionally seen as the radical wing of the right bloc, a number of elements to the FN's electoral and ideological profile do not conform to the traditional left–right map (Perrineau, 1997: 208–26, Mayer, 1999: 214–22). In particular, recent shifts in economic policy and the presence of a large number of working-class voters in the extreme-right electorate have suggested that the party no longer sits comfortably on the margins of the right.[3] Some have seen this as simply the manifestation of a protest movement with a pragmatic, reactive approach to economic policy or a populist party drawing support from all parts of the political spectrum. Gérard Grunberg and Etienne Schweisguth's influential analysis of public opinion in 1995 in *L'électeur a ses raisons*, however, suggests that a combination of shifts in the social bases of extreme-right support and significant changes in the electorate's values has resulted in the FN separating from the moderate right and consequently becoming a political orientation *sui generis* – the so-called *tripartition* of political space into left, moderate-right and extreme-right blocs (Grunberg and Schweisguth, 1997).

An implication of the *tripartition* thesis is that the left does not merit a similar separation into extreme and moderate blocs. At first glance, this bears out when we examine the second shift in the party landscape, namely the appearance of the *gauche plurielle*. Paradoxically, this change seems to have consolidated the left side of the spectrum to an extent not seen before under the Fifth Republic. Such convergence suggests that an emphasis on pluralism of views being brought into the governing fold may be matched by a convergence of mass attitudes to extent to allow this, in contrast with the fortunes of past left alliances. Put another way, a cohesive plural left cannot afford to be too plural at either mass or elite levels. We turn to look at this aspect now, before considering the *tripartition* hypothesis in more detail.

The consolidation of the *gauche plurielle*

As Hanley's chapter has shown (Chapter 5, this volume), left-wing parties have always engaged in various kinds of within-bloc alliance, although until the 1990s, these have proved for the most part fragile and short-lived. The Rocard minority government's equally doomed overtures to the centre CDS in 1988 fell prey to the inescapable logic of the bipolar blocs of left and right which the Fifth Republic's institutional and electoral framework had established. Conversely, the *gauche plurielle* has been much more stable than many commentators had foreseen, bringing together a PCF which had previously helped bring down the first PS-dominated government, a vocal Green Party previously unrepresented in govern-ment and a fiercely Jacobin MdC with an Interior Minister, Jean-Pierre Chevènement, who had resigned from the previous left government over the Gulf War.[4]

As Hanley suggests, this stability has been based firstly on the weakness of the PS and the need for its elites to compromise; and second, upon its minor partners' need of the coalition in order to enter government. The emphasis here is clearly on elite pragmatism. What has not yet been analysed is the extent to which it is matched by, if not predicated upon, a growing convergence within the left-wing electorate. The Greens of the Waechterian period placed great emphasis on the salience of Green issues, and eschewed the mainstream policy alternatives which threatened to render them a party *comme les autres*. Such isolated electoral success has not been matched, but the integrated 'realistic' Green strategy epitomised by Dominique Voynet has come close, and better still has brought the Greens into the incumbent fold. If for the Green vote the environment retains primacy in issues terms, mainstream left-wing economic and social considerations have also risen in importance.

Similarly, the reactionary idealism that returned the PCF to the wil-derness in the mid-1980s has been replaced by a more pragmatic 'liberal' programme capable of attracting and accepting a half non-communist and grudgingly pro-European list in the European elections of 1999, the edicts of democratic centralism a thing of the past. Furthermore, its electoral results may be a long way below those of its anti-system heyday, but the terminal collapse predicted since the Eastern bloc cataclysm of 1989/90 and reiterated on a regular basis since had failed to materialise by 1997 (although came a step closer after the 2002 results). Given the presence of the *gauche de gauche* LO and just as importantly the plethora of non-electoral social movements highlighted by Wolfreys in Chapter 6, less entrenched sections of the PCF electorate displeased with the ideo-logical bent of Hue's party could certainly find alternative vote receptacles or modes of political action.

Many commentators have emphasised that the party grouping of the left is solely pragmatic. They argue that it merely represents a declining PS shoring up its electoral success in 1997 with Green, PCF and MdC supporters. In return, these parties used the opportunity as a ticket out of the electoral wilderness without relinquishing their old identities.[5] Similarly, Villalba and Vieillard-Coffre have underlined in Chapter 4 of this volume that the factions vying for power and the presidential candidacy within the Greens have disagreed over the extent to which the PS had betrayed the former's demands made as a condition of their governmental support. We know of no analysis concentrating on the ideological consistency of the core electorates supporting this alliance, however. Data from 1988–97 are important because they can indicate whether the electorates were in the process of converging before the 1997 governing coalition. These data can also give hints to what extent the compromises of five years in government were challenged in the 2002 elections because of *a priori* dissatisfaction with ideological incompatibility. Future data on the 2002 elections will be crucial in determining whether the period of the *gauche plurielle*'s first incumbency resulted in convergence of the respective parties' voters. However, given the results of the 2002 legislative elections, it must be said that, if any convergence did occur after 1997, it had absolutely no cohesive effect on the left.

Thus, in looking at the success of the left bloc, we will explore whether there was a homogenisation of its electorate in attitudinal terms. This homogenisation, then, should reflect growing cultural liberalisation of the French electorate (Schweisguth, 2000) and the declining impact of the previously explosive topic of economic management. As a mirror image to this process, however, the second major partisan development of relevance to this analysis has been seen as fragmenting rather than uniting the right bloc.

Tripartition and the fragmentation of the right

The *tripartition* argument implies that the extreme right now possesses a basis for long-term stable identification. In other words, the social and ideological characteristics of its electorate should be quite distinct from the two traditional political blocs. This would, of course, give less credence to the protest and populist arguments since it implies that the basis of FN support is not solely due to socially segmented interests or the popularity of its leader.

The rise of the anti-system FN during the 1980s did not initially challenge the stability of left–right politics because it was perceived to be in proximity to its moderate-right neighbours, at least during its early years. Its early espousal of neo-liberal economic doctrine, together with an authoritarian moral and overtly anti-immigrant line placed it firmly in the right bloc. Yet by 1995, the FN's traditional petty bourgeois Catholic support had been increasingly matched by working-class and secular voters with economically more interventionist views more characteristic of the left-wing parties from which many had come. Thus, Charlot's 'double electorate' of 1988 had become implanted (Charlot, 1988: 30), apparently unified only in their socially conservative and ethnocentric views, but also, in keeping with the extreme-right trends across Europe, manifesting decreasing levels of education and being drawn increasingly from younger cohorts (Betz, 2001). In social terms too, then, the extreme-right voter decreasingly resembled his older, more educated moderate-right counterpart.

For Grunberg and Schweisguth, the change in profile of extreme-right voters reflected a reorientation of ideological concerns on the extreme right, and in particular a decline in importance of economic liberalism and the fragmenting of attitudes pertaining to the previously unidimensional cultural liberalism scale. In the case of economic liberalism, the decline in state intervention as a policy option and indeed its failure under the Socialists during the 1980s has led the left to move away from its previous position of protectionism and engage in its own privatisations (Grunberg and Schweisguth, 1997: 148). Paradoxically, the FN has moved towards the left, abandoning radical neo-liberalism and adopting a more mixed protectionist policy offering national preference in response to the demands of its disenchanted working-class voters who precisely wish to benefit from some element of economic and social protectionism. Moreover, the moderate right cannot be said to promote unfettered neo-liberal economic policies during this period either.[6]

In contrast to the convergence of bloc supporters in terms of economic attitudes, Grunberg and Schweisguth posit a more striking evolution in cultural liberalism. Although historically conceived of as a single ideological dimension, they argue that 1988 saw it explode into a number of independent subdimensions. In particular, they argue that by 1995 issues related to homosexuality, the death penalty and immigration could no longer be used to map French parties along a single cultural liberalism scale. They argue that cultural liberalism should now seen as two separate fundamental value sets: progressive–traditional and socially egalitarian–hierarchical elements. The latter of these they also refer to as the universalist–anti-universalist dimension (1997: 164). The former is closely linked to religiosity, being the ideological manifestation of the secular–Catholic conflict over attitudes on moral matters, such as homosexuality and abortion. While the extreme right had manifested a strong element of moral authority in 1988, by 1995 these issues had become the domain of the moderate-right identifiers, whereas attitudes to social authority and law and order, as well as differentiation and rejection of out-groups had intensified on the part of the extreme right. In the same way that the moral elements were characterised by high levels of religiosity, so the authoritarian and ethnocentric elements forming the anti-universalist belief system were characterised by low levels of education (1997: 168).

Thus, if Grunberg and Schweisguth are correct, a younger, more secular, less educated group of anti-universalist extreme-right voters should now be separated from the older, religious, educated traditionalists of the moderate right. This profile matches the modernisation loser or populist models of extreme-right support (Betz, 1994, Minkenberg, 1998). Grunberg and Schweisguth lay particular emphasis on the separation of political blocs, the extreme-right bloc in their formulation being in many ways as close to their left-wing counterparts as to the moderate right, at least in social structural terms. The key difference lies in the ideology, however, which as we have noted has moved in the opposite direction from the general trend in the French population towards greater cultural liberalism.

Expanding Grunberg and Schweisguth's analysis

Grunberg and Schweisguth base their findings on the SOFRES presidential surveys, using presidential vote to define political space. Such a measure of political space can be problematic because it does not take into account the various important pragmatic or non-ideological considerations which may motivate a voter's presidential choice – credibility, personality effects, economic considerations, protest, inter alia. Instead, party proximity or party identification are more suitable measures of political space because they imply a longer term psychological attachment more appropriate for defining political bloc identification. In addition the inclusion of the 1997 data, which were not available when Grunberg and Schweisguth carried out their analysis, means that the only constant variable in voting terms is that of identification – all legislative voting in the presidential surveys is recalled at two years' distance. We thus use the identification measure as our dependent variable, rather than presidential vote.[7]

To look at the shifts in political space, rather than the individual ideologies of party electorates, we group the parties into the three relevant blocs for the analysis. Mean scores and distributions of the socio-demographic indicators and attitudinal data will indicate the relative distance between the three blocs – of importance to the definition of the dimensions in political space. As concerns the homogeneity of the left bloc, standard deviations of the attitudinal items will indicate the trends in this across time. Bloc allocation of the parties is given below (Table 11.1).

As independent variables, we look first at the social indicators of bloc

TABLE 11.1 Allocation of party proximity response to blocs

	Left	*Moderate right*	*Extreme right*
1988	Extreme left	UDF	FN
	PCF	RPR	
	PS		
	Left-Radicals		
	Ecology parties		
1995	Extreme left	UDF	FN
	PCF	RPR	
	PS	MPF	
	Left-Radicals		
	'Ecology Generation'		
	Greens		
1997	Extreme left	UDF	FN
	PCF	RPR	
	PS	MPF	

belonging – age, gender, education, class and religion – and then look at the bloc positions on economic liberalism dimension, as manifested by a question on respondents' attitudes to privatisation; cultural liberalism, using support for or rejection of re-establishing the death penalty; and ethnocentrism, using a question on respondents' views on the number of immigrants in France being excessive. Lastly, because of its importance in the *tripartition* argument, we include the 1988 and 1995 data for homosexuality, the item unfortunately being missing in 1997.

Including 1997 in the analysis is important both because it provides a longer time period over which to assess trends and also for a number of contextual reasons. First, party actors remained stable from 1995, and the principal shift in voting alignment occurred between moderate left and moderate right, together with the reintegration of abstainers and generational turnover favouring the left. Indeed, the extreme right consolidated its position, with the FN winning just below what Le Pen received in the 1995 elections – 15 per cent as compared with 15.5 per cent. This was the first time that the legislative score had so closely approached the presidential equivalent. Furthermore, in 1997 the number of extreme-right identifiers jumped to 7 per cent, from less than 5 per cent as the previous ceiling (Mayer, 1999: 191). Given this appearance of the FN and the extreme right as a growing focus for identification, it seems crucial to assess the political bloc hypothesis in 1997 as well as in 1995. In particular, does the extreme-right group of identifiers manifest greater social and ideological specificity than before?

Our principal aims are two-fold: to establish whether the FN should now be separated from its moderate-right counterparts in a separate electoral bloc; and, second, to establish the extent to which the left-wing electorate has become more homogenous, in particular in ideological terms. More generally, we wish to assess the stability of support for the three alleged major political blocs – the moderate right, the left and the extreme right (essentially the FN) – in order to discern whether there have been any trends in social realignment during the 1988 to 1997 period.

Analysis

We start with Table 11.2, which displays the demographic profile of the three major political blocs as determined by a survey question measuring party proximity. Here we can see clear differences in the socio-demographic profiles of the three major groups. A couple of general observations can be made from this table. First, the profile of extreme-right identifiers is quite different from the profiles of moderate-right identifiers, but quite similar to the profile of left identifiers. Second, there has been very little change in the relationship between demographics and party proximity over time. We discuss these observations in more detail below.

TABLE 11.2 Demographic profiles (per cent) of party proximity groups in France (1988–97)

	Left bloc			*Moderate-right bloc*			*Extreme-right (FN)*		
	1988	*1995*	*1997*	*1988*	*1995*	*1997*	*1988*	*1995*	*1997*
Men	47.6	49.5	48.6	49.3	45.2	47.0	60.5	56.3	55.3
Less than 30 years old	28.2	23.8	21.0	17.6	21.0	20.0	32.2	39.3	26.7
Practising Catholics	21.2	16.2	20.6	49.1	43.4	45.5	26.5	18.0	22.0
University degree	15.1	24.8	21.0	18.2	23.8	23.7	11.8	15.8	7.3
Social class									
Managers and professionals	20.5	22.3	27.7	22.6	21.1	32.9	17.1	13.7	18.9
Self-employed	10.1	8.2	9.0	24.5	21.8	21.5	16.4	10.4	13.6
Routine non-manual	30.3	21.7	29.1	26.3	19.8	22.9	24.3	26.8	25.0
Working class	39.1	47.8	34.2	26.7	37.2	22.7	42.1	49.2	42.4
Unemployed	9.8	15.8	6.5	9.7	14.8	3.8	7.9	16.4	6.7

We shall begin by discussing how the moderate-right profile differs from the profile from the other groups. Most importantly, we notice that moderate-right voters are generally older, more likely to be practising Catholics, have university degrees and be self-employed. The age differences are not surprising given that parties under the left bloc and the extreme-right bloc have clearly more radical policies. This concurs with previous research on voting and attitudes in western societies that shows young people are generally more likely to favour radical ideologies because they have less invested in the status quo.[8]

A similar explanation can be given for the overrepresentation of Catholics in the moderate-right bloc – i.e., since religious people are more likely to be socially conservative, they are also more likely to support the status quo and moderate parties. Differences in education and occupation can be explained by considering voters as rational actors who choose parties that best reflect their economic interests. This is especially true with respect to the fact that self-employed and educated people generally have much to gain from a well-functioning capitalist economy, something the moderate-right parties uphold more than others – looking at Table 11.2, it equally applies to managers and professionals, two other groups served well by capitalist structures.

We now turn to an examination of the uniqueness of extreme-right support. Perhaps the most striking observation, albeit well documented in the literature, is the manner in which its gender profile stands out. Here we notice that the extreme right has clearly been far more attractive to men than women while both of the other blocs have slightly higher representation from women than men. Equally striking is the convergence of the party electorates across time: although men are still more strongly represented than women on the extreme right in 1997, the ratio has gradually moved towards parity since 1988. The opposite trend produces a similar effect in the moderate blocs. More at odds with 'accepted wisdom', however, is the finding that being unemployed is seemingly unrelated to party proximity and that this relationship changed little over time. Of course the marginal proportions of unemployed shifted across time, but the relative inter-group proportions remained fairly constant. Simply put, unemployed individuals are as likely to identify with the left or moderate right as the extreme right, *ceteris paribus*.

It is clear from Table 11.2 that the extreme-right and left groups find similarities in their attracting younger, less religious, working-class identifiers than the moderate right. This finding suggests that social divisions in the contemporary French electorate no longer can be divided neatly into the traditional bidimensional secular–working class and Catholic–middle-class blocs. To what extent is there evidence of similar restructuring along ideological lines? Our analysis will now try to answer this question.

To assess changes in the cultural liberalism foundations of the bloc affiliations we can explore the relationships between party proximity and three types of issues: (a) authoritarian issues; (b) ethnocentric issues; and (c) sexual issues. Authoritarian issues are tapped by asking respondents whether they thought the death penalty should be reintroduced. This item was measured using a four-point scale with high scores representing

FIGURE 11.1 Mean scores (standard deviations in parentheses) for attitudes in favour of immigration by party bloc

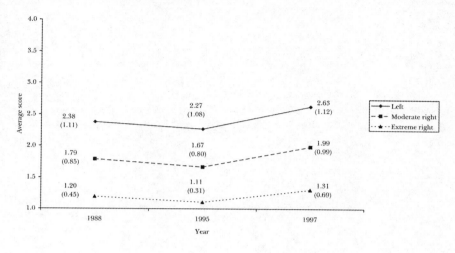

FIGURE 11.2 Mean scores (standard deviations in parentheses) for attitudes not in favour of the death penalty by party bloc

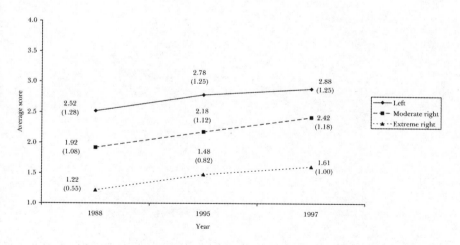

attitudes against reintroduction of the death penalty. Ethnocentric issues are tapped by a question asking how respondents felt about immigration. Low scores indicate that the respondent felt that there are too many immigrants in France while high values on this question represent disagreement with this statement. As we mentioned earlier, we only have data available for the homosexuality question pertaining to 1988 and

FIGURE 11.3 Mean scores (standard deviations in parentheses) for attitudes against homosexuality by party bloc

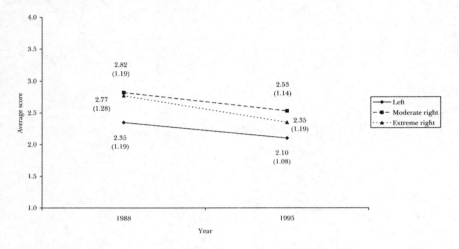

FIGURE 11.4 Mean scores (standard deviations in parentheses) for attitudes against privatisation by party bloc

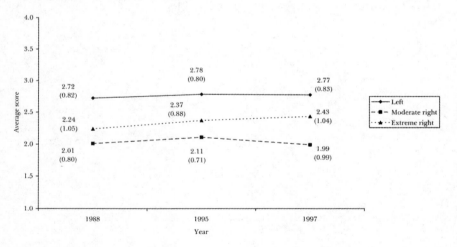

1995. The question in this case is coded so that high values represent attitudes against homosexuality.

The average scores (and standard deviations in parentheses) for the immigration and death penalty questions are shown in Figures 11.1 and 11.2. The most important point from these figures is that the profile of FN supporters is clearly on the extreme right of the political spectrum in all three years. On average, FN identifiers are far more likely to feel

that there are too many immigrants in France and to desire a reintroduction of the death penalty than those who identify with the other two
blocs. Concomitantly, left identifiers are far less likely to favour a reintroduction of the death penalty and far more likely to favour immigration
than identifiers of the other blocs. With both of these issues the moderate
right sits neatly between the FN and the left-bloc parties. Crucially, taking
the score of 2.5 as the political centre, the moderate-right party consistently falls to the right of centre in all six cases. In other words, the
moderate right resembles the extreme right in terms of direction but
not in intensity. In this sense, the two blocs are *not* distinct.

We now turn to Figure 11.3, which charts attitudes toward homosexuality of the electorate for each of the major political blocs. Recall
that high mean scores represent negative attitudes towards homosexuality.
Looking at the trend between these, and expecting to see a drop in
tolerance on the moderate right not matched by the extreme right, the
prediction does not bear out. Very simply, the two parties move almost
in parallel towards a slightly more tolerant stance.[9] Regarding this issue,
the moderate and extreme right both seem to be following the national
trend towards liberalisation on such matters in 1995.

We now explore attitudes towards the economy. As stated earlier,
Grunberg and Schweisguth argue that the FN could no longer be
accommodated within the traditional left-right spectrum with regards to
economic issues from 1995. Each of the surveys we use contained a
question regarding attitudes toward privatisation which allow us to easily
assess this argument. Figure 11.4 plots average responses to this question,
with high scores indicating negative attitudes toward privatisation and
low scores indicating positive scores toward privatisation, for each of the
major political blocs. As Grunberg and Schweisguth suggest, we find that
with respect to this issue, the FN's supporters are clearly in the centre
between identifiers of the left and moderate-right bloc.

When examining the standard deviations of economic positions, however, we see that there was considerably more variation in mean scores
for the extreme-right electorate than for the left and moderate-right
electorates. Breaking down the figures by occupation, as in Table 11.3,
it is evident that the lower social strata, represented by the blue-collar
and routine non-manual occupations, are much less favourable towards
privatisation than the managerial and the self-employed categories. The
former strata are closer to the left bloc in their views, the latter to the
right. Again, the benefits derived from free market capitalism determine
the views of the individuals towards privatisation, and it would be unwise
to see the electorate as having a single line on the subject.[10]

These findings for the right are again suggestive that political space
in France is more than one dimensional – i.e., the left–right bloc does
not neatly divide parties along a single dimension. Contrary to Grunberg

TABLE 11.3 Average attitudes toward privatisation for extreme-right identifiers, by year and social class (standard deviations in parentheses)

	1988	1995	1997
Managers/professionals	2.00 (0.76)	2.04 (1.08)	2.04 (0.88)
Self-employed	2.17 (1.04)	2.13 (1.01)	2.06 (0.99)
Routine non-manual	2.42 (0.84)	2.43 (1.07)	2.69 (1.10)

and Schweisguth's argument, this pattern is stable through the course of the years we examine. This, of course, indicates that if there was a critical change in ideological space, it occurred before 1988 rather than in 1995. Moreover, the social profile of the FN is not distinctive, suggesting that there is not a clear basis for defining it as a distinct political bloc.[11] There seems no ideological reason not to regard the FN as still on the radical wing of the right bloc *in toto*. Ultimately, the ideological disparities between moderate-right and extreme-right blocs are all a matter of intensity rather than direction.

Lastly, we return to the hypothesis of mass ideological convergence in the left bloc prior to the *gauche plurielle* incumbency. Simply, we find no support for this hypothesis. In all cases, the standard deviations remain constant, even in the cases where the position shifts across time.[12] On cultural issues such as the death penalty and immigration, there is a shift between 1988 and 1997 towards a more liberal stance. Still, there is no evidence whatsoever of a mass convergence within the left bloc. Only with regards to homosexuality are opinions converging towards a more liberal position, but this shift is smaller than that of the right-wing electorate. Furthermore, in comparison with the two right blocs, there is *greater* disparity on the death penalty and immigration issues – to this extent, the evidence is that the left merits subdivision into more than one bloc as much as the right. Such figures demonstrate that the coalition-building was indeed based upon elite pragmatism, rather than any convergence of left-wing views.

Of course, it remains to be seen from the 2002 data whether or not the *experience* of cooperation has an effect at the mass level. As we have already noted, however, the electoral campaign and electoral results suggest that this was not the case. Granted, many of the problems with the left were associated with the campaign and its 'intended' candidate at the presidential *ballottage*, Lionel Jospin. However, the intense fragmentation on the left in the presidential first round and the almost entire inability of the *gauche plurielle* to field candidates under the hastily contrived *gauche unie* banner are clear indications that policy, as well as personality, were at stake.

Conclusion

Overall, the key feature of French political space between 1988 and 1997 is its stability. While there are some trends in social and ideological profiles, these are subtle and do not indicate any major reconfiguration of the French electorate's views. In many ways, the left and the right blocs present interesting contrasts in this respect. The right, for so long fragmented by personality clashes, shows surprising evidence of homogeneity, even including the extreme right. The left, a coherent governing bloc between 1997 and 2002 because of elite compromise, shows no sign of ideological homogeneity, either empirically from its electorate's views in 1997 or speculatively from the 2002 election results. Moreover, those parties and candidates on the left trying to move the debate away from the traditional axis of competition, notably the MdC and Jean-Pierre Chevènement discussing the PRep, and the Greens pushing the environmental issues, both suffered in the legislative tally. To this extent, then, the left–right spectrum remains as valid as ever in French political life.

Most tellingly, perhaps, the 'nuisance effect' predicted to be devastating for the right in these elections [13] turned out to be entirely redundant, despite Le Pen's earlier success in the presidential elections. Where the 37 triangulaires occurred, the FN experienced considerable losses as compared with the first round, undoubtedly because of a solid cohesive moderate right. The FN only made significant gains in straight two-candidate run-offs against the left, profiting from a proportion of moderate-right support. In other words, under both scenarios, the success of the extreme right is principally conditioned by the strength of the moderate right. The separate bloc winning support from both moderate blocs simply does not match reality in 2002.

Indeed, the separation of moderate and extreme right as political blocs per se was already somewhat at odds with the experiences of the right over the past five years. First, the moderate right had itself experienced a level of fragmentation unprecedented under the Fifth Republic. While the basis to this has to a large extent been personality rather ideological politics at work, ideological differences are nonetheless present. As Evans has shown in his chapter on the European dimension (Chapter 10, this volume), some members of the UDF and of the former RPR are poles apart in their vision of France in the EU, even if there economic and cultural attitudes are close. The way the UDF can exploit this specificity in the new legislature will undoubtedly determine its survival over the next few years.

Similarly, one of the key issues in intra-UDF and UDF–RPR relations in the late 1990s – the regional council presidency support from the FN for the UDF – demonstrated diverse attitudes to relations with the extreme-right party. These feelings and conflicts were mutual – as Ivaldi has noted, one of the major sticking points between Mégret and Le Pen was precisely whether or not the FN should open to their moderate neighbours. These are all political divisions, undoubtedly, but again along the principal left–right axis, the ideologies remain similar in their direction, the socio-economic specificity of the two groups is blurred, and thus the 'third bloc' status of the FN/MNR and their presidential candidates is weak.

In conclusion, it is perhaps unsurprising to note that between 1988 and 1997, mass attitudes have changed little. After all, nine years does not represent a period sufficiently long to expect generational turnover in attitudes. However, it is clear that there has been no major sea-change in the French electorate's desires, either. Where political changes have occurred, it has been due to changes in political supply, either in shape or in quality. Indeed, it is quite revealing that the French electorate want pretty much what they wanted over a decade ago. However, from the continued alternation every election, a rise in protest voting and in abstention, they are simply still not getting what they want. That the left–right logic remains the principal axis of competition illustrates two things. First, the modern conceit that globalisation, Europe, post-industrial society and the rest are fundamentally altering the shape of politics does not find sustenance in political competition: as Cole states, these issues are undoubtedly muddying the ideological waters, but behind this the main ideological affiliations remain (see Chapter 1, this volume).

Second, and connected to this, the conceit that modern societies have solved the old conflicts that used to structure politics is also wrong. In an election campaign where the main differences between left and right parties appeared on issues of taxation and according to traditional left–right lines, the 'modern' issues have become a given for all parties rather than a new political cleavage and thus largely irrelevant in France's first-order elections. The search for something truly New in political competition continues.

Notes

The authors are indebted to the Banque de Données Socio-Politiques, Grenoble, for providing access to the 1988, 1995 and 1997 SOFRES/CEVIPOF post-election survey datasets and to CREST (Centre for Research into Elections and Social Trends) for providing funding for part of the research.
 1 For ease of accessibility for readers, we refer throughout the text to the excellent translated version published by the University of Michigan Press (Boy and Mayer, 1993).

2 On theories and interpretations of the post-industrial transformation, see in particular Dalton *et al.* (1984), Franklin *et al.* (1992).

3 On economic shifts on the extreme right, see Bastow (1997). On working-class voters moving to the extreme right, see Evans (2000a).

4 And indeed resigned once again, this time over the Corsican question.

5 Szarka is particularly vehement on this point, emphasising that 'the *gauche plurielle* represented an attempt to stabilise a crumbling electoral base, rather than a realignment of the French left' (1999: 35).

6 As Sauger recounts in this book, by 1999 DL had separated itself from the centre-right UDF, concerning itself with promoting the free market ethos (see Chapter 7).

7 Many observers have argued that party proximity/identification is traditionally weak in France (Converse and Dupeux, 1962, Percheron, 1977) but we concur with more recent literature suggesting that it has become sufficiently normalised in recent years (Converse and Pierce, 1986, Haegel, 1993).

8 On this, see for instance Inglehart (1990).

9 In fact, in a more robust testing of the *tripartition* hypothesis, the independent effect of the homosexuality issue on presidential voting and party proximity turned out to be stronger in distinguishing moderate right from extreme right in 1988 than in 1995. This element to the *tripartition* hypothesis would have been more suited to the earlier election, then – see Andersen and Evans (2003).

10 It is worthwhile acknowledging that the central position of the lower strata would be interpreted according to directional voting theory as ambivalence or indifference to the issue – see, e.g., Rabinowitz and Macdonald (1989), Merrill and Grofman (1999). Given blue-collar and lower white-collar defection to the FN and Le Pen through disillusionment with the moderate parties' competing but equally failing economic policies, such a lack of salience for this item would be unsurprising. In short, blue-collar and lower white-collar groups are not voting for the extreme right on the basis of economics.

11 We examine the theoretical role of socio-structural elements in political bloc definition in greater detail elsewhere (Andersen and Evans, 2003).

12 In the bloc codings, we realise that we have included two actors – the extreme left and GE – in the left bloc which are not included in the *gauche plurielle* government. The standard deviations remained almost identical when they were excluded from the left bloc, and so we have not excluded them for a separate analysis.

13 *Le Monde*, 2 February 2002.

Conclusion

Jocelyn A. J. Evans

Looking at the French party system in 2002 in the wake of the presidential and legislative elections, it is perhaps initially tempting to see abrupt change everywhere. An apparently successful left-wing government is overturned, all its partners losing almost half their National Assembly seats or more. A fractured moderate right, led – if one can use that word – by a president weighed down by corruption scandals and coming out of a largely inactive incumbency, wins almost 70 per cent of the seats in the Assembly, and the vast majority of those under a single-party label. For the fringes of the system, the changes seem almost more abrupt than even for the mainstream. The extreme left, so visible in the presidential elections and so vital in the left's second-round absence, disappears from view once more with no seats, as does its extreme-right opposite numbers whose combined score in the presidential elections accounted for one in five French voters. In a system renowned for its larger-than-life political figures, the names of Jean-Pierre Chevènement, Dominique Voynet, Martine Aubry, Charles Pasqua, Philippe Séguin and others have all been eclipsed during the last legislative term or by the elections themselves.

Yet, because of the primacy of the presidential race and the peculiarity of its first round – an unprecedented disarray of candidates and a *ballottage* unsurpassed by even the 1969 election – focus has been too tightly drawn onto the *éléments de rupture* so beloved of French political commentators, and has largely ignored the *éléments de continuité* which are in fact far more characteristic of a system which coasts blithely on from election to election, ignoring the howls for constitutional reform and fundamental rebuilding which have greeted some aspect of every result since 1959.

In drawing this book to a close, we wish to try to discern more exactly what represents continuity and what represents change. To do this, we turn first to some basic summary statistics which are commonly used to look at party system dynamics – the effective number of parties; individual and total volatility – in order to locate the 2002 party system at the end of a trend starting in 1978, the *quadrille bipolaire* benchmark year. Such

189

FIGURE C.1 Effective number of parties and presidential candidates in France (1978–2002)

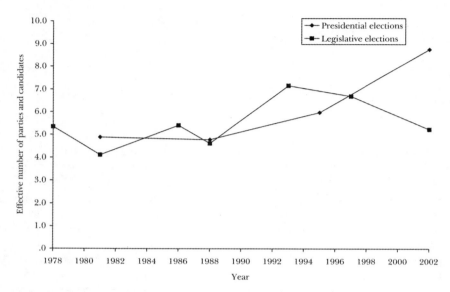

Source: Banque de Données Socio-Politiques, Grenoble, electoral archive [1]

statistics by their very nature simplify depictions of reality, but this makes them an ideal means of identifying trends across time in a system if they are used cautiously. We will then turn to consider the implications of these figures for the parties, and what they reveal about the likely prospects for the French party system in coming years.

As expected, an empirical perspective to the trends in the party system clarifies the level of continuity which the system is experiencing. Figure C. 1 shows the index for the effective number of parties and presidential candidates for elections since 1978 (Taagepera and Shugart, 1989: 79).[2] The presidential elections show a definite trend towards greater fragmentation, with the major increase between 1995 and 2002, explained by the parties' need to field presidential candidates to ensure campaign prominence prior to the legislatives, as well as a product of the lack of decidability between the two main candidates. However, the legislative elections show what we might refer to as trendless fluctuation. The implantation of the *quadrille bipolaire* between 1978 and 1981 is followed by a rise in fragmentation in 1986 due to the appearance of the FN, and another surge in 1993 with the increase in FN and Green support. The two following elections remain stable, with a decline in the effective number of parties in 2002 due to the birth of the dominant UMP. The

FIGURE C.2 Effective number of parties and presidential candidates on
the left and right in France (1978–2002)

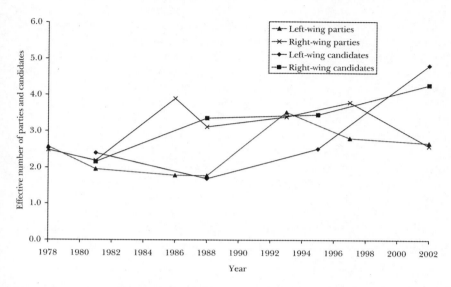

Source: *Banque de Données Socio-Politiques*, Grenoble, electoral archive

major comparison to be made between presidential and legislative trends
is clear: until 2002, the effective number of parties and candidates never
differed by more than one unit, but the fragmentation of the 2002
elections was totally at odds with the party system format.

If we look at Figure C. 2, which disaggregates the presidential and
legislative scores into left and right blocs, the 'fault' for the excessive
fragmentation in the presidential elections clearly lies with the left.
Granted, the right sees a steady increase in the effective number of
candidates between 1981 and 2002. However, given its reputation for
personality-riven politics, the increase from 3.3 in 1988 to 4.3 in 2002
is an effective increase of only one candidate. The losses in the 1980s
and 1990s were clearly unrelated to an excess of supply in the right bloc.
The left on the other hand blossoms from 2.5 candidates to 4.8 in 2002,
almost doubling the effective number of candidates. In other words, the
number of candidates standing increased, and the distribution of the
vote was more equitable.

This is quite at odds with the legislative pattern. The left bloc remains
relatively stable in terms of party numbers, with the exception of 1993,
again due to the surge in Green support. The fragmentation of the right
is far more prominent, with the FN's presence from 1986 pushing the

quadrille bipolaire more towards a five-party format. But the pattern is clear – when the right finds itself relatively close to the left in terms of fragmentation, it wins. The obvious exception here is 1986, when the proportional representation system meant that level of fragmentation was largely irrelevant. In 2002, in particular, the offer from the UMP that could not be refused by the other right-wing parties gave the right bloc a cohesion which, together with the added value of a presidential success, an ultimately failed extreme right and a divided left, secured its landslide success. The right has thus returned to a two-party bloc, the UMP and the two 'half-parties' of the UDF and the FN, plus assorted stragglers.

However, it is very noticeable that the left cannot be described as irrevocably split. Indeed it is at its lowest level of fragmentation for three elections, back to its 1978 levels. The problem for the left is the domination of a Socialist Party that cannot find that all-important partner to ensure control of its own electoral space while encroaching on the centre to win the floating voters from the right. The volatility figures between 1997 and 2002 next to the actual results tell the story all too clearly (Table C.1).

TABLE C.1 2002 legislative election results (first round) and change (1997–2002)

	2002 vote	*Change (1997–2002)*
Extreme left	2.80	0.23
Communists	4.90	–5.05
Socialists/radicals	25.71	0.05
Republican Pole/other left	2.27	0.09
Ecologist (Greens + others)	5.33	–1.19
UDF–RPR/UMP	38.16	8.16
Other right	5.34	0.66
FN/MNR/other ex. right	12.55	–2.68
Others	2.94	–0.17
Total	100.00	
Total volatility		9.14

Source: *Banque de Données Socio-Politiques*, Grenoble, electoral archive

In net terms, it appears that the new UMP won most of its support from extreme-right and Communist defections – an unlikely scenario in the latter case. What is more likely is that the Communist losses moved largely to the Socialists, who themselves lost centrally located voters more attracted by the cohesive presidential UMP than by the presidentially failed, fractionalised left and perhaps anxious to avoid another period of cohabitation.[3] But in net terms, the Socialists lost almost no support whatsoever. What caused the left to lose by such a margin was the centripetal competitive dynamic away from the extreme left partner

FIGURE C.3 Total volatility in French legislative elections (1978–2002)

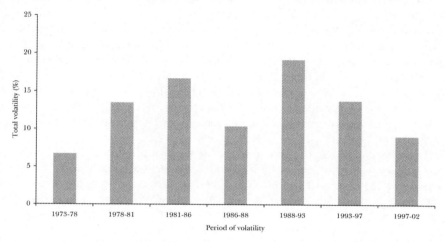

Source: Siaroff (2000: 42–3), *Banque de Données Socio-Politiques*, Grenoble, electoral archive

PCF on the left, from the extreme-right FN and MNR to the UMP, and crucially across the centre in the key area of inter-bloc competition. In these terms, a system which six months earlier had looked fragmented and which during the presidential elections had seen extremist candidates pick up a significant share of the vote, is once more displaying dynamics almost synonymous with moderate pluralism as defined by Sartori (1976) – medium fragmentation, centripetal competitive dynamics and an unoccupied central ideological space whose voters win and lose elections.

Lastly, in empirical terms, the total level of volatility is the lowest since the 1973–78 electoral period, and indeed one of the lowest in the history of the Fifth Republic (Figure C.3).[4]

The 1988 election stands out as the outlier in an otherwise relatively smooth trend in volatility. The 1986–88 right-wing government clearly made little difference to the electorate in terms of their choice – no wholesale defection to the right, no grateful return to the left, and hence the minority government of the left until 1993 when wholesale defection *did* occur. However, in the following two elections, volatility has declined despite the change in government in each case. In aggregate terms, at least, the French electorate is stabilising.

Given the findings of Andersen and Evans in Chapter 11 of this volume regarding the electorate's stability in attitudinal terms, this is of little surprise. If post-war research into the role of policy preferences and vote has agreed on anything, it is that when underlying preferences remain stable, one would not expect high levels of voting change *ceteris paribus*.[5] This is not to say that changes do not occur, but that if they are significantly common, one evidently needs to look to other sources of change. In the case of the Communist Party in 2002, for instance, the five-point drop in support was partially a result of the perceived failure of the party as an influential governmental partner, as an effective representative and certainly, given Robert Hue's individual result, as the presidential party of the extreme left. Where this support goes is key. In the case of the 2002 elections, it is clear that some support moved to the Socialists, smaller proportions to the extreme left and some was lost to generational turnover among an ageing electorate – and crucially some to abstention.

For it is clear that political parties, despite predictions of their wide-spread demise because of policy inadequacies, corruption, failing mass-elite linkage and so on, still have *potential* electorates in society – all voting patterns and survey data support this. What parties are finding increasingly difficult to do in France, as in other countries, is to mobilise these potential electorates so that they become *actual*. Party behaviour and the electorate's reaction to this over the last twenty years demonstrate this very effectively. First, abstention is rising. Arguments over whether this is due to increasing apathy among comfortable voters or increasing disenchantment among a political and social underclass both have validity, but the proximity in social and attitudinal profiles between abstainers and the FN electorate, with the key exception of xenophobic and authoritarian attitudes, suggests that the former has greater resonance.[6]

Second, party behaviour has repeatedly played into the hands of abstention as well as losing the all important centre floating voters which allow the other bloc to win. In 1988, as we have mentioned, the left's 'victory' was a race with no winner, and suffered from a lack of mobilisation accordingly. In 1993, the Socialist Party's virtual admittance of defeat before the election, epitomised by Michel Rocard's ill-timed call for a complete overhaul of the party a couple of weeks prior to the first ballot – the infamous 'big bang' – added dispirited abstention among some supporters to defection to the right by others. In 1997, it was the right's turn to demobilise its voters both with a cynical early call for elections and an unresponsive Gaullist Party fielding an arrogant and unpopular government. Lastly, in 2002 Socialist protestations that the presidential disaster should convince left-wing supporters of the need to turn out had no visible effect whatsoever, even if the PS vote did remain stable: despite a respectable first term in office, many *gauche plurielle* voters simply failed to play their part in pressing for a second.

Third, on the rare occasion that French parties *do* get their act together, the results are usually beneficial. The combined RPR–UDF lists of 1986 would have won an even greater victory had a majoritarian electoral system been in place. In 1997, the cohesion of the *gauche plurielle* at least in terms of candidates provided a newly humble alternative to the disasters of four years previously that could capitalise on the right's unpopularity. Similarly in 2002, the UMP behind the newly incumbent president presented the possibility of an effective and unified moderate right which for so long had been riven by personality disputes and subsequent party fragmentation. As both Sauger and Knapp have emphasised in their respective chapters in this volume, organisational differences have played a role in obstructing right unity (see Chapters 7 and 8). But as many parties have learned to their cost, such esoteric disputes are of no interest to an electorate. The only party that clearly understands this is the FN: given that its split was predicted to destroy the extreme right, Le Pen and his cohorts' exorcising of the *mégretistes* and their return to 'politics as normal' as far as possible proved to work in terms of electoral support, even if the possible Mégret bridge to the moderate right had been lost.[7] Perhaps the Green elites' replacement of Lipietz with Mamère might be seen in a similar light.

The attempt by the Socialists to salvage some cohesion on the left by promoting the notion – although unfulfilled – of *gauche unie* candidates in 2002 suggests that both the left and the right are relearning the underlying dynamics of the Fifth Republic institutional framework. There is a common misconception in much of the literature that party system typologies and classifications somehow inexorably set the dynamics and strategies that parties will undertake in a certain system type or class. In reality, where schemas identify such dynamics, they simply indicate which dynamics are prevalent in a certain type or class and consequently which strategies may be regarded as appropriate to exploiting these. There is nothing to say that parties can or will engage in these strategies, either due to imperfect information or due to external factors which prevent them from doing so.

The early years of any regime are largely regarded as forming a learning curve for the parties within, and the Fifth Republic was no exception (Bartolini, 1984). As a number of the contributors to this volume have mentioned, the convergence on the *quadrille bipolaire*, the ideal type of moderate pluralist competition in the Republic's institutional framework, occurred principally through the balancing of the right-wing parties, the nationalisation of the Socialist Party and the centripetal shift of the Communists. Similarly, as the effective number of parties and volatility figures show, both elite and mass levels stabilised. Yet any notion of inexorable system dynamics pulling the parties towards this bipolar bloc arrangement are quickly dispelled by the late 1980s and early 1990s which, as we have seen, manifested higher volatility levels and, more importantly from a systemic perspective, growing fragmentation. This can partly be ascribed to the entry of new relevant actors, particularly the Greens and the FN. However, new parties do not necessarily mean new poles – there is no reason *a priori* that Green parties or extreme-right parties cannot be integrated into existing blocs. What has prevented this in the French case has been splits within parties over such a possibility – the Greens hovering on the border of integration and autonomy, the FN excluded by some of the moderate right but not others, and itself split over rapprochement with the Gaullists and UDF.

Ideological divergences are most often cited as the reason for such separation, but as the chapters in this book have made clear, the extent of such divergence is largely an exaggeration by elites wanting to retain their specificity in a competitive arena. For smaller parties, merger means oblivion; for larger parties, promoting one's uniqueness remains an elite's prerogative in the fight for leadership. Yet, the experiences of both left and right from the mid-1980s onwards have shown that such stances are not only vacuous, they are often damaging in electoral terms, and no more so than in 2002. The left's conceit that somehow its eight presidential candidates all had something different to offer provided no small embarrassment when this 'diversity' led to its absence from the second round. Moreover, to criticise Jacques Chirac for only winning 19 per cent of the vote and yet still win rather misses the point: Jacques Chirac has remained remarkably stable in his vote between 1981 and 2002, always winning between 18.0 per cent and 20.7 per cent of the vote (albeit this time as the incumbent). It is the other candidates who have collapsed.

So the parties have learned that it does make sense to follow the system's dynamics and cohere even when personalities, organisations and ideologies are not necessarily conducive to this. The UMP provides the hegemonic party of the right that the UNR and its successors provided in the 1960s. The Socialists have realised that the *gauche plurielle* may have saved them from the arrogance of the 1980s but in its format to date it concomitantly promotes fragmentation which does their electoral chances no favours in the face of a cohesive right. In future, it needs to secure similar predominance on the left and try to ensure that the multifaceted candidatures or lack of electoral agreements do not sink it. But as Hanley predicts, the single party of the left – a left-wing UMP – is far from likely, given the continued rivalries and political persuasions that constitute this bloc. Whether an alliance or a single entity would be more attractive to the left electorate is unclear.

But to what extent can we expect the parties to act upon such learning where the consequences are more evident? As Knapp points out, at the time of writing DL had still not dissolved itself as promised and the UDF has no intention ever to do so. Whether the UMP proves a stable replacement for its Gaullist, DL and dissident UDF predecessors will only be shown by its founding Congress and the success of the Raffarin government in its first incumbency. With the notable addition of the prime ministerial seat, the distribution of ministerial positions has been as equitable as in previous right-wing governments, and to this extent the smaller partners have little to complain about. Whether this is the case after the end of the honeymoon period, cabinet reshuffles and the usual round of petulant resignations remains to be seen. However, it is perhaps naïvely optimistic to think that the personality politics which have riven French parties since the Third Republic are likely to disappear as of 2002.

The key test for the right in this respect will be the future selection of Jacques Chirac's successor. Assuming that Chirac does not run for a third term, commentators have already lined up Alain Juppé as the *dauphin*, no doubt because Chirac himself sees his former prime minister and Bordeaux Mayor in this light. Whether the rest of the Gaullists, UMP and the electorate regard him as such is very much another matter. For a candidate whose lack of charisma and perceived arrogance was in no small part responsible for his government's 1997 defeat, the position of right-wing *présidentiable* looks less than assured. The likes of Nicolas Sarkozy and Philippe Douste-Blazy are unlikely to sit back and allow Juppé to inherit the presidential mantle by default. Memories of the 1974 election and the worthy but dull Jacques Chaban-Delmas' trouncing by Valéry Giscard d'Estaing after a young Jacques Chirac's betrayal inevitably spring to mind.

The left's predicament is more immediate. Despite the certain knowledge that a greater show of unity might have given them a chance of the victory in both 2002 elections, the shape that such unity should now take is unclear. The Socialists' vote remained stable in aggregate and thus its dominance is assured. The question is, who will it dominate? The PS does not have an obvious partner for a governing coalition alternative. In terms of votes, the previous *gauche plurielle* partners may only be 6.5 per cent behind the new right incumbents, but to win back this support requires offering something more persuasive than simply 'more of the same – but with weakened Greens and Communists'. The old partnership needs to be revitalised to win back centre voters and to remobilise many of those who abstained in 2002.

An obvious solution for revitalisation would be a strong *présidentiable* able to gather the remnants of the *gauche plurielle* as well as inspire electoral support. Looking at the left, however, who that candidate might be is not obvious. Some of the more charismatic left-wing leaders have been on the margins – Jean-Pierre Chevènement and Dominique Voynet, for example – and their political careers are currently in decline. Laurent Fabius and Dominique Strauss-Kahn, younger members of the old guard, are lacking in cross-party and electoral appeal and have both been damaged by scandal investigations, despite neither being convicted. Lastly the likes of François Hollande, the Socialist General Secretary, and Martine Aubry, the mayor of Lille lack the charisma necessary for a successful presidential candidate.

But the left also faces an external threat from its extreme flank. Arlette Laguiller, Olivier Besancenot *et al.* may not have repeated their presidential success at the legislative elections, but they have less of a need to do so. Unlike the mainstream parties, the extreme left's success has come as much from the direct-action approach to politics highlighted by Wolfreys as through the ballot box (see Chapter 6, this volume). Increasingly, social movements in France are taking up the issues and complaints of the left-wing electorates in a way that political parties used to, but apparently no longer can. The risk for the left is that, as the electorate increasingly turns to such movements for issue-representation and focuses its limited political interest on these groups, the motivation to turn out for the parties of the left decreases. Granted, in the face of a hard-line right-wing government, such voters might turn out rationally in order to prevent the incumbency of a party or coalition which they perceive as pernicious. But the evidence to date is that such voters *decreasingly* perceive governing parties in such a light, rather the opposite – they do not see sufficient distinction between them. In which case, why bother voting?

That demobilisation is more a curse of the left than the right is understandable. The increasingly dominant new middle class and its traditional counterpart are less likely to belong to strata dislocated from politics and society, and conversely are more likely to feel that they have something to lose specifically from a left-wing government. The left will probably benefit more in the long term if the right engages in a confident hardline programme of business-friendly, growth-oriented policies, rather than a middle-of-the-road, socially oriented approach. Which path the right will take is currently unclear. On the one hand, the reaction to the questions of law and order and security has seen Minister of the Interior Sarkozy touring French *gendarmeries* promising increased funding. Similarly, this traditionally authoritarian right-wing approach has been matched by the initiation of income tax cuts, particularly for higher-income brackets, as promised by Chirac in his presidential manifesto. However, Raffarin himself is seen as a moderate whose appointment coincided with Chirac's wish to present an inclusive face to his 'republican' second-round electorate. Epitomising these two tendencies have been the economically liberal economic minister Francis Mer's clashes with the socially inclined social security minister, François Fillon.[8] Which approach wins the upper hand as the incumbency progresses will have major implications for how the left chooses to oppose the government – 'we can do social liberalism better than they can' or 'hard right policies are wrong'.

In many ways, the system and political context resemble the late 1960s in France, the right strongly implanted in the presidency and government, the left about to embark upon a long period of reconstruction to allow it into power over a decade later. Commentators have predicted that the Socialists will need a long period in opposition to be able to consolidate their strength and move back into a position to challenge the right.[9] Undoubtedly any future coalitions will be fraught by the same ideological and logistical differences which hampered the *programme commun* for so long and cost the left an earlier victory than it eventually won. Whether the cycle back to left power takes as long as predicted is a moot point – after all, the 1993 *raz-marée* proved remarkably curtailed in its after effects. That the process *is* cyclical is less in doubt. As the past twenty years have proved, the institutional framework of the Fifth Republic promotes alternation, and there is only one alternative to the right. Short of major constitutional reform, which was promised during the elections but which has now slipped down the agenda, such political cycles are destined to continue – and those parties and alternative dimensions such as Europe which currently find themselves marginalised are unlikely to find any greater saliency in future.

Overall, the French party system has displayed a number of changes since the 1990s, but these should be seen as principally conjunctural changes taking place within a relatively stable structural framework. Parties have fragmented against the competitive logic of the system and have caused the defeat of governments in elections. However, such shifts against the prevailing dynamics of the system have almost inevitably been revealed as negative in terms of electoral strategy, and the parties have reacted accordingly, albeit sometimes slowly. Where they have done so with less success, extreme parties and abstention have been the sole beneficiaries. Such continuity does not disguise the fact that the system has become host to parties which find it increasingly difficult to mobilise, let alone inspire, their electorates. An increasing tendency to ignore party politics has itself caused changes within the system. However, the electorate is still there to be mobilised. Parties which show the capacity to adapt win an electoral premium which is normally sufficiently large to ensure victory. The challenge to French parties in the twenty-first century is thus to ensure that the system does not become an elite desert where the players scrabble for ever diminishing pools of voters. Parties are secure as the means of staffing government, simply because there is no viable alternative. In this respect, the notion of a crisis of parties is exaggerated. But whether such recruitment is for a mass-oriented representative government based on a social majority or a distant oligarchic institution based on a political minority depends largely on parties' focus and performance in years to come.

Notes

1 All figures and tables in this chapter include only the 555 metropolitan constituencies due to data availability.

2 The effective number of parties or candidates is calculated as the inverse of the sum of individual party votes squared. For example, in a party system with four parties, two large (40 per cent of the vote each) and two small (10 per cent each), the index would be $1/(.40^2 + .40^2 + .10^2 + .10^2) = 1/.34 = 2.94$. In a system with four equally sized parties (25 per cent of the vote each) the index would be 4.00. Thus this index takes into account both the number of parties and the distribution of the vote between them to illustrate the fractionalisation of the party system.

3 This is supported by a more detailed analysis of volatility at the constituency level (Abrial *et al.*, 2002).

4 It should be noted that volatility can also be calculated without grouping parties which have split or amalgamated. For instance, we could have calculated volatility including the UMP as a separate party, rather than an amalgamation. In this case, volatility would have been much higher. However, this would have made no real intuitive sense.

5 This was one of the key underlying assumptions of Philip Converse's 'normal vote', the distribution of latent party preferences among the electorate (Converse, 1966).

6 For an analysis of this, see Andersen and Evans (2003).

7 Jean Marie Le Pen is keen to play down the possible succession battle between Marine Le Pen and Bruno Gollnisch, his second-in-command.

8 *Le Monde*, 23 July 2002.

9 In conversation with a member of *Le Figaro*'s political department, the author was told that the Socialists were now condemned to opposition for at least twenty years. Allowing for rhetorical hyperbole, the implication is clear.

References

Abrial, S., B. Cautrès and J. Evans (2002) 'Evolution du système de partis français: une nouvelle étape en 2002?', *Revue Politique et Parlementaire*, 1015, 228–43.

Amar, C. and A. Chemin (2002) *Jospin et Cie: histoire de la gauche plurielle, 1993–2002*, Paris, Seuil.

Andersen, R. and J. Evans (2003) 'Values, cleavages and party choice in France, 1988–1995', *French Politics*, 1:1, forthcoming.

Bacot, P. (1976). *Le Parti socialiste et le front de classe*, Lyon, Presses Universitaires de Lyon.

Bartolini, S. (1984) 'Institutional constraints and party competition in the French party system', *West European Politics*, 7:4, 103–27.

Bastow, S. (1997) 'Front National economic policy: from neo-liberalism to protectionism?', *Modern and Contemporary France* 5:2, 61–72.

Bell, D. (2000) *Parties and Democracy in France*, Aldershot, Ashgate.

Bell, D. and B. Criddle (1988) *The French Socialist Party*, Oxford, Clarendon.

Bell, D. and B. Criddle (1994) 'The French Socialist Party: presidentialised factionalism' in D. Bell and E. Shaw (eds) *Conflict and Cohesion in European Social Democratic Parties*, London, Pinter.

Bennahmias, J.-L. and A. Roche (1992) *Des Verts de toutes les couleurs*, Paris, Albin Michel.

Benoît, B. (1997) *Social-Nationalism: An Anatomy of French Euroscepticism*, Aldershot, Gower.

Bergounioux, A. and Grunberg, G. (1992) *Le Long Remords du pouvoir*, Paris, Fayard.

Berstein, S. (2001) *Histoire du gaullisme*, Paris, Perrin.

Betz, H.-G. (1994) *Radical Right-wing Populism in Europe*, New York, St Martin's Press.

Betz, H.-G. (2001) 'Entre succès et échec: l'extrême droite à la fin des années quatre-vingt-dix' in P. Perrineau (ed.) *Les Croisés de la société fermée. L'Europe des extrêmes droites*, Paris, L'Aube.

Betz, H.-G. and S. Immerfall (eds) (1998) *The New Politics of the Right*, London, Macmillan.

Birenbaum, G. (1992) *Le Front National en politique*, Paris, Balland.

Bogdanor V. and D. Butler (1982) *Democracy and Elections*, Oxford, Oxford University Press.

Boltanski, L. and E. Chiapello (1999) *Le Nouvel Esprit du Capitalisme*, Paris, Gallimard.

Bourlanges, J.-L. (1990) 'Le rendez-vous manqué de la rénovation' in SOFRES, *L'Etat de l'opinion 1990*, Paris, Editions du Seuil.

Boy, D. (1990) 'Le vote écologiste, évolutions et structures ', *Cahiers du CEVIPOF*, 6.

Boy, D. (1993) 'Ecologistes: retour sur terre' in P. Habert, P. Perrineau and C. Ysmal (eds) *Le Vote sanction: les élections législatives des 21 et 28 mars 1993*. Paris, Presses de la FNSP.

Boy, D. and J. Chiche (2002) 'Paris à contre-courant' in B. Dolez and A. Laurent (eds) *Le Vote des villes. Les élections municipales des 11 et 18 mars 2001*, Paris: Presses de Sciences Po.

Boy, D., V.-J. Le Seigneur and A. Roche (1995) *L'Ecologie au pouvoir*, Paris, Presses de la FNSP.

Boy, D. and N. Mayer (eds) (1990) *L'Electeur français en questions*, Paris, Presses de Sciences Po.

Boy, D. and N. Mayer (eds) (1993) *The French Voter Decides*, Ann Arbor, University of Michigan Press.

Boy, D. & N. Mayer (eds) (1997) *L'Electeur a ses raisons*, Paris, Presses de Sciences Po.

Boy, D. and N. Mayer (2000) 'Cleavage voting and issue voting in France' in M. Lewis-Beck (ed.) *How France Votes*, New York, Chatham House.

Boy, D. and B. Villalba (1999) 'Le dilemme des écologistes: entre stratégie nationale et diversités locales' in P. Perrineau and D. Reynié (eds) *Le Vote incertain. Les élections régionales et cantonales de 1998*, Paris, Presses de Sciences Po.

Boy, D. and B. Villalba (2000) 'Les motivations des militants Verts persistent à l'exercice du pouvoir' in *Le Monde*, 15 January.

Bréchon, P. (1999) 'L'union RPR-DL au plus bas', *Revue Française de Science Politique*, 49:4–5, 653–61.

Brochier, J.-C. and H. Delouche (2000) *Les Nouveax Sans-culottes. Enquête sur l'extrême gauche*, Paris, Grasset.

Buffotot, P. and D. Hanley (1998) 'Chronique d'une défaite annoncée: les élections législatives des 25 mai et 1er juin 1997', *Modern and Contemporary France*, 6:1, 5–20.

Buzzi, P. (1994) 'Le Front national entre national-populisme et idéologie d'extrême-droite' in P. Bréchon (ed.) *Le Discours politique en France. Evolution des idées partisanes*, Paris, Les Etudes de la Documentation Française.

Cambadélis, J.-M. (1999) *L'Avenir de la gauche plurielle*, Paris, Plon.

Capdevielle, J., E. Dupoirier, G. Grunberg, E. Schweisguth and C. Ysmal (1981) *France de gauche, vote à droite*, Paris, Presses de la FNSP.

Castel, R. (1993) *Les Métamorphoses de la question sociale*, Paris, Gallimard.

Castells, M. (1998) *The Rise of the Network Society*, Oxford, Blackwell.

Cathala, J., and J.-B. Prédall (2002) *Nous nous sommes tant haïs, 1997–2002. Voyage au centre de la droite*, Paris, Seuil.

Charlot, J. (1988) 'Le séisme du 8 mai et la nouvelle donne politique' in P. Habert and C. Ysmal (eds) *L'Election présidentielle 1988: résultats, analyses et commentaires*, Paris, Etudes Politiques du Figaro.

Charlot, J. (1992) 'Les rapports de forces electoraux entre les partis', *Revue Politique et Parlementaire*, 958, 19–24.

Charlot, J. (1993) 'Recomposition du système de partis français ou rééquilibrage limité?' in P. Habert *et al.* (eds) *Le Vote sanction*, Paris, Presses de la FNSP.

Charlot, J. (1994) 'La recomposition du système de partis français ou rééquilibrage limitée?' in P. Perrineau & C. Ysmal (eds) *Le Vote sanction: les élections législatives des 21 et 28 mars 1993*, Paris, Presses de la FNSP.

Chiche, J., and D. Reynié (2002) 'La France en dépression électorale' in SOFRES, *L'état de l'opinion 2002*, Paris, Seuil.

Clift, B. (2000) 'Towards a new political economy of social democracy?: the fall and rise of the French Parti Socialiste 1990–1998', unpublished Ph.D. thesis, Sheffield University.

Cohn-Bendit, D. (1999) *Une Envie de politique*, Paris, Découverte/Poche.

Cole, A. (1986) 'Factionalism in the French Socialist Party', unpublished DPhil thesis, Oxford University.

Cole, A. (1989) 'Factionalism, the French Socialist Party, and the Fifth Republic: an explanation of intra-party divisions', *European Journal of Political Research*, 17:1, 77–94.

Cole, A. (1995) '*La France pour tous?* The French presidential election of 23 April and 7 May 1995', *Government and Opposition*, 30:3, 327–46.

Cole, A. (1998) *French Politics and Society*, Hemel Hempstead, Prentice Hall.

Cole, A. (2002) 'A strange affair: the 2002 presidential and parliamentary elections in France', *Government and Opposition*, 37:3, 65–91.

Colombani, J.-M. (1984) 'Qui est à la droite de qui?', *Pouvoirs*, 28, 47–52.

Converse, P. (1966) 'The concept of the normal vote' in A. Campbell *et al.* (eds) *Elections and the Political Order*, Free Press, New York.

Converse, P. and G. Dupeux (1962) 'Politicisation of the electorate in France and the United States', *Public Opinion Quarterly*, 26:1, 1–23.

Converse, P. and R. Pierce (1986) *Political Representation in France*, Cambridge (MA), University of Harvard Press.

Coupé, A. and A. Marchand (eds) (1999) *Sud: syndicalement incorrect? SUD–PTT une aventure collective*, Paris, Syllepse.

Crozier, M. (1970) *La Société bloquée*, Paris, Seuil.

Dalton, R., S. Flanagan and P. Beck (eds) (1984) *Electoral Change in Advanced Industrialised Societies*, Princeton, Princeton University Press.

Dalton, R. and M. Kuechler (eds) (1990) *Challenging the Political Order: New Social and Political Movements in Western Democracies*, New York, Oxford University Press.

de Gaulle, C. (1970), *Mémoires d'espoir*, Paris, Plon.

Dolez, B. (1997) 'Les "petits" partis au regard de la réglementation du finance-ment de la vie politique' in A. Laurent and B. Villalba (eds) *Les Petits Partis. De la petitesse en politique*, Paris, L'Harmattan.

Dolez, B. (1999) 'La liste Bayrou ou la résurgence du courant démocrate-chrétien?', *Revue Française de Science Politique*, 49:4–5, 663–74.

Duhamel, O. (1997) 'Derrière le brouillard, le bipartisme' in O. Duhamel and J. Jaffré (eds) *SOFRES: l'état de l'opinion*, Paris, Seuil.

Duhamel, O., and G. Grunberg (1992) 'Référendum: les dix France' in SOFRES, *L'état de l'opinion 1992*, Paris, Editions du Seuil.

Duhamel, O. and J. Jaffré (eds) (1997) *SOFRES L'état de l'opinion 1997*, Paris, Seuil.

Dumont, R. (1974) *A vous de choisir. L'écologie ou la mort*, Paris, Pauvert.

Dupin, E. (1991) *L'Après-Mitterrand: le Parti Socialiste à la dérive*, Paris, Calmann-Levy.

Dutreil, R. (1993) *Le Coq sur la paille*, Paris, Editions Quai Voltaire.

Duverger, M. (1951) *Les Partis politiques*, Paris, Armand Colin.

Duyvendak, J. (1994) *Le Poids du politique. Nouveaux mouvements sociaux en France*, Paris, Harmattan.

Evans, J. (2000a) 'Le vote gaucho-lepéniste. Le masque extrême d'une dynamique normale', *Revue Française de Science Politique*, 50:1, 21–51.

Evans, J. (2000b) 'Contrasting attitudinal elements to Euroscepticism amongst the French electorate', *Electoral Studies*, 19:4, 539–61.

Evans, J. (2002) 'Political corruption in France' in M. Bull and J. Newell (ed.) *Political Corruption in Contemporary Politics*, Basingstoke: Palgrave.

Evans, J. and G. Ivaldi (2002) 'Les dynamiques électorales de l'extrême-droite européenne', *Revue Politique et Parlementaire*, 1019, 67–83.

Favier P. and M. Martin-Roland (1991) *La Décennie Mitterrand*, volume 2, Paris, Seuil.

Fillieule, O. (1997) *Stratégies de la rue. Ordre et désordres des manifestations dans la rue*, Paris, Presses de Sciences Po.

Filoche, G. (1999) *Le Travail jetable non, les 35 heures oui*, Paris, Ramsay.

Fondation Copernic (2001) *Un social libéralisme à la française?*, Paris, La Découverte.

Franklin, M., T. Mackie and H. Valen (eds) (1992) *Electoral Change*, New York, Cambridge University Press.

Frémontier, J. (1984) *Les Cadets de la droite*, Paris, Seuil.

Furet, F. (1999) *The Passing of an Illusion*, Chicago, Chicago University Press.

Furet, F., J. Julliard and P. Rosanvallon (1988) *La République du centre. La fin de l'exception française*, Paris, Calmann-Lévy.

Futur antérieur (1996) *Les Coordinations de travailleurs dans la confrontation sociale*, Paris, L'Harmattan.

Fysh, P. and J. Wolfreys (1998) *The Politics of Racism in France*, New York, St Martin's Press.

Gaffney, J. and E. Kolinsky (1991) (eds) *Political Culture in France and Germany*, London, Routledge.

Gallagher, M., M. Laver and P. Mair (2001) *Representative Government in Modern Europe*, New York, McGraw-Hill.

Gaxie, D. (1996) *La Démocratie représentative*, 2nd edn, Paris, Monchrestien.

Gerstlé, J. (2002) 'Les campagnes électorales', communication to the French Political Science Association one-day conference on '*L'Election presidentielle entre deux tours*', 26 April, IEP, Paris.

Giacometti, P. (1998) 'Les nouveaux profils des "peuples" de gauche et de droite', *Commentaire*, 82, 429–36.

Goguel, F. (1946) *La Politique des partis sous la Troisième République*, Paris, Fayard.

Grunberg, G. and E. Schweisguth (1993) 'Social libertarianism and economic liberalism' in D. Boy and N. Mayer (eds) *The French Voter Decides*, Ann Arbor, University of Michigan Press.

Grunberg, G. and E. Schweisguth (1997) 'Vers une tripartition de l'espace politique' in D. Boy and N. Mayer (eds) *L'Electeur a ses raisons*, Paris, Presses de Sciences Po.

Guyomarch, A. (1995) 'The European dynamics of evolving party competition in France', *Parliamentary Affairs*, 48:1, 100–24.

Habert, P. (1991) 'Les cadres du RPR' in SOFRES, *L'Etat de l'opinion 1991*, Paris, Seuil.

Habert, P., P. Perrineau and C. Ysmal (eds) (1993) *Le Vote Sanction: les élections législatives des 21 et 28 mars 1993*. Paris, Presses de la FNSP.

Haegel, F. (1993) 'Partisan ties' in D. Boy and N. Mayer (eds) *The French Voter Decides*, Ann Arbor, University of Michigan Press.

Hanley, D. (1999a) 'France: living with instability' in D. Broughton and M. Donovan (eds) *Changing Party Systems in Western Europe*, London, Pinter.

Hanley, D. (1999b) 'Compromise, party management and fair shares: the case of the French UDF', *Party Politics*, 5:2, 171–89.

Hanley, D. (2002) *Party, Society and Government: Republican Democracy in France*, Oxford, Berghahn.

Hardt, M. and T. Negri (2001) *Empire*, Cambridge (MA), Harvard.

Hazan, R. (1997) *Centre Parties: Polarization and Competition in European Parliamentary Democracies*, London, Pinter.

Hecht, E. and E. Mandonnet (1998) *Au Cœur du RPR: enquête sur le parti du Président*, Paris, Flammarion.

Hincker, F. (1997) 'French Socialists: towards post-republican values' in D. Sassoon (ed.) *Looking Left. European Socialism after the Cold War*, London, I. B. Tauris.

Hine D. (1982) 'Factionalism in West European parties: a framework for analysis', *West European Politics*, 5:1, 36–53.

Hue, R. (1995) *Communisme, La Mutation*, Paris, Stock.

Inglehart, R. (1990) *Culture Shift in Advanced Industrial Society*, Princeton, Princeton University Press.

Ion, J. (1994) 'L'évolution des formes de l'engagement public' in P. Perrineau (ed.), *L'Engagement politique, déclin ou mutation?*, Paris, Presses de la FNSP.

Ivaldi, G. (1998a) 'The National Front: the making of an authoritarian party' in P. Ignazi and C. Ysmal (eds) *The Organization of Political Parties in Southern Europe*, Westport, Greenwood-Praeger.

Ivaldi, G. (1998b) 'Le Front national à l'assaut du système', *Revue Politique et Parlementaire*, 995, 5–22.

Ivaldi, G. (1999a) 'La scission du Front national', *Regards sur l'actualité*, 251, May, 17–32.

Ivaldi, G. (1999b) 'La liste Pasqua-Villiers aux élections européennes du 13 juin 1999', *Revue Française de Science Politique*, 49:4–5, 643–52.

Ivaldi, G. (2001) 'Les formations d'extrême-droite: Front national et Mouvement national républicain' in P. Bréchon (ed.) *Les Partis politiques français*, Paris, La Documentation Française.

Ivaldi, G. and M. Swyngedouw (2001) 'The extreme-right Utopia in Belgium and France. The ideology of the Flemish Vlaams Blok, the French Front National and the Belgian Front National', *West European Politics*, 24:3, 1–22.

Jaffré, J. (1997) 'La décision électorale au second tour: un scrutin très serré', *Revue Française de Science Politique*, 47:3–4, 423–35.

Jaffré, J. (2002) 'Le vote des droites', communication to the French Political Science Association one-day conference on the parliamentary election, 19 June, IEP, Paris.

Kalyvas, S. (1996) *The Rise of Christian Democracy in Europe*, Ithaca, Cornell University Press.

Kirchheimer, O. (1990) 'The catch-all party' in P. Mair (ed.) *The West European Party System*, Oxford, Oxford University Press.

Kitschelt, H. (1988) 'Left–libertarian parties: explaining innovation in competitive party systems' in *World Politics*, 40:2, 194–234.

Kitschelt, H. (1995) *The Radical Right in Western Europe. A Comparative Analysis*, Ann Arbor, University of Michigan Press.

Kitschelt, H. (1997) 'European party systems: continuity and change' in M. Rhodes *et al.* (eds) *Developments in West European Politics*, Basingstoke, Macmillan.

Kitschelt, H. and S. Hellemans (1990) 'The Left-Right semantics and the new politics cleavage', *Comparative Political Studies*, 23:3, 210–38.

Knapp, A. (1999) 'What's left of the French Right? The RPR and the UDF from conquest to humiliation, 1993–1998', *West European Politics*, 22:3, 109–38.

Knapp, A. and V. Wright (2001) *The Government and Politics of France*, 4th edn, London, Routledge.

Knutsen, O. (1995) 'Value orientation, political conflicts and left-right identification: a comparative study', *European Journal of Political Research*, 28:1, 63–93.

Kriesi, H., R. Koopmans, J. Duyvendak and M. Giugni (1995) *New Social Movements in Western Europe: a Comparative Analysis*, London, UCL Press.

Lancelot, A. (1998) *Les Elections nationales sous la cinquième République*, 3rd edn, Paris, PUF.

Lane, J.-E. and S. Ersson (1987) *Politics and Society in Western Europe*, Newbury Park, Sage.

Lavabre, M.-C. (1994) *Le Fil rouge*, Paris, Presses de la FNSP.

Laver, M. (1989) 'Party competition and party system change: the interaction of coalition bargaigning and electoral competition', *Journal of Theoretical Politics*, 1:3, 301–24.

Lazar, M. (1999) 'La gauche communiste plurielle', *Revue Française de Science Politique*, 49:4–5, 695–705.

Le Gall, G. (1993) 'Une répétition des élections du printemps 1992', *Revue Politique et Parlementaire*, 964, 6–19.

Le Gall, G. (1998) 'Cantonales et régionales: quand 1998 confirme 1997', *Revue Politique et Parlementaire*, 993, 5–23.

Le Gall, G. (2002) 'Consultations électorales du printemps 2002: enseignements et spécificités', *Revue Politique et Parlementaire*, 1019, 35–43.

Lucardie, P. (2000) 'Prophets, purifiers and prolocutors. Towards a theory on the emergence of new parties', *Party Politics*, 6:2, 175–85.

McAna, M. (2001) 'The Front National in Municipal power', unpublished Ph.D. thesis, Bradford University.

Machin, H. (1989) 'Stages and dynamics in the evolution of the French party system', *West European Politics*, 12:4, 59–81.

Mair, P. (2000) 'The limited impact of Europe on national party systems', *West European Politics*, 23:4, 27–51.

Martin, P. (2001) *Les Elections municipales en France depuis 1945*, Paris, La Documentation Française.

Mayer, N. (1983) 'L'ancrage à droite des petits commerçants et artisans indépendants' in G. Lavau *et al.* (eds) *L'Univers politique des classes moyennes*, Paris, Presses de FNSP.

Mayer, N. (1999) *Ces Français qui votent FN*, Paris, Flammarion.

Méchet, P. (2000) 'Européennes 1999: entre démobilisation et dispersion' in O. Duhamel and P. Méchet (eds) *SOFRES: l'état de l'opinion 2000*, Paris, Gallimard

Mendras, H. (1989) *La Seconde Révolution Française*, Paris, Gallimard.

Mény, Y. (1992) *La Corruption de la République*, Paris, Fayard.

Mény, Y. (1995) 'The reconstruction and deconstruction of the French party system' in G. Flynn (ed.) *Remaking the Hexagon: The New France in the New Europe*, Oxford, Westview Press.

Mercier, A.-S. and B. Jérôme (1997) *Les 700 jours de Lionel Jospin*, Plon, Paris.

Merrill, S. and B. Grofman (1999) *A Unified Theory of Voting*, Cambridge, Cambridge University Press.

Minkenberg, M. (1998) *Die Neue Radikale Rechte Im Vergleich*, Wiesbaden, Westdeutscher Verlag.

Moreau, J. (1998) *Les Socialistes français et le mythe révolutionnaire* Paris, Hachette.

Mossuz-Lavau, J. (1998) *Que veut la gauche plurielle?*, Paris, Odile Jacob.

Mouriaux, M.-F. (1998) *Une Potion magique, la flexibilité? L'année sociale édition 1998*, Paris, Editions Ouvrières.

O'Neill, M. (1997) *Green Parties and Political Change in Contemporary Europe*, Aldershot, Ashgate.

Offerlé, M. (1987) *Les Partis politiques*, 3rd edn, Paris, PUF.

Ottenheimer, G. (1996) *Le Fiasco*, Paris, Albin Michel.

Parodi, J.-L. (1989) 'Le nouvel espace politique français' in Y. Mény (ed.), *Idéologies, partis politiques et groupes sociaux*, Paris, Presses de la FNSP.

Parodi, J.-L. (1997) 'Proportionnalisation périodique, cohabitation, atomisation partisane: un triple défi pour le régime semi-présidentiel de la Cinquième République', *Revue Française de Science Politique*, 47:3–4, 292–312.

Percheron, A. (1977) 'Ideological proximity among French children: problems of definition and measurement', *European Journal of Political Research*, 5:1, 53–81.

Perrineau, P. (1995) 'La dynamique du vote Le Pen: le poids du gaucho-lepénisme' in P. Perrineau and C. Ysmal (eds) *Le Vote de crise: l'élection présidentielle de 1995*, Paris, Presses de Sciences Po.

Perrineau, P. (1997) *Le Symptôme Le Pen*, Paris, Fayard.

Perrineau, P. and C. Ysmal (eds) (1998) *Le Vote surprise: les élections legislatives des 25 mai et 1 juin 1997*, Paris, Presses de Sciences Po.

Pingaud, D. (2000) *La Gauche de la gauche*, Paris, Seuil.

Pitts, J. (1981) 'Les Français et l'autorité' in J.-D. Reynaud and Y. Grafmeyer (eds) *Français, qui êtes-vous?* Paris, La Documentation Française.

Poguntke, T. (1993) *Alternative Politics. The German Green Party*, Edinburgh, Edinburgh University Press.

Rabinowitz, G. and S. Macdonald (1989) 'A directional theory of issue voting', *American Political Science Review*, 83:1, 77–91.

Rémond, R. (1982) *Les Droites en France*, Paris, Aubier

Rémond, R. (1988) 'Jacques Chirac et son parti', *L'Express*, 9 September.

Richardson, D. and C. Rootes (eds) (1995) *The Green Challenge. The Development of Green Parties in Europe*, London, Routledge.

Rihoux, B. (2001) *Les Partis politiques: organisations en changement. Le test des écologistes*, Paris, L'Harmattan.

Rioux, J.-P. (1987) *The Fourth Republic*, Cambridge, Cambridge University Press.

Rose, R. (1964) 'Parties, factions and tendencies in Britain', *Political Studies*, 12:1, 33–46.

Ross, G. (2000) 'Europe becomes French domestic politics' in M. Lewis-Beck (ed.) *How France Votes*, London, Chatham House.

Safran, W. (1998) *The French Polity*, New York, Longman.

Sainteny, G. (2000) *L'Introuvable Ecologisme français?*, Paris, PUF.

Sartori, G. (1976) *Parties and Party Systems*, Cambridge, Cambridge University Press.

Sauger, N. (1998) 'La sélection des candidats à l'UDF (1996–1998)', DEA dissertation, IEP Paris.

Schild, J. (2000) 'Wählerverhalten und Parteienwettbewerb' in S. Ruß *et al.* (eds)

Parteien in Frankreich. Kontinuität und Wandel in der V. Republik, Oplanden, Leske und Budrich.

Schlesinger, J. and M. Schlesinger (2000) 'The stability of the French party system: the enduring impact of the two-ballot electoral rules' in M. Lewis-Beck (ed.) *How France Votes*, London, Chatham House.

Schonfeld, W. (1981) 'The RPR: from a Rassemblement to a Gaullist movement' in W. Andrews and S. Hoffmann (eds) *The Fifth Republic at Twenty*, Albany, University of New York Press.

Schonfeld, W. (1986) 'Le RPR et l'UDF à l'épreuve de l'opposition', *Revue Française de Science Politique*, 36:1, 14–29.

Schweisguth, E. (2000) 'The myth of neo-conservatism' in M. Lewis-Beck (ed.) *How France Votes*, London, Chatham House.

Seiler, D.-L. (1984) *De La Comparaison des partis politiques*, Paris, Economica.

Sferza, S. and S. Lewis (1987) 'French Socialists between state and society: from party building to power' in G. Ross *et al.* (eds) *The Mitterrand Experiment*, Oxford, Oxford University Press.

Siaroff, A. (2000) *Comparative European Party Systems*, New York, Garland.

Sjöblom, G. (1968) *Party Strategies in a Multiparty System*, Lund, Studentlitteratur.

Sommier, I. (2001) *Les Nouveaux Mouvements contestataires à l'heure de la mondialisation*, Paris, Flammarion.

Szac, M. (1998) *Dominique Voynet. Une vraie nature*, Paris, Plon.

Szarka, J. (1999) 'The parties of the French "Plural Left": an uneasy complementarity', *West European Politics*, 22:4, 20–37.

Taagepera, R. and M. Shugart (1989) *Seats and Votes. The Effects and Determinants of Electoral Systems*, New Haven, Yale University Press.

Taggart, P. (1998) 'A touchstone of dissent: Euroscepticism in contemporary Western European party systems', *European Journal of Political Research*, 33:3, 363–88.

Urvouas, J.-J. (1997) 'La mutation du PCF: fiction ou veilléité?', *Regards sur l'actualité*, March, 3–14.

Vialatte, J. (1996) *Les Partis Verts en Europe Occidentale*, Paris, Economica.

Vieillard-Coffre, S. (2001) 'Les Verts et le pouvoir. Regards géopolitiques sur les écologistes français: stratégies et représentations', *Hérodote*, 100, 120–50.

Villalba, B. (1995) 'De L'Identité des Verts: essai sur la constitution d'un nouvel acteur politique', unpublished Ph.D. thesis, University of Lille 2.

Villalba, B. (1999) 'La rose et le myosotis. La gauche plurielle aux élections régionales de 1998' in B. Dolez and A. Laurent (eds) *Des roses en mars. Les élections régionales et cantonales de 1998 dans le Nord/Pas-de-Calais*, Lille, Presse Universitaire du Septentrion.

Voynet, D. (1995) *Oser l'écologie et la solidarité*, Paris, La Tour d'Aigue.

Waters, S. (1998) 'New social movements in France: the rise of civic forms of mobilisation', *West European Politics*, 21:3, 170–86.

Williams, P. (1964) *Crisis and Compromise: Politics in the Fourth Republic*, London, Longman.

Witkowski, D. (2001) 'Jacques Chirac: la popularité captive' in SOFRES, *L'Etat de l'opinion 2001*, Paris, Seuil.

Wolfreys, J. (1999) 'Class struggles in France', *International Socialism*, Autumn.

Wolfreys, J. (2000) 'In perspective: Pierre Bourdieu', *International Socialism*, Summer.

Wright, V. (1989) *The Government and Politics of France*, London, Unwin Hyman.

Yanai, N. (1999) 'Why do political parties survive?', *Party Politics*, 5:1, 5–17.

Ysmal, C. (1989) *Les Partis politiques sous La Ve République*, Paris, Montchrestien.

Ysmal, C. (1992) 'Les cadres du CDS et du Parti républicain: l'UDF en proie à ses divisions' in SOFRES, *L'Etat de l'opinion 1992*, Paris, Seuil.

Ysmal, C. (1998) 'Le second tour: le prix de l'isolement de la droite modérée' in P. Perrineau and C. Ysmal (eds) *Le Vote surprise*, Paris, Presses de Sciences Po.

Ysmal, C. (2000) 'Face à l'extrême droite, la droite existe-t-elle?' in P. Bréchon, A. Laurent and P. Perrineau (eds) *Les Cultures politiques des français*, Paris, Presses de Sciences Po.

Index

Note: 'n.' after a page reference indicates the number of a note on that page.

Act Up, 98, 100
Agir ensemble contre le Chômage
    (AC!), 98, 107
Air France, 39, 95, 97
Algerian crisis, 32
Alliance, 130
Alliance pour l'Ecologie et la
    Démocratie (AED), 75 n. 17
Alliot-Marie, Michèle, 128, 131, 132
Alternance 2002, 115, 132
Alternative Rouge et Verte (AREV),
    66
Amsterdam Treaty, 157–8, 163
Andersen, R., 187 n. 9, 200 n. 6
Anger, Didier, 63, 68
Annual General Meeting (AGM,
    Green Party), 57
Antony, Bernard, 143
Arditi, Maryse, 72, 75 n. 21
Aschieri, André, 75 n. 20
Assises de la transformation sociale, 51, 52
Association des Amis de Jacques
    Chirac, 130, 131
Association pour l'Emploi dans
    l'Industrie et le Commerce
    (ASSEDIC), 39
Association pour l'Emploi,
    l'Information et la Solidarité
    (APEIS), 98
Attac, 91, 101, 102, 103
Aubert, Marie-Hélène, 75 n. 20
Aubry, Martine, 95, 189, 198
Auchedé, Rémy, 79
Austria, 139
Autrement les Verts, 166

Bachelot, François, 143
Balladur, Edouard, 51, 97, 119 n. 20,
    123, 125–6, 127, 132, 164
Bariller, Damien, 143, 148, 151 n. 11
Barnier, Michel, 115, 132
Baroin, François, 132
Barre, Raymond, 119 n. 20, 123
Barrot, Jacques, 115, 132, 134
Bastow, S., 187 n. 3
Baylet, Jean-Michel, 16
Bayrou, François, 10 n. 1, 16, 23, 123
    centre/moderate right, 126, 132,
        133, 135
    Europe, 163, 164
    plural left, 86
    UDF, 108, 111, 113, 114, 115, 118
Belgium, 139
Benoît, B., 169 n. 1
Bérégovoy, Pierre, 55 n. 5, 55 n. 6
Bergounioux, A., 44
Bernstein, Eduard, 47
Berstein, Serge, 126
Besancenot, Olivier, 7, 30, 91, 102,
    103, 134, 198
Billard, Martine, 68, 72, 75 n. 21
Blandin, Marie-Christine, 66, 71, 72,
    75 n. 21
Blot, Yvan, 143, 151 n. 11
Boltanski, L., 98–9
Bompard, Jacques, 146, 151 n. 11
Bouge l'Europe!, 159, 160
Bourdieu, Pierre, 91, 100–1
Bové, José, 91, 101
Boy, Daniel, 53, 171
Brière, Jean, 68

Buchmann, Andrée, 63
Buffet, Marie-George, 37, 82
Bussereau, Dominique, 132

Cambadélis, J.-M., 51, 80, 87
Caron, Jean-François, 75 n. 17
Cassen, Bernard, 101, 102
Centre des Démocrates Sociaux
        (CDS), 4
    Europe, 163, 166
    moderate-right dynamics, 113,
        116, 117
    modification in political space,
        109, 110
    plural left, 174
    and UDF, 112, 118 n. 1, 118 n. 2,
        119 n. 15
Centre National des Indépendants
        (CNI), 119 n. 17, 120 n. 28
Chaban-Delmas, Jacques, 123, 197
Charlot, J., 46, 176
Chasse Pêche Nature Traditions
        (CPNT), 14, 169 n. 2
Chevènement, Jean-Pierre, 3, 6, 16,
        17, 18, 26 n. 4, 185, 189, 197
    centre/moderate right, 134
    Europe, 157, 158, 169 n. 2
    far left, 93
    plural left, 78, 82, 84, 85–6, 88, 174
Chiapello, E., 98–9
Chirac, Jacques, 6, 17, 18, 20, 23, 25,
        196, 197, 198
    centre/moderate right, 121, 122,
        123, 125–8, 130–3, 134, 135
    Europe, 168
    far left, 95, 100, 102
    far right, 141, 145
    Green Party, 62
    plural left, 86, 89
    UDF, 111, 112, 113, 114
Christian Democrats, 76, 77
Christlich–Demokratischen Union –
        Christlich–Soziale Union
        (CDU–CSU), 121, 133
Cochet, Yves, 53, 68, 75 n. 20
Cohn-Bendit, Daniel, 61, 67, 69–70,
        160
Colombani, Philippe, 143
Coluche, 98

Comité de Vigilance, 101
Communist Party, *see* Parti
        Communiste Français
Comparini, Anne-Marie, 113
Confédération Française
        Démocratique du Travail
        (CFDT), 97, 98, 100
Confédération Générale des
        Travailleurs (CGT), 31, 41
Confédération Paysanne, 101
Conservative Party (Great Britain),
        121, 133
Convention pour une Alternative
        Progressiste (CAP), 66
Convergence Ecologie Solidarité
        (CES), 66, 75 n. 17
Converse, Philip, 200 n. 5
Co-ordination Communiste, 38
Coordonner, Rassembler, Construire
        (CRC), 97
Corsica, 5, 60, 84, 187
Crété, Alice, 71

Dalton, R., 187 n. 2
Debré, Jean-Louis, 127, 130, 132
de Charette, Hervé, 127
de Gaulle, Charles, General, 12, 13,
        32, 33, 43, 120 n. 28, 123,
        125, 130
de Gaulle, Charles (FN MEP), 151
        n. 12
Delevoye, Jean-Pierre, 131
Démocratie Libérale (DL), 2, 5, 6–7,
        16, 17, 23, 187 n. 6, 196
    centre/moderate right, 113,
        114–15, 116, 120 n. 26, 126
    Europe, 163, 164, 165, 166
    far right, 143
    and GE, 66
    plural left, 86, 89
    and UDF, 107, 108, 109–11, 118,
        118 n. 2, 119 n. 10
    and UMP, 132, 133, 134
Démocratie Libérale et Indépendants
        (DLI), 115, 157
de Villiers, Philippe, 10 n. 3, 14, 16,
        93, 118 n. 5, 126, 157, 160,
        161–2, 163
Dialogue et Initiative, 115

Dolez, B., 160
Donzel, François, 75 n. 17
Douste-Blazy, Philippe, 132–3, 134, 197
Dreyfus affair, 95
Droit au Logement (DAL), 98
Droite, 14, 111
Droite Libérale et Chrétienne, 119 n. 11, 119 n. 17
Droits devant!! (DD!!), 98, 102
Duhamel, Olivier, 167
Dumont, René, 56, 62, 75 n. 11
Duthu, Françoise, 72, 75 n. 21
Dutreil, Renaud, 131, 132, 134
Duverger, M., 122

Ecologie Autrement (EA), 75 n. 17
Ecologie Bleue, 67
Ecologie et Démocratie, 166
Ecology Entente, 66
Emmanuelli, Henri, 93
Entente Radicale Ecologiste pour les Etats-Unis d'Europe, 62
Erika petrol-tanker, 75 n. 10
Esprit, 100
Estates General of the European Social Movement, 100–1
European Central Bank, 158
European Popular Party, 110, 119 n. 10
European Union 4–5, 24, 155–6, 168–9, 185
  Euroscepticism, 156–65
  factionalism, 16
  institutional context, 165–8
  PCF, 35, 36, 39
Evans, J., 10 n. 4, 169 n. 1, 187 n. 3, 187 n. 9, 200 n. 6
Executive College (EC, Green Party), 57

Fabius, Laurent, 48–9, 50, 51, 82, 157, 197
Federal Assembly (FA, Green Party), 57
Fédération Solidaire, Unitaire, Démocratique des PTT (SUD–PTT), 97–8, 102, 103
Fernex, Solange, 58
Fillon, François, 132, 198

Fini, Gianfranco, 148
Force Démocrate (FD), 108, 116, 117, 118 n. 2, 163, 165
Fraisse, Geneviève, 160
Franklin, M., 187 n. 2
Frémion, Yves, 71
Front National (FN), 3–4, 13, 20, 25, 137–8, 185–6, 190, 193, 194, 195–6
  absorptive capacity, 22–3
  centre/moderate right, 108, 126
  electoral strength and party system after 2002, 145–7
  emergence, 14, 15–16
  Europe, 156, 162–3, 165
  factionalism, 16
  far left, 92, 93, 97, 101
  fragmentation of right, 175–6, 191–2
  growth, 171, 173
  isolation, 21
  legitimacy of party politics, 17, 18
  and MNR, new balance of power between, 147–8
  organisation, 22
  party system change in mid-1990s, 138–42
  and PCF, 35, 36, 37
  plural left, 81, 86, 89
  prospects, 149–50
  and PS, 49
  split, 17, 142–5
  supporters, 24, 179, 182–3, 184, 187 n. 10
  and UDF, 111, 119 n. 19
Front National de la Jeunesse (FNJ) 143
Futurs, 37

Gaudin, Jean-Claude, 134
Gaymard, Hervé, 132
Gayssot, Jean-Claude, 90 n. 6, 95
Génération Ecologie (GE), 48, 64–7, 74 n. 4, 187 n. 12
Germany, 25, 121
Giscard d'Estaing, Valéry, 107, 112, 119 n. 15, 123, 163, 197
Gollnisch, Bruno, 143, 146, 149, 151 n. 11, 151 n. 12, 200 n. 7

Great Britain, 25, 121, 133
Green Party, 2, 3, 5, 6, 13, 25, 56,
    72–4, 173, 185, 190, 191, 192,
    195–6, 197
  absorptive capacity, 22
  electoral journey, 20, 60–8
  emergence, 14, 48, 77
  Europe, 158, 159, 161, 166–7
  far left, 93, 102
  organisation, 22
  and PCF, 39
  plural left, 68–72, 73, 77, 80–1,
    82–3, 84, 85, 86
    consolidation, 174, 175
    contradictions, 88
    integration into party system, 92
  and PS, 54, 61, 67, 69, 70, 73–4,
    75 n. 17
    factionalism, 48, 49, 51, 52–3
    Vedel Commission, 55 n. 5
  structure and membership, 56–60,
    96
  and UDF, 113, 114
Gremetz, Maxime, 38
Grofman, B., 187 n. 10
Groupe des dix federation, 97
Grunberg, Gérard, 44, 150 n. 6, 173,
    176–7, 183–4
Guidoni, Pierre, 52
Gulf War, 174

Hage, Georges, 38, 79
Hanley, D., 44, 116
Hardt, M., 99
Hascoët, Guy, 68, 69, 71, 75 n. 20, 75
    n. 21, 82, 83, 84
Hermier, Guy, 37
Herzog, Philippe, 51, 160
Hine, D., 47
Hollande, François, 53, 85, 89, 198
Holleindre, Roger, 151 n. 11
Honecker Committees, 38
Hue, Robert, 18, 194
  Europe, 159, 160
  far left, 95, 102, 103
  PCF, 30, 31, 36, 37, 38–40, 54
  plural left, 85, 88, 174
Humanité, L', 31, 39
Hungary, 33

Ievoli Sun petrol-tanker, 75 n. 10
Inglehart, R., 187 n. 8
Italy, 25, 32, 82, 148
Ivaldi, G., 10 n. 4, 144, 150 n. 7, 151
    n. 13, 161

Jospin, Lionel, 1, 5, 15, 17, 18, 19,
    20
  centre/moderate right, 133
  Europe, 167
  far left, 94–5
  Green Party, 60, 62, 69
  PCF, 36
  plural left, 77, 78, 79, 81, 82–4,
    85–6, 92, 94, 184
  PS, 48, 51, 52–3, 54
  UDF, 114
Juppé, Alain, 15, 197
  centre/moderate right, 127, 128,
    132, 133, 134, 135, 136
  far left, 100

Karman, Jacques, 38
Kautsky, Karl, 47
Keynes, John Maynard, 94
Khrushchev, Nikita, 32
Kirchheimer, O., 43, 44
Kitschelt, Herbert, 104, 155
Knapp, A., 170 n. 8
Kosovan crisis, 160
Kouchner, Bernard, 98

La Droite, 14, 111
La Droite Libérale et Chrétienne,
    119 n. 11, 119 n. 17
Lafargue, Paul, 95
Laguiller, Arlette, 7, 30, 91, 99,
    102–3, 134, 198
Lajoinie, André, 36, 80
Lalonde, Brice, 62, 64
Lang, Carl, 143, 151 n. 11, 151
    n. 12
Lazar, M., 159, 160, 170 n. 7
Lecanuet, Jean, 123
Le Gall, Gérard, 50, 150 n. 2
Le Gallou, Jean-Yves, 143, 148,
    151 n. 11
Lenin, Vladimir Ilyich, 30
Léotard, François, 108, 130

Le Pen, Jean-Marie, 3, 6, 15, 17, 18,
25, 137, 150 n. 1, 151 n. 12, 178
centre/moderate right, 133, 134
challenge posed by, 173
conciliatory phase, end of, 141,
150 n. 7
electoral strength, 145, 146
Europe, 162–3
far left, 92, 101, 104
issue-voting, 146, 147
MNR and FN, balance of power
between, 148
party cooperation, lack of, 147, 186
PCF, 35, 36
plural left, 85, 86, 89
prospects for far right, 149, 150
split of FN, 142–4, 195
supporters, 139, 140, 147, 187
n. 10
UDF, 113
Le Pen, Marine, 146, 149, 163, 200
n. 7
Lewis, S., 44
L'Humanité, 31, 39
Liber/Raisons d'Agir, 100
Ligue Communiste Révolutionnaire
(LCR), 18, 91, 102, 103, 156,
160
Lipietz, Alain, 71, 73, 195
Lucardie, P., 109
Lutte Ouvrière (LO), 14, 18, 39, 91,
102, 103, 156, 160, 174
Lyonnaise des Eaux-Dumez, 131

Maastricht Treaty, 157–8, 159, 161,
163, 164
centre/moderate right, 125, 126–7,
128–9
PCF, 35, 39
Macdonald, S., 187 n. 10
Machin, H., 44, 45
Madelin, Alain, 16, 17
centre/moderate right, 113, 118
n. 2, 123, 126
DL's split, 109, 110, 114
Europe, 163
FN, 111
UDF, 127
UMP, 115, 132, 133

Mair, P., 155
Mamère, Noël, 38, 75 n. 20, 195
CES's formation, 75 n. 17
Dynamiques vertes, 75 n. 21
electoral journey, 61, 68, 72, 73
far left, 102
influence, 74 n. 4
plural left, 71, 83, 88
Manifeste contre le Front National, 97
Maoism, 99
Marchais, Georges, 33, 36, 38, 159
Marchand, Jean-Michel, 75 n. 20
Maréchal, Samuel, 143
Martelli, Roger, 37
Martinez, Jean-Claude, 146, 151 n. 12
Marx, Karl, 31, 94
Marxism, 31, 98
Mauroy, Pierre, 12, 48–9, 93
Mayer, N., 171
McDonalds, 101
Médécins sans frontières, 98
Mégret, Bruno, 137, 186, 195
centre/moderate right, 119 n. 12,
119 n. 19
electoral strength, 15, 145, 151
n. 11
far left, 92
FN and MNR, balance of power
between, 148
ideology, 146
issue voting, 147
prospects for far right, 149
split of FN, 7, 17, 142–4
Mélenchon, Jean-Luc, 82
Mény, Y., 45
Mer, Francis, 198
Merrill, S., 187 n. 10
Millon, Charles, 14, 113, 118, 119
n. 11, 157, 165
Mitterrand, François, 23, 24
centre/moderate right, 125, 126,
128
Europe, 157, 167
far left, 93–4, 96, 97
PCF, 29, 33, 34, 35
plural left, 76, 78
PS, 43–4, 45, 47–8, 51, 52, 54
UDF, 112
Monde Diplomatique, Le, 101

Monod, Jérôme, 131–2
Monory, René, 163
Moreau, Jacques, 93–4
Mouvement des Citoyens (MdC), 16,
    17, 30, 185
  Europe, 157, 158, 161, 169 n. 2
  plural left, 77, 78, 79, 82, 84, 86,
    88, 174, 175
Mouvement des Entreprises de
    France (MEDEF), 85
Mouvement Ecologiste Indépendant
    (MEI), 14, 66
Mouvement National Républicain
    (MNR), 7, 15, 17, 20, 137,
    192, 193
  centre/moderate right, 119 n. 19
  electoral strength, 145, 146
  Europe, 156
  and FN, balance of power
    between, 147–8
  ideology, 146
  issue-voting, 147
  party cooperation, lack of, 147, 186
  prospects, 149
  split of FN, 17, 142–5
Mouvement pour la France (MPF), 10
    n. 3, 16, 118 n. 5, 119 n. 17,
    156, 161–3, 178
Mouvement Républicain Populaire
    (MRP), 12, 32
Movimento Sociale Italiano (MSI), 148
Mutuelle Nationale des Etudiants
    Français (MNEF), 84

National Inter-Regional Council
    (NIRC, Green Party), 57
Negri, T., 99
North Atlantic Treaty Organization
    (NATO), 160
Norway, 139
Notat, Nicole, 100

Olivier, Philippe, 143

Pacte Civil de Solidarité (PACS), 38,
    110
Partido Popular de Espana (PPE),
    121, 133
Parodi, Jean-Luc, 4, 150 n. 8, 165

Parti Communiste Français (PCF),
    1–2, 5, 6, 26, 29–30, 40–1,
    192, 194
  alliance politics, 32–4
  anti-system to system politics, 35–6
  centre/moderate right, 136 n. 2
  centripetal shift, 195
  continuities in party system, 20
  decline, 24
  Europe, 156, 157, 158–61
  evolution of party system, 12, 13,
    14
  factionalism, 16
  far left, 95–6
  and Green Party, 69, 74 n. 8
  membership, 96
  municipal government, 21–2
  party system possibilities, 36–40
  plural left, 76–7, 79–80, 81, 89, 197
    consolidation, 174–5
    decline, 78, 88
    in government, 82, 83, 84–5, 86
    Jospin's nurturing, 92
  and PS, 34, 35, 36–7, 38–9, 41,
    44, 47, 52–4, 111
  three aspects of Communism, 30–1
  and UDF, 113, 114
  un passé que ne passe pas, 31–2
Parti Ecologiste, 66
Parti Populaire pour la Démocratie
    Française, 118 n. 2
Parti Radical de Gauche (PRG), 6, 16,
    53, 69
  plural left, 76, 77, 78, 79, 82, 85,
    86, 88
Parti Républicain (PR), 108, 109, 110,
    112, 117, 118 n. 1, 118 n. 2,
    134, 163
Parti Social Démocrate, 118 n. 2
Parti Socialiste (PS), 2, 5–6, 12, 13,
    14, 16, 21, 22
  competing institutional and
    electoral logics, 44–6
  Europe, 157, 158, 161, 164,
    166–7, 170 n. 7
  far left, 92, 93–6, 97
  and Green Party, 48, 49, 51, 52–3,
    54, 55 n. 5, 61, 67, 69, 70,
    73–4, 75 n. 17

membership, 96
and PCF, 34, 35, 36–7, 38–9, 41,
    44, 47, 52–4, 111
plural left, 76–7, 78–81, 82–5,
    86–8, 89, 90 n. 6, 174, 175,
    196
rassemblement, 44
and UDF, 113
and UMP, 133, 135
union de gauche, 44
Pas-de-Calais, 38
Pasqua, Charles, 10 n. 3, 14, 16, 17,
    188
    centre/moderate right, 126
    Europe, 157, 160, 161–2
    far left, 93
    far right, 144
Perben, Dominique, 115, 132
Perrineau, P., 150 n. 2
Phénix nuclear reactor, 83
Piat, Yann, 137
Pocrain, Stéphane, 71, 72
Poher, Alain, 123
Pôle Républicain (PRep), 6, 20, 185,
    192
Pompidou, Georges, 34, 122, 123
Poncelet, Christian, 132, 163
Pons, Bernard, 130, 132
Popular Front, 76, 95
Portelli, H., 88

Quilès, Paul, 80

Rabinowitz, G., 187 n. 10
Radical Party, 112, 118 n. 1, 118 n. 2
Radicaux–Citoyens–Verts (RCV), 75
    n. 20, 157, 158
Raffarin, Jean-Pierre, 108, 115, 116,
    132, 133, 135, 196, 198
Raisons d'Agir, 100
Ras l'Front, 97
Rassemblement du Peuple Français
    (RPF), 12, 26, 122
Rassemblement pour la France (RPF),
    10 n. 3, 14, 16, 17, 89, 126,
    156, 161–2, 164
Rassemblement pour la France et
    l'Indépendance de l'Europe
    (RPFIE), 161, 162

Rassemblement pour la République
    (RPR), 2, 5, 6, 12, 14, 15, 16,
    17, 21, 22, 23, 25, 46, 185,
    192, 194
    centre/moderate right, 113, 114,
        115, 116, 117, 122, 123, 124
    convergence, 125–8, 129–30
    Europe, 156, 157, 161, 162, 163,
        164, 165–6
    and European People's Party, 119
        n. 10
    far left, 92, 93
    far right, 140, 141, 143, 144
    modification in political space, 111
    plural left, 86, 89
    and UDF, 107, 108, 112, 119
        n. 14, 135
    and UMP, 130, 132, 134
Rémond, René, 121–2
Rennes Congress, 48
Républicains Indépendants (RI), 118
    n. 4
Restaurants du coeur, 98
Revenue Minimum d'Insertion, 97
Rivasy, Michèle, 75 n. 20
Rocard, Michel, 4, 47, 50–2, 194
    Europe, 166
    far left, 93, 94, 95
    plural left, 77, 174
    Union du Centre, 119 n. 18
Rochet, Waldeck, 33
Rosanvallon, 87
Rose, R., 48
Ross, G., 155
Rufenacht, Antoine, 132

Saint-Josse, Jean, 14, 18, 169 n. 2
Sarkozy, Nicolas, 126, 127, 132, 135,
    148, 197, 198
Sarre, Georges, 86
Sartori, G., 47, 193
Schengen Agreement, 159
Schild, Joachim, 23
Schlesinger, J., 44, 119 n. 14
Schlesinger, M., 44, 119 n. 14
Schweisguth, Etienne, 150 n. 6, 173,
    176–7, 183–4
Section Française de l'Internationale
    Ouvrière (SFIO), 12, 32, 76, 77

Séguin, Philippe, 6, 126, 127, 128, 130, 189
  Europe, 157, 158, 161, 162, 163, 165, 169 n. 3
  UMP, 132
Sève, Lucien, 37
Sferza, S., 44
Siméoni, Max, 60
Single European Act, 125
Socialist Party, *see* Parti Socialiste
SOS Racisme, 96, 97
Soviet Union, 30, 33, 35, 37, 38
Spain, 121
Stirbois, Jean-Pierre, 150 n. 1
Stirbois, Marie-France, 146, 151 n. 11
Strauss-Kahn, Dominique, 19, 197
Swyngedouw, M., 144
Szarka, J., 85, 187 n. 5

Tapie, Bernard, 51
Tête, Etienne, 71, 75 n. 21
Thorez, Maurice, 32, 33
Timmermans, Franck, 143, 151 n. 11
Tobin tax, 101, 102
Todd, Emmanuel, 93
Touraine, Alain, 100
Trotskyism, 81, 86, 89, 92, 99, 160

Union du Centre, 119 n. 18
Union en Mouvement (UEM), 132–3
Union of Soviet Socialist Republics, 30, 33, 35, 37, 38
Union pour la Démocratie Française (UDF), 46, 107–8, 117–18, 185–6, 192, 196
  absorptive capacity, 22
  centre/moderate right, 122–3, 124
  convergence, 125, 126, 127, 129–30
  corruption, 16
  Ecologie Bleue, 67
  electoral journey, 2, 14, 194
  Europe, 156, 157, 160, 161, 163–6
  evolution of party system, 12
  far left, 92, 93
  far right, 4, 15, 140, 141, 143
  fragmentation of right, 187 n. 6
  isolation, 7
  municipal government, 21
  plural left, 86, 89

  and RPR, 5, 15, 107, 108, 112, 119 n. 14, 135, 194
  split and modification of parties in political space, 17, 107–8, 109–12, 128
  tensions, 6–7
  and UMP, 7, 10 n. 1, 23, 132, 133, 134
Union pour la France (UPF), 123
Union pour une Majorité Présidentielle/ Union pour un Mouvement Populaire (UMP), 9, 115–17, 118, 192, 193, 195, 200 n. 4
  centre/moderate right, 5, 121, 128, 129, 133–5
  challenge posed by, 15, 17, 189
  continuities in party system, 20, 23
  Europe, 162, 163–5, 167
  far right, 148, 150
  hegemony, 196
  launch, 133
  plural left, 86, 89
  prospects, 196–7
  and UDF, 7, 10 n. 1, 23, 132, 133, 134
Union pour un Mouvement Populaire (UMP), *see* Union pour une Majorité Présidentielle
Union pour la Nouvelle République (UNR), 43, 120 n. 28, 196
United Kingdom, 25, 121, 133
United States of America, 160

Vaillant, Daniel, 84
Vedel Commission, 55 n. 5
Veil, Simone, 119 n. 15, 125
Vendredi, 51
Viansson-Ponté, Pierre, 91
Voynet, Dominique, 53, 60, 66, 68, 69, 71, 72, 74 n. 9, 75 n. 20, 75 n. 21, 189, 197
  plural left, 77, 80, 82–3, 90 n. 6, 174

Waechter, Antoine, 14, 58, 60, 63, 66, 68, 69, 174
Workers' International, 159
World Trade Organisation (WTO), 101, 103

Yanai, N., 95